Travelling o   Highway

MANY THANKS

DOUGIE

PREFACE

Helen has always said that when I meet or speak to someone for the first time I tell him or her my life's story, so here it is! I feel very grateful to have grown up in a period where it was safe to go camping at thirteen, to cycle around Scotland when there weren't many cars on the roads, to play in a band in the sixties, and to work in Fairfield's shipyard at the time of the UCS crisis. I have also been fortunate to be in the position to leave my job in the shipyard at 42 to pursue my two great loves, art and music. I could not have done this without the support from my wife Helen, our daughters Tracey and Pauline, and especially Helen's dad Bert. He did so much for us from the time we moved in with him in 1989 after the sudden death of his wife Nellie. I am also glad to have had the pleasure of watching my granddaughter Louise growing up, and when we thought she would be our only grandchild, along came Rosslyn, Zander and Helenna. This is for all of them!

Travelling on Life's Highway

Jim Collins

Published by Jim Collins

Printed by Book Empire
www.bookempire.co.uk
Unit 7, Lotherton Way, Garforth, Leeds, LS25 2JY

Printed in Great Britain

First Edition

ISBN 978-191-3319-89-2

Acknowledgements

I could not have published my story without help from others. Back in 2002, my schoolfriend Bob McGoran, English teacher gave me advice and corrected my many grammatical errors etc. When my Mother passed in 2003, I put my memoirs on hold. At the beginning of 2021 after being in Lockdown for most of 2020, I decided to finish what I had started in 1998. Then in February 2021, my good friend Bill Kerr took over the task that Bob started nearly 20 years ago. Thank you Bill for making sense of my nonsense. I could not have done this without the lifetime of support from my wife Helen and daughters Tracey and Pauline. I would like to thank Frank Donnelly for putting up with me while playing music together and driving me to and from gigs for 48 years.

Photographs

I would like to thank the following for allowing me use their photographs. John Keachie, Charlie Gilmour, Anne Oldfield, Susan Steel, Willie Scott, Steve Hunter and David Rees. Thanks also to David Reid for giving me permission to use the photograph of his oil portrait of me.

Poems

Thank you Polly Hamilton and Dr Anne Lorne Gillies for the poems you both wrote for me, and also for allowing me to publish them here.

Thanks also to musicians, Joe Short, Allan Craig, Andy Neil, Johnny Campbell, Frank Sutton, Dougie Henderson, jackson Clarkin, Ian (Busby) McCallum, Alex Stenhouse, Ronnie Young and George Nimmo. Thank you mum and dad, Pauline Collins, Martin Tierney, John Young, Iain Morrison, John Gray, Bill Gallagher, Eric Mackie, David Millar, Ron Culley, John McLaughlin, Mick Gallagher, Ben Donnelly, Ian Cooper, Polly Hamilton, Bill Kerr and Sam Stellard.

Contents

Travelling on Life's Highway.

As you travel on along life's highway
Keep in close contact with your family,
It's a strange strange road but you have to push on
Travelling on life's highway.

Always wear a smile even though you frown
Have a friend to turn to when you're down,
A friend in need is a friend indeed
Travelling on life's highway.

Sometimes you're happy, sometimes you're sad,
Don't worry 'bout a thing it's never quite as bad

You may struggle on with a heavy load
Don't despair as the burden, will ease, instead
Keep your thoughts upon the road ahead,
Travelling on life's highway.

The road can be short; the journey can be long,
Sometimes you're right, sometimes you're wrong,

Do not be afraid to admit your mistakes,
Travelling on life's highway.
You'll survive if you've got what it takes,
To travel on life's highway.

Chapter 1

"Now then" as my sculptor friend Ian Cooper would say. Last month I turned forty two and today, after twenty one years, I am walking out of the shipyard gates for "New Beginnings". It was Friday 16 June 1989 and we had moved from Glasgow to Irvine at the end of the month. Helen's dad had asked us if we would consider moving in with him after the sad loss of his wife Nellie in April, and as I was leaving the yard, we used my redundancy money to purchase his house from the council. I had also promised my sister Chris that if I left the yard we would come to visit her in the Caribbean, so we booked flights for the month of July. The yard had made an agreement with Social Security that anyone who took voluntary redundancy would go on unemployment benefit immediately, so I signed on and informed them that I intended to start Enterprise Allowance as a self employed artist. You had to be in receipt of benefits for 3 months before starting but they sent me to an awareness day where you would get all the information and application forms you required. I discovered that if you had a business account then you should close it and apply one year from the date of closing. Although I had an account to which held the sales from my hobby I could not apply for Enterprise Allowance for another year. This was a major setback for me at this time as I had organised three exhibitions for the following year. Putting it behind me for the time being, I contacted my friend Jim Nelson to get the names and contact numbers for hotels in London which were near the tube stations for the line that goes to Heathrow Airport. We booked a hotel for the third of July and arranged for Jim and Maureen to meet us there for dinner. We spent a lovely evening catching up with all the gossip, as we had not seen Jim and Maureen since they had moved to London many years before. We flew out to Antigua the next morning. It was a nine and a half hour flight to Antigua where we would catch the connecting flight to Anguilla. It was very hot and windy when we stepped off the plane and also quite a walk to the terminal building. We relaxed in the bar drinking rum punches to pass the time until our next flight. My sister had forewarned me that if it was delayed, not to worry as it was a usual occurence in the Caribbean. We got talking to a man who had come on the same flight as us. His mother was dying and he was going to visit her in the Dominican Republic. He was also going to meet his brother who he had not seen for forty years. I bought him a drink and after a few more, he asked us how much we had paid for our flight with British Airways. When we told him, he went spare as he had paid double the price and his connecting flight was also delayed. His flight arrived before ours and as he staggered along the tarmac he shouted abuse at British Airways. Eventually our Liat airline flight arrived and we were given a complimentary drink on board as an apology for the delay. It was a small plane, which hopped from one small island to the next until it finally arrived at Anguilla. After we went through customs, Chris and Paul were waiting to take us to their home, which was on a cliff top overlooking Sandy Ground and Road Bay. It was

dark when we arrived so we didn't have the benefit of the view until the next morning. We also met our nephew Jonathan for the first time. He was a sweet child of sixteen months who strolled around naked most of the time and could swim like a fish in the sea with his eyes open. The Mariner was the only hotel on the island at that time, and as Chris and Paul knew the manageress, we had access to the swimming pool and open air

jacuzzi. We went to a party at a friend's house on our second night where there was a local man playing keyboards and an electric guitar which sat there awaiting my arrival. I must say that I was impressed with the soca music which was played in the bars and on the radio. Chris and Paul had our itinerary laid out for the four weeks we were to spend there. Wherever I went, I had a need to explore and as Paul owned a bicycle, I went off on a run to Island Harbour one morning. It was very easy going there as it was downhill, but on my return, the wind was been blowing in my face, so when I arrived at the house, my hair was standing straight up and my face was like a beetroot. To avoid sunstroke I was given three pints of diluting orange, which I devoured in no time at all. My face was covered with aloe vera and I went to bed for the rest of the day. Luckily I was fine the following day. We always ate outside on the verandah where huge lizards would cheekily come seeking food. We also watched crabs coming right up the cliff where there was running water. As soon as you went near them they would go in their shells and tumble back down the slope. In the evenings there were also huge land crabs.

On the fourteenth of July we all went to Nevis for four days. Our accommodation was like a Swiss Chalet on a hillside with its own small swimming pool and a view of St Kitts across the sea from us. Have you ever tried to open a coconut? Let me tell you it's not easy, even with a cleaver. One had fallen from a tree where we were staying and it took me forever to get the nut out. I went into a record store in Nevis and ordered a tape of Bob Marley. I paid for it and they said it would be delivered to our accommodation. I was surprised when it arrived by police land rover the following evening and handed to me by the policeman who was in the shop when I placed the order. Nevis is a small Island so most of our time was spent relaxing by the pool. Back to Anguilla for another five days before Helen and I travelled to Puerto Rico for three days. Our accommodation in San Juan was lovely and quite central. We took a trip into the rain forest where we drank a coconut liqueur from the shell of a coconut. The scenery was amazing. Back in San Juan I remember turning a corner to see the huge bow of a cruise ship in front of me. I have never seen ships as beautiful as the two, which were in that harbour. One was The Sovereign of the Seas and the other, Jubilee. We had dinner one evening at a restaurant and were entertained by a flamenco dancer. While we were in San Juan my three weeks of mosquito and sand fly bites were getting me down as

my ankles were covered in blisters and I had to visit a pharmacy to get something for them. During our four weeks we went twice to St Martin, which is partially owned by France and Holland, so we managed to see different cultures in all the islands we visited. One day I went into the Valley with Paul, and while he visited his dental surgery I went wandering. I heard the sound of steel drums coming from what looked like a community hall. I walked up and saw that they were making steel drums. The making of a beautiful musical instrument from an oil drum is a really skilled task. Each area, which will result in a musical note, is chalked and beaten until the required note is achieved. The person who was in charge of the workshop came from Trinidad and went to the Royal Academy of Music in London. He played Beatles tunes for me before I left. As I strolled along after stopping at a little roadside bar for a passion fruit drink served by a Rastafarian, I heard this drumbeat. When I arrived at the source of this wonderful sound, there was a small boy banging away on a cardboard box. I carried on to Crocus Bay and introduced myself to a couple of Chris and Paul's friends who had a bar there. I had a beer and a chat before making my way back to the surgery to get a run home. On another day out on Paul's bike I came across an art gallery in the middle of nowhere. I walked in and the walls were covered in paintings from floor to ceiling. In a corner sat an artist painting away. His name was Ben and he charged two US dollars for entry. For this, you got a drink as he has a small bar tucked away. I spent hours with him talking about art and music and sinking umpteen rum punches, free of course. After a while two of his friends arrived with a case of beer and we had a right ding-dong. I'm afraid I was a little unsteady riding the bike back home that afternoon but that's OK man, we're in the Caribbean. The highlight of my holiday was playing with the local reggae band in Jonno's beach bar at Sandy Ground. I did "Knocking on Heaven's Door" and "No Woman No Cry" and I don't know how the guitarist played that instrument as the strings were about a centimetre from the fretboard. On a previous visit to this establishment we were sitting next to the American martial arts actor Chuck Norris who had a holiday home on the Island. My worst experience was at a party where all the women sat together and the men were sat at the opposite end of the verandah. The Attorney General was at this and I was not involved in their highbrow conversations. I felt like a wallflower and the more wine I drank, the more I wanted to uproot and take off. I managed to keep my cool and survived this terrible evening. We went to a birthday party and I did a painting as a present. I hadn't taken my paints with me so one of the local ex pat's had loaned me theirs in order to do this, so I have left my mark on Anguilla. During our stay, a British warship arrived and anchored out from the Island. When this happened, any British residents got the opportunity to either visit the ship on a certain evening, or go to a party at the Governor's residence where the ship's officers were. We decided to visit the ship and were taken out in a small boat to embark on the portable stairway, which was lowered down the side. We had a great evening and stayed longer than anyone else as Paul had been talking to the Captain. When it came time to leave we had to disembark over the side on a rope ladder and then jump on to the launch. You can imagine Chris and Helen with their high-heeled shoes, which they had to throw on to the launch before jumping. We left Anguilla on the first of August and I had the runs all through the flight including the shuttle to Glasgow. Our daughter Pauline went to stay with Chris and Paul for the month of August. When we arrived back in Irvine Helen's dad had spent the last month flooring the attic so that I could work there. We bought Tracey a second hand car so that she could commute to her job in Glasgow.

Helen's dad drove her to Glasgow to her work for a year before she got a transfer to Fencedyke Primary School, which is only a five-minute walk from our house. I had to sign off the unemployment register while we were away so I signed back on

when we returned. I began painting in the attic, as I had to prepare for my three exhibitions in 1990. I wrote the following song in 1994 as an account of my musical Caribbean adventure. In reality, the man teaching the locals how to make steel drums was from Trinidad and attended the Royal Academy of Music in London. The steel drum player in the band at Jonno's was the best player on the Island.

The Trinidad Man

Far across the ocean, over the sea
Me play music with 'e' Trinidad man, in the caribbee

Me go on a Caribbean holiday
Play the guitar at a party
Soca music reggae music come from an organ
African music played by African man
Me stay with I sister on Anguilla Island
Looking across to St. Martin highland
Down at Jonno's bar were a local band
That where me play with the Trinidad man

Me walk down the road one day
Me hear the steel drum play
Go to investigate what go on
That when me meet the Trinidad man
E teachy local man to makey drum
Makey makey music bum bum bum
Studied at the Royal Academy
He played Beatle music just for me

Strolling along in the Valley
Me hear a rhythm come from far away
Inquisition makes I follow that sound
Me see a little boy sitting on the ground
He play a soca music on cardboard box
Me listen and watch, lying on the rocks

Just a little boy, who can
One day play like e Trinidad man

     I got a call on the first week of September 1989 from a researcher for STV. She wanted to know if a film crew could come and visit me to do a piece on me for the daily six o'clock news program Scotland Today. They came the following day and it was put out on Friday the eighth. It was a bit of a squeeze in my small attic as there were camera, sound, lighting men, along with the interviewer Stephen Jardine and I. While the technical crew was setting up, Stephen was keeping me calm by firing questions at me. When they were ready, I was to climb up the straight ladder to the attic, walk over to my easel, pick up my palette and brush and begin painting. I climbed the ladder and hit my head off the overhead beam. Someone shouted, "Cut!" I replied, "Is it?" I have never done that before, or since, and I've been up and down thousands of times but it'll be 'Alright on the night.' I was chuffed when I saw what they had done to make the interview more interesting to the public. It began with newsreader Angus Simpson talking about me before showing black and white footage of the yard with Stephen Jardine's voice in the background talking about the decline of the shipbuilding industry. It then went on to show the yard as it was at present before moving to me climbing up the ladder and being interviewed. Angus Simpson phoned me a couple of days later to say that Sydney Devine was interested in my work and would it be alright if they gave him my phone number. Well I got the call and there was no doubt who was on the other end. I told Sydney that I didn't want to sell just now as I was building up work for next year's exhibitions. Months later I went down to see him at the Harbour Lights pub that he owned at the time. He was looking for bargains and I wasn't giving away any! It bothered me that I could not apply for enterprise allowance because of my honesty in declaring my earnings so I went to their place in Kilmarnock and asked to speak to the Manager. I had taken my accounts for previous years and after explaining my position, since I had been to the awareness day I was told to start on the following Monday. This meant that I would be self-employed and get £80 every fortnight for the next year. I still had to have £1000 in a business account or an overdraft facility of the same amount. I had been using the TSB bank for years and thought that it should be no problem getting an overdraft facility but I was proved wrong. Being rather annoyed with this situation I went to the Royal Bank and after speaking with the Business Manager, I went back to the TSB and drew all my money from my personal account. I used my credit card to draw out what was needed to make it up to £1000 and returned to the Royal to deposit it in a Business account.

On Monday October 30 1989 I began my first day as a full time artist, forty-two years old and excited about my future. I worked steady, seven days a week at various times of the day and got a call from Frank Little of Glasgow's Transport Museum to discuss the possibility of an exhibition. I met with him on Monday November 27 and he said that he was proposing to the Directors that I have an exhibition mid January through to February. He phoned on Wednesday December 13 to let me know that the Directors had agreed and could he come to Irvine the following day for a preliminary selection. He came along and selected the exhibition but there was still no date as it could get squeezed out if anything major came along. On the fifteenth of January Frank came and took away seven paintings and photographs of my work for approval. I finally got the decision on the nineteenth of January that my exhibition would open on February 15 and close on the first of April. This was a fine start to my new career. John McNeil, Production Director at Kvaerner Govan phoned and asked me to do an artist's impression of yard redevelopment. This was a new challenge for me and I met with him at the Govan yard the following day. He gave me a model and photographs of the new tank assembly shop and told me what was required to be included in the painting. I began working on it that evening until 2am the following morning. It took me forty-one hours

10

to complete and I delivered it to Mr. McNeil on the thirtieth of January 1990 for the fee of £300. Ian Lang, Minister of State for Industry and Education in Scotland unveiled my impression on February12, which was shown on Scotland Today that evening. The impression was reproduced in a handout, which was distributed to the workforce to let them know the improvements that were being made in the yard to increase production. My exhibition "The Art of Shipbuilding" opened at The Transport Museum with The Scotsman and Glasgow Herald attending. I then had two interviews at Radio Clyde with Jimmy Mack and Mike Lloyd. Both Interviews were recorded to be put out later, so I had no fear about being live on air. I found that I was more fluent with Jimmy Mack as he was laughing all the time where as Mike Lloyd was dreary. This reflected on my interview, as I couldn't get into the spirit of my impressive subject. I was happy with the exhibition layout as it had models of the Norsea and a crane to complement my paintings. I got a call from a researcher at Radio Scotland on 27 February to go over questions for an interview with Jimmy Mc Gregor on "McGregor's Gathering" which would be live on Thursday 8 March. While I was on the air someone

called the station to commission me to do a painting of Lobby Dosser from a statue, which would soon be erected in Glasgow, but it came to nothing in the end. I went to the Transport Museum on the last day of my exhibition to get the reaction from visitors. I met many interesting people and all comments were positive. I took Frank Little for lunch on April 12 as he was leaving the Museum to work at Summerlea Industrial Heritage Museum, Coatbridge. On Thursday 26 April 1990 I went to a press conference for Bill Bryden's epic production "The Ship" which would be opening later in the year in the old engine shop of the former Harland and Wolff yard in Govan. I had spoken the previous year to Eddie Jackson who was to be the Producer of "The Ship". I thought that with my background and present circumstances that I should have some involvement in the project. It was quite exciting that day as the conference was held in the engine shop, which would be turned into a theatre. A model of "The Ship" was presented and the engineering of it described by the show's designer Bill Dudley. The engine shop was split in two, as there was a row of beams in the middle. "The Ship" would be constructed in one half of the engine shop by ex shipyard workers who would also act in the promenade production. The stage in the centre would be stationary and occupied by an agreed number of the audience, which would be determined by health and safety. On either side of the stage railway sleepers were laid at an incline with a single track on each side. The three-decked ship would rest on these rails allowing it to be launched but leaving the central stage behind. The members of the audience occupying the ship would disembark and assemble in the other half of the engine shop to view the launch. Those in centre stage, including the band, would remain stationary as "The Ship" left them behind gently moving down the ramp to the sound of music. The cast would perform among the audience, both on centre stage and at various points of the structure. The prospect of being involved in something as ambitious as this was exciting. I had a chat with Bill Dudley, and Eddie said he would be in touch. I Collected paintings from the Transport Museum on Saturday 28 April and took them to the Scottish Amicable insurance building in the city centre for my next exhibition. My paintings hadn't been for sale at the Transport Museum but they would be here so I stayed all day on Monday 30 April and sold nothing. "What a waste of time!" The show closed on Friday 11 May and I had sold nothing. Before collecting my work that evening I went to pay insurance for my next exhibition in the Pearce Institute, Govan. I also went to Framemaker Gallery in King Street to ask for an estimate of my picture-framing bill, which was £1300. So here I was with two exhibitions under my belt, sold nothing and £1300 in debt. My new career did not look as if it was going to be prosperous although I had received a lot of publicity.

12 May. 43 today and a little unsure of my future!

My exhibition in Govan's Pearce Institute opened on Saturday 26 May 1990. I had a really good turnout and two paintings were reserved. The show ran until 9 June and was well received and

14

attended by shipyard workers, most of whom I knew. I was in attendance every day, working on a five foot by four oil painting titled "Links". The Managing Director of Kvaerner Govan Steinar Draegebo had purchased my painting "The Art of Shipbuilding II" and I delivered it to his home following the closing of the exhibition. Bobby Carey, a friend of mine from my time in the Govan yard had said to me at my Transport Museum exhibition that when his wife Mary saw my painting of the Norsea titled "Homeport", she said to him, "I want that". I wanted to show the painting at Govan so I also delivered that painting to Bobby and Mary after the show. My fourth exhibition that year at the Harbour Arts Centre Irvine opened on Sunday 24 June and I sold a pastel portrait of a shipyard worker to

Douglas Tharby and Joan Fraser. It was a painting of one of my friends in the yard, Dougie Noble. They bought it because Douglas said that it reminded him of his grandfather. I actually titled it "Noble Dougie" because I thought that he looked distinguished. Mr. Tharby was the marketing consultant I had while taking business seminars as part of the agreement for being on Enterprise Allowance. On 18 July 1990 Steinar Draegebo commissioned me to do a painting of the first liquid gas tank carrier built by Kvaerner Govan. The first ship was to be named Helice and the painting would be a panorama of the yard with the ship sitting on the slipways. The QE2 visited Greenock on Wednesday 25 July 1990. I was there all day. It was a wonderful sight as the Waverley paddle steamer went to meet "The Queen" as she sailed into port. Greenock was buzzing all day and the sun shone for them all.

Feeling a lot happier now that my finances were in a better state Helen and I went off to Paris for a week. We stayed at a hotel in the student area, just off the Boulevard St. Michel. All the major attractions were within walking distance. Notre - Dame Cathedral was just down the hill from us, and The Louvre not much farther. We went right to the top of the Eiffel Tower where the viewing platform was surrounded in wire mesh so that no one could jump off. I managed to squeeze my head through the mesh so that I could take photographs looking straight down to capture the splay of the tower's legs. I would drag Helen for miles every day and we would always end up cooling off our feet in the fountains at the foot of the tower. We spent a day at Monmartre visiting the impressive Sacre Coeur church and watched the street artists at work in the square round the corner from it. We found that it was not as expensive in Monmartre as it was in central Paris so we returned one evening to have dinner and catch the sights like the Moulin Rouge at night. Unfortunately the poor artist and his wife could not afford to go in and see the show. We could not be in Paris and neglect a visit to the Louvre. Going by the size of queue in front of us it looked as if we would be waiting for hours to get in but we didn't have to wait too long. It was hot and humid at that time of the year and after going to the room which housed the Mona Lisa, I had to get out. I couldn't believe the sight before me as hundreds of tourists, camera held arms stretched in the air, were trying to take a photograph of the small painting behind a glass cage. I'm afraid I lost interest and walked out without seeing it. We enjoyed our break in Paris and would hope to return sometime in the future.

I dismantled my exhibition at the Harbour Arts Centre on Thursday 16 August and brought the paintings home. I met with

Eddie Jackson on 21 August and The Ship's Company had agreed that my work would be hung for sale in the two hospitality rooms for the duration of the play. Eddie also said that they would commission me to do a painting as a gift to the main sponsor GEC. By then the construction of The Ship was well underway and Eddie said that I should be seen sketching so I had the freedom of the massive temporary theatre. There had been a need for artist's studio space in Cunninghame District so a group of artists and craftworkers, including myself, had our first meeting on 27 August 1990. I spent four hours sketching at The Ship on my first visit on Thursday 30 August 1990. On one of my sketching days I was sitting on the stage drawing when Roy Fitzsimmons appeared. I hadn't seen him for years and he was now teaching art in a secondary school. He was surprised to see me as he thought I was still working in the shipyard. I took my paintings to the hospitality rooms on Wednesday 5 September and began to position where they would hang. I had gone to the toilet and when I returned, Jimmy Logan was standing over my paintings that were laid on the floor. He thought they were wonderful and asked me if I had been in the Glasgow Art Club. As I hadn't, he said that he would take me for lunch one day. On Friday 7 September 1990 the first ship Helice was launched along at Kvaerner Govan so I went along to take photographs before hanging my work at "The Ship". I watched the first dress rehearsal of "The Ship" on Monday 10 September and took notes of certain scenes that I should photograph for reference. The following day I purchased 1000 a.s.a. film for my camera and got permission to photograph that night's performance. I delivered my commission on the 12th to Steinar Draegebo at Kvaerner Govan and he was delighted with it so I took it away to be framed. I attended another meeting regarding studio space in Irvine on Monday 17 September and photographed the matinee of The Ship on the 19th September, got the film developed and returned to photograph the evening's performance.

THE SHIP

The Epic Story of a River and it's People.

Written and directed by Bill Bryden
Designed by Bill Dudley
Produced by Eddie Jackson
Music composed by John Tams
Musical Director: Phil Cunningham
Lighting: Mark Henderson

The play opened with The Ship's band accompanying the voice of Rod Paterson. The cast appeared centre stage happy that they had an order for a ship. I did a painting of the next scene "The Dummy's Bunnet", which included James Grant as the yard foreman, John Murtagh, and Neil McKinven. John played a moving part in portraying the dummy, and also the young Neil as a Catholic boy who had just started in the yard. The laying of the keel was a marvelous piece of artistic direction and also my favourite scene. An H beam was lowered down slowly from above two rows of actors facing each other and in between them; a channel in the stage had been opened up to receive the beam which represented the keel. The cast raised their arms up and inward to steady the beam and guide it through the channel. James Grant was like Christ on the Cross as he stood at the centre of the bandstand with a whistle in his mouth and his arms outstretched to guide the operation. When the beam had been put in position he jumped on to it and walked it's length, and behind him, the stage panels were closed alternately left then right, bang bang bang bang, until the beam was concealed below. The late Jimmy Logan played the shipyard boss and Tom Watson gave his usual excellent performance as the elderly, but not retired unemployed worker, in a pub scene where he met with the shipyard workers at lunchtime and gave them his worldly patter. Derek Lord was the Black Squad foreman and Boys Brigade Master. Each performance had boys from various BB troupes around Glasgow marching throughout the stage and causing the audience to move aside to avoid them as they changed direction. Topics such as religion, industrial injuries, and the type of passengers who would sail on this magnificent vessel were discussed. There was a humorous New Year scene when the women appeared at various levels of the ship, representing them hanging out of the windows of tenement buildings. The shipyard was to close after this order was completed and every time I experienced the launch of "The Ship", a single tear would run from an eye. Andrew Byatt, Jake Darcy, Brian Pettifer, Joe Mullaney and Freddie Boardley were The Black Squad. Phil McCall, William McBain, Billy Armour and Joe Brady played joiners. Hugh Martin played the publican. Juliet Cadzow, Mary Riggans, Jan Wilson, Sandra McNeeley and Victoria Nairn played both wives and workers. It was an exciting time for me as I mingled with all these famous Scottish actors. The band was Phil Cunningham, keyboards and

accordion, Wendy Weatherby, cello, Taj Wyzgowski, guitar, Mike Travis, drums, Neil Hay, bass, (deseased), and Rod Paterson, vocals.

I sold pastel portraits to Jake Darcy, John Murtagh, Derek Lord, Hugh Martin and Joe Mullaney. Mary Riggans had asked me to do her in a scene with Victoria Nairn. I spent twenty-seven and a half hours on it and it cost £50 to have the oil framed. When I presented it to her, she said that she had a huge tax bill to pay from her time in Take the High Road and she couldn't afford it. This was the only disappointment I had. I was impressed with the effect the rays from the welder's arcs had in the darkness of the theatre. In the shipyard it was always lit wherever anyone worked and you did not see this magical experience. I would employ this effect into my future shipyard paintings and include it in my commission for The Ship's Company. I also did paintings of The Laying of the Keel, and Reminiscing, which saw Hugh Martin, Phil McCall and Joe Brady talking about what was once the shipyard. I also did pastel portraits of Jimmy Logan, Andy Byatt, and Tom Watson, which they did not buy but that was fine. On October 25 I took a colour sketch to Eddie Jackson as my study for the commission but he didn't like it. He said that the ideal picture would be from the bar area looking over to the ship's side. I watched that evening's performance from the viewpoint he mentioned and understood what was required.

After the meeting with Eddie I met with Ron Culley, the Director of Govan Initiative Ltd. He said that the Company would like to use 12 of my works for their 1991 calendar. I took slides of my work along to Govan Initiative the following day and left them. That evening I tried to paint the scene from the bar area. I had done a sketch from that position before the play began and when there was light. I had a torch in one hand and a brush in the other trying the impossible.

Meanwhile, Deliverance had been playing in Finlay's at Burns Statue Square, Ayr on Thursday's during September and October 1990. One of those evenings, a guy came to us at our break and asked us if we could play any Kinks, as his mate was the drummer in the band. We looked over the bar and sure enough, it was Mick Avery. He came over and had a chat with Dougie as they were both drummers and with Dougie's past success in the Marmalade, they had more to talk about than the rest of our band. When we went back up to do our second set we did You Really Got Me and Mick sent us up a round of drinks.

I was invited to exhibit my paintings from The Ship in Cunninghame Arts Council road show at Barrfields Pavilion, Largs on Sunday 28 October. This was a one-day annual event, which went to a different Town within Cunninghame district each year. I joined Cunninghame Arts Council that day. They had formed a year earlier in 1989.

I began the commissioned painting of The Ship on Tuesday 30 October. After showing it to Eddie, he said it was required for the middle of the following week. I finished the painting by the following Wednesday at 2pm after 63 Hours work and took it through to "The Ship" for Eddie's approval. The next day was a busy one as I had an appointment at 9am with Govan Initiative to decide on the 12 works that were to be used for their calendar. From there I went to "The Ship" to pick up my commissioned painting as it was being presented to Sir Robert Easton in Yarrow's at 11.30am. My wee legs were shaking, as there were photographers from the Glasgow Herald, Daily Record, Scotsman, Evening Times, and Clydebank Post. And there I was, dressed in white boiler suit and helmet with Eddie Jackson, Bill Bryden and Sir Robert Easton with the workers shouting at me, including one of Helen's cousin's husband, big Sam Mooney. After the press left we all went up to the boardroom for lunch. When we finished eating Sir Robert looked at his watch, he left the table and returned with Yarrow's ties and golf umbrellas for us all, which was a slight hint for our dispersal. "The Ship's" last performance was to be on Saturday 10 October 1990 and as I couldn't be there due to playing a gig at Nitshill Bowling Club, I went on the previous night. As this would be the last time I would see the performance, when it came to the launch the tears flowed from my eyes. Bill Bryden must have felt good, as he turned round to see the state I was in. I actually had to walk from the platform and find a dark corner until I pulled myself together. I explained to him that I could not make the following night but he saw me on the Saturday afternoon matinee when I was delivering portraits to members of the cast and he said to me, "I thought you wouldn't be back." I told him why I was there and that I would return with Helen, our daughter Tracey and Bert for the party after the night's performance. We had a brilliant night as the place and everyone that was there were buzzing. A Cajun band was playing on "The Ship" and the drink flowed into the small hours. I had taken my guitar and went up to play during the band's break. I wouldn't think anyone was impressed as I was rather pissed, but then again, so was everyone else. I took my paintings down from the hospitality rooms on the Monday and brought them home. I took some of them to Framemaker Gallery at King Street, Glasgow on Thursday 15 November, collected Mr Draegebo's framed commission, and delivered it to him at Kvaerner. I also took the information on the twelve works that were being used in Govan Initiative's calendar to them so that it could be passed on to the printer.

I had got friendly with Billy Armour who used to play Hamish in Take the High Road. We arranged to meet up in Glasgow on Monday 19 November at lunchtime. He took me to the Queens Club, which was in a basement in Queen Street. We descended a steep flight of stairs to enter the premises, and by luck, it was the president's birthday. Caterers were laying out the tables for a slap up meal. The starters were half melons filled with fruit, and a half bottle of vodka was equally poured into each portion. We remained there all afternoon and then went to a pub at The Barras where Billy's son in law worked until contacting Bert to pick us up. We went to Billy's house in Rutherglen where Bert had a coffee while we had a whisky. Billy tried to hypnotise Bert and he said he felt himself going before telling me it was time to go home.

I collected my cheque from The Ship on Thursday 22nd November and went to Govan Initiative the following day to have my photograph taken for the calendar. Helen's brother Raymond had been working in Millport so Bert and I went over with him on 5 December. This was the first time I had been on Cumbrae. We used Raymond's van to drive round the island while he worked, then spent the rest of the day in the pub. While I was doing the business seminars for Enterprise Allowance, I met Pamela Beattie who had just graduated from Art School and was like-minded. She had an exhibition opening on Friday the seventh at The Jougs, Kilmaurs, where she lived. I went along and discovered that the exhibition was shared with her mother who ran the local Art Club. Pamela's mother was originally from Irvine and her dad was putting a book together. I took the paintings whose images were used for the calendar along to Govan Initiative on 13 December and collected some calendars. I sold a painting of Kvaerner's first ship Helice on 20th to Lief Nordbo who was taking it to Norway. Ron Culley had arranged for me to display my calendar paintings at Strathclyde Regional Headquarters the following day as all the councilors were being given calendars. Govan Initiative bought three of the paintings. I cleared my picture-framing bill on 22 December so that I would go in to the next year with no debt. I must say that I could not have framed the paintings I had been exhibiting that year without receiving the credit and trust from Sandy, Sheila, Richard and John at Framemaker Gallery, King St., Glasgow. I had produced 59 paintings mostly oils in that busy time since November1989 until the end of December 1990. Iain Murray bought my painting of **The Shipwright** whose image was used for the 1991 calendar. This was a tribute to Davy Welsh, another of my shipwright friends, who had sadly died of cancer.

I visited Tom McKendrick's Submarine exhibition at the MacLaurin Gallery in Ayr on 23 January 1991. I was aware of Tom's work but this was the first exhibition of his I had been to and I was amazed at the quality and sheer scale of his project.

Billy Armour called me on the phone and asked me to bring Helen and a bottle to the end of Panto' party at the Tron Theatre on

Sunday 27 January. We met Dorothy Paul, John Stahl, Eric Cullen, Dean Park, Jan Wilson, Phil McCall and his wife Kate. Helen had too much drink and Jan Wilson took her into a garden area in the middle of the Tron and told her to stick her fingers down her throat, "and you'll feel a lot better hen. I've been here often". Big John Stahl ended up carrying her out to the car over his shoulder. We both thought Dorothy Paul was a wonderful person and so friendly.

Tom's Submarine exhibition had moved to the Dick Institute in Kilmarnock and I went along on Saturday 16 February in the afternoon. It was looking much better than it did in the MacLaurin, as Tom was able to erect the large framework which surrounded the submarines with water tanks at its top and lights shining through to throw reflected light onto the vessels.

Much of February 1991 was spent at Irvine's Ravenspark Academy constructing the hull of a ship in clay under the supervision of art teacher Jerry Hendeson.

I met Tom McKendrick and his wife Christine for the first time at the Dick Institute on Thursday 7 March. He said that he would send me an invitation to the preview of his exhibition on the Clydebank Blitz. This was his previous major show and was being brought together for the fiftieth anniversary of the "Blitz". It was being shown in Clydebank Town Hall on 13 March. Here was another opportunity to view the talents of this fine Scottish artist.

One of my cousins, Ronnie Collins, had been separated from his wife at this time. She was living in Bourtreehill with their son David. David was tragically knocked down and killed by a car on the Towerlands Road. The funeral was on 16 April 1991.

I saw another fine Scottish artist's work at his preview in the Visitor's Centre, Eglinton Country Park on 18 April. He was Stuart

Miller of Kilwinning. Stuart had been living successfully in London as an artist since his graduation.

The two paintings I had submitted to the Royal Scottish Academy in 1991 were both rejected. Oh well, try try again!

I was invited to Cunninghame Arts Council's AGM on Sunday 28 April and was talked into joining the executive committee by Cunninghame District Council's Director of Leisure Mick Gallagher. I was also invited by the Ayrshire Leader to preview the exhibition "Clyde Built" in the Scottish Maritime Museum Irvine on Thursday 2 May.

Steinar Draegebo bought my painting **Taking the Strain** on the 18th, and allowed me to exhibit it in my next exhibition at The Valley Arc, Glengarnock.

I went to see the Stanley Spencer exhibition **Canvassing the Clyde** at Glasgow's Kelvingrove Art Gallery on 21st May. Being a shipbuilder myself I noticed some misrepresentation in his work, but on the whole, he did a fine job of depicting shipbuilding on the lower reaches of the Clyde during the Second World War.

My preview was well attended on Friday 24 May and Billy Armour came through from Rutherglen armed with his camera which I thought was so kind. My exhibition was to open the second Cunninghame Arts Festival. The following morning local photographer Vinnie Walker and I were to occupy for the next two weeks, the former Paige shop at the corner of Bridgegate and High Street Irvine. This venue would be used as an information point for the festival and included an exhibition of paintings by local artists, along with woodcarvings and ceramics. Vinnie had been photographing Queens and Marys for the District Council during the annual Marymass Festival. He filled the window on the High Street with his entire Marymass photo collection and got a good response from the community. Alex Quigg came in every day and sat with his work while I worked on two paintings, **Bow Assembly** and **The**

Caulker. Alex had a nephew, Stephen Quigg, who was a renowned folk singer from Saltcoats. The response from the public to our project was so great that after an announcement about it by Willie Freckleton on Westsound Radio's Cunninghame Close Up, a journalist from the Ayrshire Leader appeared the following day resulting in a fine article about the place finally being used as it was an eyesore when closed.

The artists exhibiting were Louise Turmine, Susan Porteous, Hugh Loney, Pamela A. Beattie and I, with ceramics by Marianne Paterson and wood carving by Alex Quigg. Most days we would get a visit from Ron Smart's dad Arthur. Like Ron, his father was a fine artist and a well-respected gentleman in Irvine. We used to make him a coffee and he would sit and watch me painting and throw in a little criticism now and again. This public display led me to meeting a six-year-old girl called Cherylanne Glen. Her drawings and paintings were excellent and she could grasp perspective at that early age. We had a party in the shop the day after the festival closed and Hugh Loney brought along these huge chalk drawings to cover the windows and give us some privacy. Sarah Proudler was the Community Arts Officer for the Council at that time. Louise and Susan moved to Australia in late 1992. The shop we were in became The Stationery Box and is now Council Offices that include the Irvine Registration Office.

Chapter 2

I was born at sixty four Braidcraft Road, Pollok, Glasgow, on the twelfth of May 1947. My mother's maiden name was Bremner and her family came to Pollok from Thistle Street in the Gorbals in November 1939. Her father came from Edinburgh and her Mother was brought up by her sisters after their parents died. Her grandmother on her father's side remarried and had two sons, John and Andrew Brown. My mother's first job at fourteen was in Miller & Lang's at Maxwell Drive where she put inserts into Christmas cards for the weekly wage of forty pence. She then moved to the Glasgow Bonding Company at 80 Duke Street making up orders for sixty-two and a half pence a week. She moved into the material department until she was seventeen when she was offered the job of supervisor. When she was twenty-one, she was advised to give up her job there because of the deterioration of her eyesight. When she left the Bond she worked once again at Maxwell Drive packing army rations for a short time before moving to a garden nursery, which became the MacDonald Hotel at Eastwood. There was an Italian P.O.W. camp along the road and my mother worked with three Italians in the nursery. During the Second World War she told me they had a corrugated Nissan hut in the living room of the house to shelter in during bombing raids. My father came from a large Irish family and was born and brought up in Newtoncunningham, County Donegal, Ireland. He was the oldest in a family of eleven. He had five brothers and the same number of sisters. They were Willie, John, Michael, Harry, Patsy, Grace, Gertie, Mary, Kathleen, Theresa, and dad, James. My granny's Collins' name was Grace McKeever and my grandfather's was Henry. I can't remember my granny Agnes Albert on my mother's side as she died in 1950 but I can vaguely recollect memories of my grandfather George. My mother had three sisters who were Jean, Peggy, and Jessie, and an adopted sister, Nan. She also had two brothers Arthur and George. George's wife Mary was my father's cousin. Mary's mother Kate Mc Bride was my granny's sister. George and Mary brought my dad over here when he was fifteen and he worked on a farm in Lanarkshire while staying with his Aunt Kate at Provanmill. As we lived in my mother's family home with her father and aunt Peggy, our family grew. My sister Gladys was born on 28 January 1951, Fred, 29 June 1953, and Christine 29 September 1957.

One of my earliest memories is going in my cowboy suit to see Roy Rogers, Dale Evans, and Trigger their palomino horse, at the Empire Theatre in 1954. I took boxing lessons at my first primary school, Damshot Road, as two brothers, John and Andrew Martin who lived next door to us at Braidcraft Road were bullying me.  They eventually moved to Airdrie. While at Damshot Road School I was knocked down by a briquette lorry that reversed as I ran behind it. Fortunately I only cut my head and did not require hospital treatment. Friends from primary school were Chris Paterson, Peter McInnes, Ian MacKinnon, Davie McColvin, Ian Stewart, Bob McGoran, Frank Sweeney, Frank Fitzpatrick, John Delaney, and Tony Scanlon.

 We used to play cricket on the central reservation of Maidland Road under guidance from an older lad, Headley Crowther. By climbing the railings at Damshot Road, we would make our way through fields and woods to Pollok Estate, eventually coming to Pollok House. This was one of my favorite places as it was my first taste of art appreciation. I especially liked an El Greco portrait and two small Goya's. One of the rooms had murals round it, which I used to admire. On a visit later in life, they had gone. I have returned many times over the years. We used to play a game in the dark nights called Chicky Melly at the houses in Damshot Road that were only on one side of the road with woods on the opposite side. We would tack black thread on to the wooden window frame with a small stone tied a couple of inches from the anchor and then hide in the woods. By pulling the thread

taught and letting it go the stone would tap the window. Then we would pull it taught again so that when the occupier came to the window they saw nothing. As soon as they closed the curtain again we would repeat it until they came out to discover our trick.

On seeing a film called "Run of the Arrow", we would paint our bodies and chase each other with sharpened bamboo arrows. It's just as well none of us were skilled archers as I am quite sure an arrow on target could have maimed, or even killed it's recipient. With my long legs, and fear, I was always well out of reach. One day while chasing Peter McInnes outside his home at Langton Road, I slipped on sand and the soda syphon I was carrying smashed, covering my arms and legs with shards of glass. In the autumn we would gather chestnuts at Barrhead Road and Pollok Estate. Damshot primary school was the annex of Braidcraft. We moved into Braidcraft for our last couple of years of primary education. The site where the school was is now a community centre. While there I used to buy three

penny gummed label pads and draw on them during lessons. I was always drawing at home and Chris Paterson's father used to say I was tracing and it used to annoy me. I suppose I was competent enough on leaving primary school as I went into the second highest class in secondary. I received a book from the headmistress Miss Flavin in the centre of the photo, for being top of the class once. I played football for the primary school. As I was tall, I wanted to be a goalkeeper. On my eleventh birthday I was playing outside my house when my father came off a bus and kicked a leather bladder [football] across the dual carriageway. When he crossed the road he gave me a goalie's strip. I was happy with my present but the school team had a keeper,

Joe Butler, so they made me centre half because of my height. I can only recall two hard boys from primary school, Peter Kenny, and Tommy Mac Donald. I had no problems with either of them but there was a boy called Leslie Winfield who challenged me to fight after school. I beat him and never had any problems with anyone after that. Some years later I read in the papers that he had been charged with the manslaughter of his girlfriend's child and was sent to prison.

My mother informs me that we went to granny's cottage in Ireland three times when I was young. I have a large scar on my right ankle where it was caught in the spokes of a bicycle while getting a

backie from my Uncle Harry when I was three or four years old. I was ten on my third visit so I must have been a baby the first time I went to Ireland. The cottage was in the country. Daily chores were, washing yourself in the morning from a tin bath, which sat under the drainpipe to catch rainwater, walking to a stream with buckets to get drinking water, and to a farm for milk. I remember feeding piglets and them licking my legs as I had short trousers on. One of the neighbouring farmers had a hay barn where I used to play along with his kids. Swinging from the top floor of the barn and landing on hay at the bottom was exciting. We always had fresh eggs and the odd chicken as granny had a chicken coup at the side of the cottage. One day my dad tied a hen's legs and hung it up in an outhouse. When he returned later to wring it's neck and pluck the feathers, it ran out of the door when he opened it. We took ages to recapture it as it ran up and down between hedging in the front garden. There were two castles nearby, Grianan, and Dunnan. While visiting one of them I reurned to the cottage with my legs covered in cleg bites. Granny covered them with kaolin poultice and I was laid up for a couple of days. I caught eels from Lough Swilly using a bent pin tied to fishing line. Granny was a wonderful baker and I'm sure my mum got a few tips from her. Buncrana was the nearest holiday resort to Newtoncunningham so we went there for the beach. We sailed to Londonderry on the cattle boat from the Clyde. I remember nearly everyone on the ship being violently ill on our last trip. It was surprising to see the police carrying guns when we disembarked the ship. I used to enjoy it when my dad took me to play snooker when he was based at Larkfield garage. In later years we would go for a drink after the game.

My first guitar was a plastic one, which had a contraption you strapped onto the neck. By pushing one of several buttons, it formed a chord on the guitar's four nylon strings. Chris Patterson was nine days older than me. He had got one of these guitars for his birthday on the third of May and I got mine on the twelfth of May 1959. Chris lived across the back from me in Binend Road and our parents were good friends. After a few months messing with my guitar, it lay for a couple of years until I was fourteen. When I heard the sound of The Shadow's "Apache", I was hooked, as were many other youngsters who would eventually become famous guitarists. Bob McGoran had moved from Carnock Road to Libo Avenue and I remember us trying to work out the chords to most of the songs from Elvis' GI Blues as his older sister Ellen had the album. I did the early morning milk run with Frank Fitzpatrick and Tony Scanlon, which gave me money to buy a cello acoustic guitar, and months later, an electric Harmony solid and an amplifier. By then I was fourteen. Frank used to annoy me on the milk round and I was never in the mood for fun at five o'clock in the morning.

Four of us left on the midnight bus from George Square to Drumchapel on the eve of Easter Sunday 1960 to go on our first camping trip. We got off the bus at Knightswood and began walking the Great Western Road, heading for Loch Lomond. We were trying to hitch a lift, but with four of us walking together, no one would pick us up. I strode out in front of the others and managed to get a lift to Dumbarton. I walked to Luss before my next lift, which took me all the way to Tyndrum. I arrived there around seven thirty on a cold Easter morning. I had a primus stove with me and was able to get a heat and make myself something to eat. Tony damaged his leg in an accident while doing the milk run so he arrived by bus from Glasgow around mid-day. I had the tent but one of the other three who had not made it yet to Tyndrum had the tent poles. Tony and I made temporary poles from branches until the others finally arrived on the Tuesday. They had walked all the way from Glasgow. Ian Stewart's sister lived there so we were looked after. Unfortunately parents think the world is full of weirdoes now and children, as young as we were would not be safe doing what we did then! One day we all went up one of the mountains and by the time we reached patches of snow there was only Frank Fitzpatrick and me left. I told him to remain there until I returned from the summit but when I got back he had gone and it was getting dark. Luckily there was a fence which went all the way down one side and I just clung to that as I made my descent, keeping my eyes on the lights of Tyndrum so that I knew which direction to walk when I finally got down. There was a path at the bottom that took me back to where we were camping and I laid into Frank for leaving me up on the mountain alone. We spent time searching through the dense forests for deer antlers but never found any.

I used to visit my Aunt Jessie and Uncle Harry when they lived in the Gorbals. By the time they moved to Castlemilk I had three cousins, Irene, Ronnie, and Derek. They lived at Ardencraig Road and facing them were the Cathkin Braes. Harry was my dad's brother and Jessie, my mum's sister. When I was thirteen Uncle Harry gave me a bicycle. It was a Sun with no gears, good for building up the leg muscles but not for climbing hills. My first cycle run was with my friends to Irvine where I live now. At that time it was a straight run from Pollok via Lugton, through Girdle Toll and into the town, over the old bridge to the harbour that was really dirty then. I believe colliers sailed out of Irvine in 1960. It took us a long time on our return journey to Pollok, as we were all shattered and nursing sore bottoms.

Another hobby was golf in my early teens along with Ian Stewart and Bob McGoran. The nearest public courses were Deaconsbank and Barshaw in Paisley. You had to be there early in the morning, or wait for hours to get a round in. One morning at Deaconsbank while we were waiting on the tee, Headley Crowther got hit on the face with the back swing from another golfer's driver while he was practicing. Bob informs me that he may be the culprit. We took him to the Victoria Infirmary and waited until he was stitched up before taking him home. Bob also remembers being hit between the shoulder blades and winded by a ball off the tee as we walked up the First fairway at Deaconsbank.

Fishing was also a passion at that time. Most times I would just go on my own on my bicycle and listen to my radio while fishing. I used to tie my rod to the crossbar of my bike and cycle to Loch Libo, Lochwinnoch, the dams at Barrhead, and Neilston Mill. When the pool at the back was serving the Mill, there were loads of trout in a small puddle. Rich pickings! I brought a pike home one day, which my mother ate and enjoyed. None of my friends had ever heard of anyone eating a pike.

I used to enjoy it when my dad took me to play snooker when he was based at Larkfield garage. In later years we would go for a drink after the game.

At fourteen we didn't have a record player at home. When I took up the guitar seriously I used to listen to the radio all the time. I learned every new Shadows instrumental by ear, picking up a little bit more each time it was played. The station everyone listened to at that time was Radio Luxembourg whose signal would disappear just as your favourite record came on. My mates and I would hang around the Stadium Café and sit for hours sipping a coke while older youths fed the jukebox.

Our family doctor's surgery was a house on Peat Road at the corner of Brock Road. Every time you visited Dr Cowan, he would get your file out and say you were due an injection for something. After giving your jag, he would then give you free tickets for Larry Marshall's "One o' Clock Gang". He was also a dental surgeon, or should I say, "A butcher". Once, after having a tooth pulled, I bled for three days. I had to return to have the wound packed and he told me if I went to any other dentists, to tell them I was a bleeder. To our surprise, he was convicted for reset in the late sixties.

One evening in 1961 while crossing the road outside our house with my cello guitar over my back, I heard someone shout, "Can you play that thing?" There were two men at an open window of the house directly facing mine. They invited me in as they had an electric guitar and amplifier in an empty room, which made the sound reverb. Joe Short and his friend, Joe, were both twenty and impressed with my playing. They said I could come over anytime as they were decorating the house for Joe Short's sister Connie, and would be there for some time. I visited that house often while they were there as that was my first taste of an electric guitar. While waiting for the milk float in the mornings I got talking to a guy who was eighteen and used to leave for his work as we were waiting outside his home. His name was Reginald Fulegar and he played the guitar. I told him about Joe Short and vice versa. We got together at Joe's sister's house for a jam and when I introduced Reginald, he said, "Call me Billy", I wonder why!

My classmate Mick McGowan had moved from Govan to South Nitshill and played the drums. Mick, Joe, Billy and I, used to practice in Mick's bedroom at 436 Parkhouse Road. Dr Cowan arranged our first gig, which was for pensioners in the Gorbals. We also hired halls at Househillwood and Brock Road to practice, where all our friends could drop in and hear us. We really played for fun and were not a gigging band. With me playing with guys of eighteen and twenty, and my interest in the guitar, I'm afraid school was a necessary hindrance to my musical development. I must say, my music teacher at school Mr. Kerr was encouraging and once translated all the tunes in a Shadows music book in to the tonic soh fah of each key, as I could understand it that way. Also at the beginning of each music lesson we had to sing, noo nay nee nah, which I found out later were the first, third, fifth, and eighth notes of a major scale and played together form a major chord. On my last day at school I took in my guitar and amp to play for my classmates in the art room. While still at school I used to go to the Flamingo Ballroom on a Tuesday evening just to listen to the band who were called the Raiders. As everyone danced, my eyes would be fixed on the guitarist Stewart Dool all night. John Mc Guinness was the pianist in the band, Alex Scott on rhythm guitar, Henry Wright on drums and Dave Watson on bass. The saxophone player always did a vocal solo; he left to form his own band, Sol Byron and the Impacts.

On leaving school, Mick Daly and I wanted to be artists but our principal art teacher Mr. Millar advised us against trying to get into art school. He told us that printing was a better career but none of us had any luck finding a job as a printer. Mick served his time as a refrigeration engineer. I got to the final interview stage for an apprenticeship in furniture making but failed at the last hurdle. I began my working life as a grocery assistant with Massey's at Cessnock. Before we began our jobs, Mick and I decided we would go hitch hiking up north camping. Mick had a small two-person tent. We took the bus from Glasgow to Balloch as that would give us a head start. We began walking from Balloch in the pouring rain and got as far as Inverbeg before deciding to camp for the night. We erected Mick's tent in a wooded headland where I believe used to have a clinker ferry which took passengers across the loch to Rowardennan. After climbing in the tent to eat a huge scone my mother had baked for us, we realized that it would be foolish to stay in there as all our gear including sleeping bags was soaking wet. Being sure there was a Youth Hostel at Inverbeg, we went in search of it. Fortunately, Inverbeg only had a hotel and the hostel behind it on the hill. We booked in, which meant we had to join the Youth Hostels Association as well, so it was a costly exercise for two fifteen year olds not yet working. We returned immediately to collect the tent and our belongings. It took three days for our sleeping bags to dry so we were really stranded there and spent our time walking the hills. Leaving

Inverbeg, we hitched a lift to Ardlui at the head of Loch Lomond. By this time the weather was beautiful so we spent a few days there. I had left my huge primus stove in the hostel, as it was too awkward to carry if we didn't get a lift so we cooked on an open fire. Deciding it was not so easy getting lifts, we waited at Ardlui until we got one, this time heading south to Tarbet and walking across to Arrochar, then on to Ardgartan by the shores of Loch Long. We spent two days there and really enjoyed walking the hills and forests around the 'rest and be thankful'. We caught the bus from Arrochar to Glasgow, so our highland holiday only got as far as the top of Loch Lomond.

I began my first job at Massey's grocer's shop in the Cessnock branch where the manager was an elderly Aberdonian called Mr. Berry. He lived in Greenock and used to commute to work. He introduced me to Aberdeen rolls, which are kind of flat with a slight salty taste and are delicious with loads of butter. Mr. Berry's hands were all swollen and his fingers curled inwards but he could still show me how to bone ham and cut meat. The oldest assistant Jean Hollywood came from Arthurlie Street in Govan. Gary Hollywood, the actor in 'Take The High Road' is related to her. Jean and Mr. Berry taught me all I needed to know. Eventually the delivery boy left and for quite some time I had to go out on the bike delivering customers orders. There was an old boy that used to phone an order nearly every day. He would only order one or two things, as it was just an excuse to get me up to his flat. After sending me for a half bottle of whisky he would give me two shillings as a tip, if he was really tipsy I sometimes got ten, and you couldn't argue with him. Another customer I used to deliver to paid me two hours a week to look after her garden. Her house was in Bellahouston. It was while doing her garden and listening to the radio that I first heard The Beatles' 'Love me do'. This new sound really stuck in my head and that is why I know where I was when I first heard it. My artist input to the shop was doing window displays and price cards. Mr. Berry gave me tips on sign writing. The one thing that upset me in the shop was having to clean maggots from the sides of bacon before boning them, and then having to sell the bacon to our customers. You would have thought knowing what goes on I would not eat bacon, but my taste buds won the battle with my conscience. My first date was with the fish shop owner's daughter who used to work in the shop along the road on a Saturday. We went to the cinema and then I took her home to Nicholson Street in the Gorbals. She was sixteen and I was fifteen. I don't think my inexperience impressed her, as she would not go out with me again. Some days at lunchtime I used to go to the nearby park with the butchers next door to play football. One day I fell on the gravel, grazing my elbow. I had to go to the hospital to have it scrubbed with a hard brush.

Mick Daly and I took up cycling after we began our jobs and our training was quite strenuous. Every weekday in the evenings I

would cycle from Pollok to Drumoyne, pick up Mick and go through the recently opened Clyde tunnel. We would then head for Lennoxtown and over the Campsies to Fintry where we would buy a packet of digestive biscuits and a bottle of orange each. After our snack we would return home. This was really hard on me as Mick had bought a Flying Scot and I was stuck with my Sun, heavy and no gears. At weekends we would go farther afield. I had to work every Saturday, so after work I would go home, get my gear together and head for Inverbeg Youth Hostel where Mick would have arrived earlier. On the Sunday we would go to Inveraray, Arrochar, Ardlui, or over to Aberfoyle and then home. Sometimes we would do our usual run to Fintry, carrying on to Aberfoyle, over the Duke's Pass to Calendar and home. In the early sixties there wasn't much traffic on the roads so you felt safe. I wouldn't like to cycle now as motorists consider cyclists a hazard and cars are a lot faster.

One memorable weekend was when Bob McGoran and I decided to go to Loch Lomond Youth Hostel. I think we were sixteen but may only have been fifteen. We took a bus to Balloch and I was drinking a bottle of cheap wine on the way. Somehow we managed to get into a pub in Balloch where we met a crowd of boys who were staying at the hostel. After closing time I was rather the worse for wear and we were refused entry to the hostel. The crowd we had been drinking with told us there was a guide's camp in a field behind the hostel and the wash tent would be vacant. You can imagine the confusion when two drunken teenage boys turn up at a camp full of girls but after a fair bit of screaming and the realisation that we only wanted a place to sleep, the girls eventually pointed out the wash tent. We had to move basins of water around to make space for us to lie down and left early the next morning before the girls got up. We left the wash tent as we found it, had a wash in a stream and headed back to Balloch. We spent the day strolling around Balloch and at night, being too embarrassed to return to the hostel; we went in to Balloch Park. Near the loch, down the hill from the castle, there was a boat shed with a protruding roof and seating round three sides. It was raining but we got our sleeping bags out and spent the night there. The next morning we were starving and couldn't light a fire because of the rain so we opened a tin of beans and ate them cold before catching the next bus back to Glasgow.

The reason Mick and I had been doing all the training was our next attempt to go north, this time on our bikes. I had bought a

Raleigh sports bike with five speed gears and found it easier to keep up with Mick. On a beautiful Saturday morning in July 1963, we set off for Fort William. It really was a glorious day as we made our way up Loch Lomond to Crianlarich, through Glencoe, arriving at Fort William in the evening. We erected Mick's tent in Glen Nevis and chained our bikes together, one on either side of a tree. It had rained through the night and was still on in the morning. Every thing in the tent was wet, as Mick hadn't checked it for proofing since our previous holiday the year before. There was a youth hostel nearby so before leaving, we rejoined, ditched the tent and made our way to Altsigh hostel near Drumnadrochit, Loch Ness. We booked in for three days and spent them walking the surrounding countryside and cycling to Inverness. As we had no planned schedule for a camping trip, we would now have to depend on the youth hostel's map and hope wherever we ended up; there would be vacancies. Aviemore was our next port of call. This was a hard run as it rained all day and was also windy. We had rain capes on which slowed us down and filled with rainwater, but we were fit and on reaching Aviemore, booked in for three days. This gave us a base to work from and time to take in the Cairngorms. Mick and I got friendly with the warden who wore the kilt and he loaned us one each for a day. We were Aviemore's tourist attraction for that day as Americans were stopping their cars and getting us to pose for photographs. When we left Aviemore it was a nice day as we headed south. Passing through Kingussie it became freezing, and rained hailstones. "Typical Scottish summer weather!" The sun returned on leaving Kingussie as we made our way to Strathtummel. Passing through Killiekrankie we stopped off at Pitlochry to see the salmon ladders, and also at the 'Queen's View' overlooking Loch Tummel. After a good night's sleep, our next day was an easy run to Killin. The following day we went across country to Crianlarich, Tyndrum, Dalmally, and Inveraray. The weather had been miserable that day and when we got to Inveraray the hostel was full, so we had to carry on over the 'Rest And Be Thankful' to Ardgarten at Loch Long. We spent two nights there before returning home. Mick had an uncle who was a long distance lorry driver and as we still had some days left before returning to work, we got him to put our bikes in the back of his lorry and drop us off at Carlisle so that we could cycle back. On our return I got a puncture near Bellshill and with no repair kit with us, we decided Mick would cycle holding my bike by his side and I would try to get a lift from a car. I got a lift to Rutherglen, then another to Bridge Street, Glasgow. I met two policemen who wanted to know why I was walking the streets at two in the morning dressed in shorts, T-shirt, and cycling shoes. When I told them my story one of them stopped a taxi and paid the seven and sixpence fare to get me home to Pollok. Not long after returning to work following our holiday, I was crossing over the Corkerhill on my way there on my bike one morning. Going over the brow of the hill I had moved in to the middle of the road without looking behind me as I was intending to turn first right at the other side. Realising my mistake I turned round just as a car hit me. It braked before hitting me but I went up in the air and when I landed, the car's wheel was right at my head. I jumped up immediately telling the driver that it was my fault for not looking. I was more concerned for my bike but it seemed undamaged. The driver of the car said he would take me to my doctor and a witness who said he was the groundsman at Nethercraigs Sports ground would look after my bike. I got in the car and as it turned to head for Pollok I noticed the pain I had in my shoulder meant something wasn't right. Obviously I was in shock and required hospital treatment. On our way to the Southern General I had to hold my right arm with my left as the pain was excruciating. I had dislocated my shoulder and fractured my collarbone. They had me lying in a bed face down with my arm dangling and every now and then someone would come along and swing it, hoping it would drop into place. The hospital had been trying to contact my parents as one of them would have to sign a form before I could be operated on as I was only sixteen. For me that was 'The Longest Day' as my dad was at work and my mum at the shops. Eventually my mum came and when I awoke from the

Me and Mick

unaesthetic it was six o'clock in the evening, and my arm was strapped to my chest. I was put out of the hospital two days later as they would need beds for casualties from the forthcoming Rangers and Celtic game. Dad had retrieved my bike and after I was home a day or so, when no one was there, I had to check it out. The only repair required was to straighten some spokes on the back wheel. I could not believe that after doing all those miles a week or so before that I could be so stupid to do what I had done.

Chapter 3

Frank Cusack, another friend of mine from secondary school worked as a grocer in a shop at Ladymuir Crescent, Pollok. In the latter recovery stage of my injury Frank appeared at my door to tell me the butcher's assistant from the shop next door to his played in a band. If I was interested, they were looking for a guitarist. I certainly was, so that evening Frank helped me with my guitarand amp to the scout hall at Lochar Crescent where they were practising. The band members were Frank Sutton, Allan Craig, Andy Neil, and Johnny Campbell. I played my Shadows' tunes and an instrumental I had composed and I was in! We practised in the hall Tuesday and

Thursday evenings and Sunday afternoons, at no cost. In return we played to an audience on Sunday evenings with the proceeds going to the hall. At first Frank Andy and I were all banging away on six string guitars; Allan was the drummer and Johnny the singer. I had still been playing with Joe Short's band and after appearing late for practise one Sunday afternoon as I had been to a party, I was given the ultimatum, "Them or us?" It was a hard decision to make, as I didn't want to desert my friends. Mick McGowan had recently joined The Cameronians as a boy soldier and tried to talk me into joining, but my music was more important to me or I may well have, as I was always the outdoor type until then. Reluctantly, I decided to stay with Frank, Alan, Andy, and Johnny as they were more my own age and seemed determined to succeed. On giving my answer it was decided that I would be lead guitar, Frank bass, Andy rhythm, and we would call ourselves, "The Interns". From then on we practised at every opportunity outwith our Tuesdays, Thursdays, and Sundays. At that rate it didn't take us long to be quite proficient. Apart from the scout hall our first gig was at Leven Beach Pavilion, Fife. It was a variety show with many other acts. We opened our spot with the Surfaris' 'Wipe out'. Allan played the drums as the curtain opened and when we struck our guitars, there was no sound. We had forgotten to plug the main's extension in, so the curtain closed and we solved the problem by putting the mains plug in. We carried on this time with sound to be well received by the audience. Now that music had taken over my life I did not see much of Mick Daly and only used my bike to go to work. Although I had left Joe Short's band I still went to rehearsals when I could and have a jam. Joe invited me to a party at Ibrox in the New Year of 1964. We took our instruments and were the entertainment for the night. There were two guys at the party who were great singers, John and George McGinley, who's sister Jean was our hostess. There was a gorgeous girl there who it turned out, lived above John and George at Brockburn Road, Pollok. Late in the evening they had a game called 'Find the garter.' All the males were sent out of the room, a female put the garter on and a certain male's name was called to go in and find it in darkness. My name was called and when I found the garter it was on the gorgeous girl whose name was Helen Morrison. Helen was born on the thirtieth of April 1947 so we were the same age. I got quite friendly with John and George after that night as Helen used to visit their house. They lived with their sister Marion and her husband Duncan. One evening when I called at their house, which was on the ground floor below Helen's, she was already there and as she left, the McGinleys told me to go after her so I did. After talking for a while, Helen invited Joe; Billy and I to come to her house some weeks later as her Mum and Dad were going to a family wedding. That evening there were also Helen's friend Winifred Strawhorn and the McGinley's sister, Mary. It was quite late when Helen heard her dad's minibus draw up and as they lived on the top flat, there was no

escape for us. Joe Billy and I went into the bathroom with Helen as the window opened on to the verandah. When we heard the door open and close, Joe opened the window and as he climbed out, Helen's mum was standing there telling him to get back in. After a telling off from Helen's parents, we were told to leave. We felt so bad about it that we returned the following night to apologize. We had a good laugh about the previous night, as we were 'Hooligans from the Bundy.' We left on good terms, but Helen was grounded. From then on Helen and I were a couple.

Meanwhile the band was doing fine. The following is an article from the 'Lennoxbank Beat News', issue 9, May 1964.

'INTERNS QUALIFY'

"Although they have only been together for six Months, The Interns have qualified music-wise as a bright, up and coming Glasgow group. The boys, who come from Pollok, are playing regularly in the City, and in June they are expected to be the first band to open Sunday night dance sessions in the new St. Conville's church hall in Pollok. Line up is – Jim Collins [lead guitar], Andy Neil [Rhythm], Frank Sutton [bass], Allan Craig [drums], and John Campbell [singer]. The boys got together last year when Andy and Frank played in a local hall. The others joined them and they became 'The Interns'. At present they wear blue Ben Casey style tunics on stage but they will be changing to dress suits soon. Guitarist Jim Collins has written an R. and B. number, 'Tell me' which they feature often in their act. Jim, who has also written two instrumental numbers, says: "We feel it's essential to have original material to get ahead these days".

Our agent at the time was John Mc Gowan from Pollok who ran the Universal Dance Agency. We went to a recording studio in Paisley to record my song 'Tell me'. The studio was the interior of a small garage behind a church, across the road from the ice rink. The engineer introduced us to the producer whose name was Graham Lyle. Graham made his name in the seventies along with fellow musician Benny Gallagher as the duo, 'Gallagher and Lyle'. We recorded my song, and then with the intention of doing Del Shannon's 'Answer to everything', Graham asked if anyone could play the piano. Frank could, so he played piano while Graham did the bass work. We got six copies, one each and one to send to a record company. While watching the records being cut we handed over the fee that was fifteen pounds with Graham getting two for his contribution. In the summer of 1964 we played in Archie McCulloch's 'Costa Clyde' clubs. Archie was a journalist with the 'Evening Citizen' newspaper. In August that year the paper sponsored a band contest at the Queens Hall, Dunoon. Each of the six bands represented one of Archie's Costa Clyde clubs. There was 'The Blue Panthers', representing El Flamenco, Rothsay, 'The Tulsans', El Toro, Millport, 'The Road Hogs', La Caverna, Gourock, 'The Valiants', El Picador, Largs, 'The Flatters', El Bolero, Dunoon, and us representing St. Tropez, Girvan. We were told to report to Gourock where our gear would be transported across the Clyde estuary to Dunoon. On arriving at Gourock, what we saw shocked us as other bands were having their gear lowered by ropes on to small boats. After getting our gear aboard we climbed down a ladder and crossed over to Dunoon where the gear was offloaded safely and taken across the road by trolley to the Queens Hall. At that time my guitar was a Hofner Galaxy and I played through the p.a. system via a Watkins Copycat echo unit. We had changed our name to The Five Interns as a Welsh group called The Interns had a record out. As we listened and watched the other bands performances we thought we didn't stand a chance, as their gear was far superior to ours, although we looked smart in our new suits. When they announced third, Mark Val and The Valiants, second, The Flatters, and first, The Five Interns, we couldn't believe it! Alan was pushed out on to the stage to receive a cheque for seventy-five pounds. Part of the prize was a recording test with George Martin, The Beatles' recording manager. The average price for a gig then was twenty-five pounds. Previous to winning, Archie had us playing two nights in the same club for thirty pounds, sleeping in the club to save accommodation costs. After winning the contest Archie contacted us to play in one of his clubs. We said we would if he put the money up but he refused and that was the end of our recording test. The prize money went as a deposit for three Vox AC.30 amplifiers, a fifty-watt p.a. with Vox column speakers, and a kit of Rogers drums with a Ludwig snare. I remember that we got the gear through the Co-operative, but had to go to McCormack's music shop to collect it. By now we were getting quite a name and playing all over Scotland.

Helen and I fell out for five months and met up again at a gig in the scout hall at Drumcross Road, Pollok, where our rivals 'The Verdicts' were playing. I had gone to hear them and Helen was there with Winnie Strawhorn. She had been considering going to America as a child minder, but thankfully she changed her mind and our romance was back on. That episode inspired me to write the song, 'After you have gone'.

After You Have Gone

I know I'm kissing, the lips I'll be Missing, after you have gone
I may be sighing but I'll keep myself from crying, after you have gone

Forever when away you go, In my heart you'll stay I know
For I always will remember you
Hope will always be with me, as you sail across the sea,
For I hope that someday soon, I will join you

To be yours only, let none of us be lonely, after you have gone
Come tomorrow my heart will fill with sorrow, after you have gone

It's well seen a romantic seventeen year old wrote that song! Upon winning the band contest, we were approached by Billy Grainger while doing a gig at Strathclyde University. Billy invited us to hear his top band 'Dean Ford and the Gaylords' at Bearsden town hall as he also wanted to manage us. We thought they were excellent and became good friends after signing with Billy. In the sixties gay meant happy! Dean was Tommy McAleese from Coatbridge, and the Gaylords

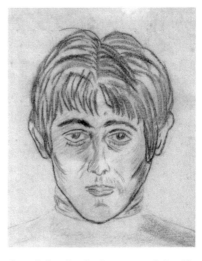

were, Junior Campbell [lead], Pat Fairley [rhythm], Raymond Duffy [drums], and Bill Irving [bass]. Bill was an electronics engineer and did the techy work. Junior played a strat upside down as he was left handed and seemed to play strange chords. He told me he learned by tuning a guitar to open e, turning it upside down and working out the chords. He was an amazing guitarist. On Tuesday the thirteenth of October 1964 we were the opening band at the second anniversary of the Lennoxbank Sunday club, Balloch. Other bands that night were Dean Ford and the Gaylords, The Senators, The Royal Crests, Phil and the Flintstones, and Tony Rivers and the Castaways. We were really impressed with the Castaways as they played Beach Boys, Jan and Dean, Surfaris, the new surf sound. Another band we supported at the Lennoxbank hotel was The Fenmen, minus Bern Elliot. They played similar material to Tony Rivers. As we were a close harmony band, Billy thought we should be doing that kind of material as there were no other Scottish bands playing surfing music. It took a lot of rehearsing; we would work out the harmonies in Johnny's bedroom and give the songs the final treatment in a hired hall. We had long given up the hall at Lochar Crescent and practised in Barnbeth Church hall. When we eventually got the surfing set together we would do our first set of contemporary chart and pop songs dressed in suits, then for the second set we changed into jeans and T-shirts to perform Beach Boys etc. Dean Ford and the Gaylords already had a single out called 'Twenty Miles' and performed their second, 'Mr. Heartbreaker's Here Instead', at the Lennoxbank anniversary gig. Glasgow gigs at that time were The Maryland, Elizabethan, Pink Panther, Lindella, and Picasso. On Tuesday evenings at the Picasso there would be a band playing and members from other bands would

meet up. We used to meet up with our friends 'The Poets' who had signed with The Rolling Stones manager, Andrew Loog Oldham. They had their first single 'Now we're Thru' released by Decca on the ninth of October 1964. Poets' singer, George Gallagher sung with 'The Blues Poets' in the Scotia bar Glasgow, every second Sunday in the nineties. Fraser Watson played with 'Dave Hunter and the Arrows in the early sixties before joining 'The Poets', and eventually 'White Trash'. He was also a member of the Blues Poets. We supported 'The Poets' at the Center club in Sauchihall St., Glasgow, and also at Dundee Art School. A strange gig at that time was the Drill hall at Dumfries where a band played at each end of the hall. The first time we played there, an English band dressed in leather occupied the main stage while we were on the floor at the far end. I'm sure their singer was Cat Stevens. The next time we went we commanded the stage. The Lennoxbank Sunday club had grown so popular that the hotel had another building erected to cater for music. This was called The Lido and managed by Billy Grainger. Because Billy was our manager we had the benefit of supporting all the big acts. The Small Faces, Spencer Davis Group, Mindbenders, Major Lance, Tommy Quickly, and The Symbols were some I can remember. When we were in the dressing room with the Spencer Davis Group Stevie Winwood's white Fender Strat was lying in its case with the lid open. I noticed that it had three unwound strings when a usual set had two. When I asked him the reason, he told me it was to bend the notes. He had substituted the third string for another second. At that time there were no custom gauge strings, so with Stevie's inf.' I had another string to my bow as you might say. Bob McGoran informs me that according to legend': Joe Brown of "Bruvvers" fame got the double second from Eddie Cochrane by asking him how he could bend the notes so well. The Moody Blues also appeared at the Lido and we went to see them with our girlfriends. When Donovan brought out 'Catch the wind' I had learned it using an acoustic guitar. The rest of the band thought I should do a solo spot and I'll never forget my first experience of knocking knees. We were really popular at Bellshill YMCA so that would be the ideal venue for my inauguration. The dance floor was full as Johnny set up a mike for my acoustic and as I began I could feel my knees knocking.

Masseys had moved me to their branch at Gauze Street, Paisley. Working on Saturdays was really inconvenient as I was travelling a lot with the band. Sometimes I went straight in to work from a Friday night gig. I left Masseys in the summer of 1965 to work in Bellahouston Park as a labourer. The money was better and I didn't have to work at weekends.

We did a gig at Whitehaven in Cumberland and travelled back to Carlisle to stay the night as we were playing at Haltwhistle the following night. The accommodation was organised by the agent. When we found it, the door was opened by a camp little man who introduced us to his male friend. He made us tea served in tiny coffee cups before showing us to our rooms. Three of us were to go in one room and two in another. As Alan Frank and Andy went into the first room Johnny said jokingly, "I've got you tonight Jim". The wee guy replied, "And when you're finished with him throw him in to me". When we closed the door of the room there was no lock, and in the bedside cabinet where you would expect to find a bible, there were porn books. I didn't sleep much that night but was still a virgin when we left for Haltwhistle in the morning. Helen's father Bert used to drive us most of the time. One weekend we played Buckhaven Fife on the Friday. After the gig we all slept in the van parked in a fan's back garden and were invited in for breakfast the following morning. That night we did the American base at Edzell and stayed at Brechin with the barman who was Scottish. We paid for that one but I remember the silk sheets were warmed by an electric blanket and we slept like logs. We arrived at HMS Condor Arbroath late on Sunday afternoon to set up the gear for the evening gig. Condor was a British Naval base then and the guys said that if we had arrived earlier we could have had a flight in a glider. American bases were good to play as we were always well treated. While playing at the US Air Force base at Prestwick I remember a guy pouring spirits into our mouths from a bottle as we played. Alan's father and Bert were at that gig.

In 1965 Susan Patron started a fan club for us. The following is her letter to them.

No 2 June 1965

"Hi again
Since last month we've got a lot of new members so the boys and I would like to say thank you for your support.

Collars

During the last month the boys got new collars put on their suits. As you know they wear light blue suits, well now they all have dark blue velvet collars.

Anyone found a chicken:

The group was playing up north in a place called Kirriemuir one Saturday night. They were tearing along a narrow country road, late as usual, when they ran over a chicken. Frank was very disappointed because there wasn't time to stop. He was determined that this was going to be his Sunday dinner, and he would get it on the way back. However on the way home, the chicken, or what was left of it was nowhere to be seen. "Anyone got a chicken they don't want"?

The Gaylords

Dean Ford and the Gaylords, in fact they rate them the best Scottish group. The Gaylords new record is released this month on Columbia and as you know the boys are great friends of Dean it's 'The name game', 'That lonely feeling'. The boys ask you all to listen to it and if you like it, buy a copy and support Scotland's top group and get 'The name game' in the charts".

Bill Irving left the Gaylords and was replaced by Graham Knight. They broke up with Billy Grainger and moved to London. They changed their name to the Marmalade in late 1965.

In the summer of 1964 we played at a Crookston Castle school dance at St. Christopher's church hall in Pollok. There was a boy who sat all night staring at our drummer Allan. I remember that scene well from my Flamingo days; it was obvious that he played the drums. When we finished playing Allan let him use his kit and we were all impressed with the young man. His name was Dougie Henderson and he lived in Damshot Crescent, which was just around the corner from me. Dougie began his musical career with The Verdicts, then The Insteps; he was still only fifteen. He then joined The Madhatters and went to Germany with them. When they returned, Davie Agnew left them to join The Senate who also had Bill Irving playing bass. Dougie left the band not long after Davie, as they wanted to return to Germany. He then had a spell with The Chevlons before auditioning for Studio Six. Poet's drummer, Jim Breakey got the job with Studio Six and Dougie walked in to The Poets. They moved to London and Hugh Nicholson left them to join Marmalade. Dougie followed him in 1971 appearing on Top of the pops, World tours, and everything else that goes with being a rock star. Marmalade was now a rock band and had many hit records. Dougie stayed with them until they split in1974.

One Monday night we did a gig at the Denniston Palais with another band. The other band played regular support to the resident band that we were replacing for one night. They thought that since we were only there for one night, we should toss a coin to see who went on first. We lost and had to go on first and third. When we did the first set there were a crowd of girls at the front of the stage that kept singing a song about the band we were replacing. Every time we finished a song they would sing, so we worked out the chords for it and Johnny sang along with them. This action got them on our side. The Palais had a revolving stage so when we finished our set the stage took us behind, and the other band to the front already playing. While they were on their first set the girls were all chanting for us. When we went on for the second time they were up on the stage trying to get the laces from our shoes and any other souvenirs, like spare plectrums and drumsticks. It was a complete turnaround to when we first went on. When we ended our second set and the stage turned round the management wouldn't let us leave for about ten minutes, as the girls were hysterical by then. The dressing room was down a flight of stairs from the stage and we were mobbed all the way. They followed us in to the dressing room and were trying to snatch anything they could get their hands on. The stewards got them out eventually and we were asked to go on again at the end to do a couple of numbers so we had to wait in the dressing room for the whole of the other band's second set. That was certainly a night to remember, as I can't recall another one like it in my career as a musician. I had been playing a Fender Duo Sonic when we played the Grand hall Kilmarnock. When it came to practise early the next week

I discovered my guitar was missing. I phoned the Grand Hall and no one knew anything about it and our agent said the same. I had to have a guitar for the following weekend so my dad signed the higher purchase agreement for a new sunburst Fender stratocaster from Mc McCormack's music shop. My Fender Duo Sonic guitar turned up two weeks later; it had been left in the Grand Hall after all. My dad never believed me that it had gone missing; he said it was just a move to get a strat. Another time we were coming back from a gig, driving along the Edinburgh Road before the M8 was built. We were overtaken by a van, which sped on down the dual carriageway. Quite a bit further on this van was parked and there were five guys out on the road with a ball. It was Dean Ford and the Gaylords, so we had a kick around in the middle of the night, on the road. We used to meet them and other bands at the hot dog stand near Eglinton Toll and talk about the night's gig as it was open until three or four in the morning. We played with Dave Berry and The Berries before Dave left to go solo with 'The crying game' and they became The Rocking Berries. Russ Abbot was their drummer. We also supported The Mojos at the Elizabethan in Glasgow. Sometime in 1965 I had a nervous breakdown. While I was laid up my mum bought me painting by numbers. I liked the feel of the oils and when I completed the two pictures supplied, I messed around with the paint that was left in the small pots. This venture inspired me and got me drawing again.

Helen and I got engaged on the twenty seventh of November 1965. I put the ring on her finger in the front seat of the top deck on a Glasgow Corporation bus. On the night of our engagement I was playing in Glasgow. After the gig we all went to Helen's house where the party was in full swing. Now that I had arrived, Helen's friend Rosemary came in with the cake and it slid from its base onto the floor. We're still together fifty six years later so it was no omen.

Johnny left the band at the end of 1965. We auditioned singers at the Lido where Billy Grainger was present. Our new singer was to be a guy called Tommy Smith who looked like Herman from The Hermits. I would not have chosen him but Billy cast the winning vote. Being the manager he was probably thinking of the image aspect and the fact that he also came from Pollok but the guy couldn't sing. We rehearsed for five months and emerged with a complete new programme. Every gig Tommy's voice would break, as he was not used to singing all night. I suffered this for two months and at a rehearsal said I wanted to leave the band. The words were hardly out of my mouth when Andy said he was also leaving. We had changed our name to The Batmen when Tommy joined. Our dress was short velvet capes with silk lining, each one a different colour, and hipster trousers. "Real mod Batmen"! We didn't split until we had seen out our commitments. Our last gig, at Bellshill YMCA was a sad night for both our fans, and us. On our way home we saw Johnny Campbell waiting for a taxi on the London Road and gave him a lift.

Chapter 4

A week or two after our last gig Helen and I went on holiday with her family in her dad's minibus. On our first night we camped in Glencoe. The next day we travelled up through Inverness to Dingwall where we stayed for a week. We watched The World Cup every evening in a pub at the railway station. This was the unforgettable year of 1966 when England won the World Cup. Our second week was spent in Lossiemouth. Every evening depending on the tide, we would watch the locals ripping salmon. Working as a team, one guy would throw a wooden block riddled with triple fishing hooks across the river and pull it back. There was no rod involved, only a length of fishing line tied to the wooden block, and there were that many salmon in the river that it worked nearly every cast. When a salmon was caught, it would be buried under rocks immediately so that when the police came they would drop their lines and scarper, returning later for their spoils. One evening Helen's brother George appeared at the campsite with a salmon as big as himself which he had nicked from under the rocks as the police chased the poachers. The booty was shared with fellow campers. The weather had been good that year; I remember my shoulders were nearly black. I felt rather lost after three hectic years playing with the band but Helen and I saw more of each other. We set the date of our wedding for October 1967 and in October 66 Andy Neil, his brother Alistair and I left our jobs to make the big money in London. An ex neighbour of theirs was already living in a flat next to Clapham Common. We took the overnight bus to London and were met by him at Victoria bus station. He had a red convertible car, so we piled in and made for his flat. When we arrived we entered through a window as it was a basement flat and we were introduced to his flat mate who was in bed with a girl. There was another room with two single beds and a girl lying out of it in one of them. He said we could sleep there until we found somewhere and not to worry about the girl as he would get rid of her. Sure enough she was taken away later that day and dumped somewhere. This was not for us but we did stay that first night. The following day we moved

into a hotel round the corner from Earls Court tube station. We paid two weeks in advance to give us time to find work. We hunted for a week and I was the only one to secure a job at a college labouring. After a week our money had run out so Andy and I decided to return home. This caused a big argument with Alistair. We got enough of a rebate from the hotel for leaving a week early to get us back to Glasgow. So here I was, skint and no job. I managed to get a part time job at the Co-operative wines and spirits factory at Shieldhall. It was supposed to be only for the festive period making up orders for Co-operative shops. My foreman at Bellahouston Park was called Frank Gilmour. Early 1967 I went to Bellahouston to see him and ask if it would be possible to get my job back. He had been promoted to assistant superintendent at Rosshall Park, Crookston. Frank got me into Rosshall in the spring and I was fortunate to hold on to the job at Shieldhall until then. I loved the job in the summer of 66, as I was my own boss. I was cutting grass in Pollok, Cardonald, Mosspark, Penilee, and had keys for each area's lock up. The first hour of each day was spent maintaining your machine, a cup of tea then you were off, and wherever you finished at the end of the day, went to the nearest lockup. Frank went around the areas on a scooter noticing the work you had done and when he saw you he would trust the overtime figures you gave him for the week. During this time I had began painting in oils and Frank would ask me to bring them in so that he could see them. They were small paintings and he would say, "I'll give you a pound for this, two for that, and so on". He really encouraged me. A week before Helen and I were married he appeared one day, told me to switch off my machine and get on his scooter. He took me to Paisley Road along from the Flamingo and said, "Pick a present". I'm not sure but I think I picked an iron. Frank was one of the best! Helen and her family had moved from Brockburn to Templeland Road before we were married and we got our first flat at 155 Crossloan Road five months before the wedding. We gutted the place and as we stripped off the many layers of paper, the plaster on the walls came away. Joe Short was a plasterer and he repaired all the walls for us. The flat was a rented room and kitchen with an outside toilet. It was on the ground floor and the door opened on to the pavement. Our summer holiday in 1967 was with Helen's family once again, to Fraserburgh this time. We left on fair Friday early evening, arriving after midnight and it rained all the way. We all tried to sleep in the minibus, as there was no way we could have erected a tent in the wind, rain, and darkness. I couldn't sleep so as soon as it was daylight I was off discovering Fraserburgh. I returned with a bag of my favourite Aberdeen rolls (butteries) just in time to erect the tent. It rained most of the time we were there but we stuck it out. We noticed a poster advertising Chris McClure and The Fireflies who were to appear while we were there so we went to see him. Chris was from Ibrox and we knew him as we used to go to see his band at the Black Man pub in Govan.

We were married on the twenty eighth of October 1967 at St.Convals chapel, Pollok. A friend of mine Jim Nelson married his wife Maureen just prior to us. Jim was also a singer. As soon as we left the chapel we went straight to see Helen's elderly Granny at Leverndale hospital so that she could see her grand-daughter on her wedding day as she couldn't be there. Helen lived with her Maw as she called her due to shortage of space in the family home. She had an older brother Jim, who was our best man, and four younger brothers, Robert, David, George and Raymond. David died when he was eight due to a burst appendix. Our best maid was my sister Gladys. Our wedding reception was in the Kingston halls and it was a free bar. Helen's mum Nellie phoned a taxi for us at nine o'clock so that we would escape any embarrassment. As the taxi turned to head for Govan I realised that I had left my coat behind. I managed to sneak in and retrieve it. We couldn't afford a honeymoon so we were sitting in our wee flat at half past nine on the night the clocks went back. "That was well worked out"! Many people went back to Helen's mum and dad's after the reception. On the Monday we phoned her dad to take the empty beer keg back so that we could get our deposit returned to buy food. Everyone says our wedding was brilliant; it was probably because of the free bar.

The winter months in the park were spent stripping and cleaning all the grass-cutting machines before they were sent to the mechanics department for maintenance and repainting. Small trees were planted around the area, and a lot of digging, planting bulbs, and generally tidying up. In February 1968 there was a terrible storm that lasted all night. We couldn't sleep as there were objects flying around the streets. It was really scary, as we were expecting something to fly through the window with us being on the ground floor. When morning came, Govan was like a battle zone. Trees were down everywhere, across roads, rivers, and in woods many trees were uprooted, leaning against others. For many months following the storm I was out with a chainsaw cutting up and cutting down trees, which were unsafe. We began clearing the roads, then working with the army. There were huge trees, which had fallen across the river Cart that we couldn't deal with as we did not have the equipment. We would go out on a boat in the river and attach a chain round the tree, which would be pulled out by an army vehicle. We used to get paid at lunchtime on a Friday and one week I lost my wages while cutting grass at a school in Mosspark. We were not long married at the time and panicking I went to the social security to see if they could help me. I was offered a loan, which had to be paid back the next week, so I declined. Brian Corr worked with me at Rosshall. He lived in Calf hill, which was across the river from the park. He told me that he used to go to see The Five Interns when we played at Barnbeth hall. Helen was expecting our first child and I told Frank Gilmour that I would have to find another job. I even had him looking for me. Tracey was born on the tenth of October 1968. When Helen came home from the hospital she asked for my wages but they were gone, I had spent them on things for our new baby. Helen's dad worked in the Fairfield shipyard, which was Upper Clyde Shipbuilders in 1968. He was a sheet ironworker to trade and at that time he was an Industrial engineer. He organised a lunchtime interview for me with the ironworks manager Jim Paul who gave me a start after telling me, "You have to work hard in here son". I started work in Fairfields shipyard that was Upper Clyde Shipbuilders on the twenty fifth of November 1968 and nearly caused a strike on my first day. My title was sheet ironworker's helper. While standing on the shop floor as everyone was given their jobs for the day, the shop foreman Willie Coleman asked me if I had just started. On my reply he then told me to wait until every one else had been attended to. Eventually he took me over to a guy called Willie Hart and said to him, "This is Jim, he's just started, he can work along with you". After standing around like a statue for ten minutes or so while Willie had his head down studying a drawing he said, "Do you want something to do". I said," Yes" as he handed me a drawing and said, "Make up these lugs, and there's the flatbar". I looked at the drawing and asked Willie for a scriber. He went into his toolbox and gave me a scribe. I then said, "Can I have a rule". He shook his head and fumbled once again in his toolbox before giving me a rule. He didn't look too pleased and I didn't know why. I began marking off the lugs on the flatbar when Bert came up and said, "What are you doing, you'll cause a strike". I didn't know what was wrong as I would have been quite happy working away. Bert turned to Willie and told him that I was a helper and not a sheet ironworker. We all had a good laugh about it, including Willie Coleman. Three of Bert's brothers, also sheet ironworkers worked in the yard at that time, Jim, George, and Thomas.

Our wee flat was getting damp by this time; it had fungus growing on the walls of the kitchen, as the flat on the other side of them had lain vacant for years. It was not a nice environment for a little baby. Luckily a flat became available on the first floor of the close next to us at 153 Crossloan Road, so we took it. Helen's brother Robert and his fiancé Rita were getting married on the twenty first of

December 1968 so they moved in to our flat when we moved next close. Robert knew Dougie Henderson from school.

My duties in the sheet iron shop included assisting tradesmen, clearing away scrap from the guillotine, and keeping the workshop tidy. Ships in the basin at that time were US Survey ships Harkness and Chauvenet and HMS Antrim for the Royal Navy. Some of the shop tradesmen would get a lift make and fit job where they would go to one of these ships lift the sizes of a job, return to the shop to make it, then take it to the ship and fit it. Sometimes I got to work with a sheet ironworker on one of these tasks. Months after I started in the yard I was asked to work a Sunday on the container ship Jervis Bay that was on the slipways. You never forget the first time you go aboard a ship in the stocks, especially one this size. Everything is huge and open so that large pieces of machinery could be put into place before being closed in. While working on that Sunday I got a message that my dad had been taken into the Southern General Hospital with pleurisy. I had to work the Glasgow fair of 1969, as I hadn't worked there long enough to accumulate my holiday pay. Helen was expecting our second child by this time. Her Mum and Dad had sited their caravan at Battlefield Caravan Park Inveraray so Helen and Tracey went with her parents and I joined them after the fair, as I had to take the days I had been due. I stayed up painting through the night of the twentieth of July 1969 to watch Neil Armstrong put his foot on the Moon at 3.56am on the twenty-first. During the holiday I worked with Bert's brother George on the 'Cornish City' at Alexander Stephen's wharf, Linthouse. This ship was one of many Cardiff Class ships we built for Cardiff based Reardon Smith shipping line who carried an Indian deck and engine room crew. One job we had was to fit mosquito gauze nets on the portholes of the two galleys. The crew arrived while we were there as the ship was due to be handed over which was the reason for us working the holidays. While we were working in the officer's and crew's galleys the Indian crew hands would give us packets of cigarettes for small pieces of gauze which they used as tea strainers. The galley crew fed us curries for the same. When you arrived on the ship in the morning you had to step over crew hands that had slept in the passageways. They all had nice cabins but would not sleep in the beds. The crew's toilets had two footpads, one on each bulkhead on either side of the receptacle and level with it. Above the pads were handles so work the rest out for yourself! There was no toilet paper, just a large tin with water in it. Whichever hand they rolled up their curry and rice and ate with would always have a rag in it or be gloved. The other hand would be for the toilet so although they wouldn't use the beds they thought of their hygiene. To get to Stephen's wharf in the morning you had to walk through a lane at the side of Shieldhall sewage works. It wasn't the smell of sewage, which nearly made you ill, but the perfume they put in to kill the smell. I did a painting of the 'Cornish City' and Reardon Smith's commissioning engineer Captain Vaughn purchased it for five pounds. Two weeks after giving him the painting I still hadn't received my fiver so I accosted him on the gangway to remind him and when he took out his wallet it would have choked a horse. I don't think I would have been paid if I hadn't asked him. I enjoyed my two weeks on the ship and the extra allowance you got so when I returned to the shop after the holidays I approached our department ship's manager Alfie Blunt and asked to be transferred. I learned to sling, and assisted in the erection of engine room ventilation which was to be my main job for many years.

Bert, his brother George and I went to the caravan at Inveraray fishing that September weekend. Before we left Helen said she thought our second child would be born that weekend but I did not take any notice and went away. When we returned Helen's Brother Robert came out of his flat to tell me I had another daughter. I ran up the stairs, opened our door and hunted all over looking for Helen, as I did not believe him. When I couldn't find her, it was straight to the hospital. Pauline was born on the twenty ninth of September 1969, the same date as my sister Chris. Our flat was gradually becoming like an art gallery as I had been painting a lot since we moved upstairs. It shames me to tell this story that my dad told me a few years later. He said that one night while he and mum were visiting us, I just sat and painted all night and never said a word. Obviously I hadn't even thought about it until he mentioned it. My only excuse would be the fact that it shows how dedicated I have been to my art. My main influence at that time was the English landscape painter John Constable 1776-1837. I had read many books about him and thought that reproductions of his work showed him to be a detailed painter. A visit to the Scottish National Gallery in Edinburgh to see his painting 'Dedham Vale' proved he was really an impressionist. This realisation made me distrust small reproductions of large paintings and made me want to see more of Constable's work. I had already done copies of 'The Haywain', 'The Cornfield', and 'Dedham Lock and Mill'. I had kept in contact with Frank Gilmour who came to our flat early in 1970 to see how my work had been developing. He really liked 'The Haywain' and knowing that I wanted to go London to study Constable's work; he offered me forty pounds and a trip there in his car at Easter. I took him up on his offer so armed with my street plan of London, Frank, his partner Jean and I set off late on the Thursday to travel overnight. Using my street plan I got them to drop me off near a tube station at the London ring road. They were carrying on to Broadstairs in Kent. I stayed three nights at a hostel off the Tottenham Court Road, just around the corner from the British Museum. All the galleries I visited in the three days I was there were within walking distance of each other. In the library of the British Museum I had Constable's watercolours in my hands. The day I went to the Royal Academy it was closed to the public but fortunately for me the receptionist was from Glasgow. I explained that I couldn't manage back and she got a security guard to take me round and show me Constable's study for 'The Leaping Horse' and his palette. I also saw his work at The Tate, National Gallery, and visited the Victoria and Albert Museum twice. London is a lonely city if you are on your own. The only time I spoke to anyone was at the

69

breakfast table each morning. Frank and Jean picked me up on the Monday morning where they had dropped me off and we got home late that night. That weekend made me want to go to Constable Country but it would be another eleven years before I got there.

While I worked at Rosshall Park, when I was in the Pollok area I used to meet Jim Nelson who worked at the Rootes car factory in Linwood. He was also a singer and hated going to work in the factory. He asked me to back him on a demo and booked a recording studio in Glasgow where he did The Beatles' 'And I love her'. Within days of sending it to Major Minor Records he got a call from Norman Solomons asking him to come down for a recording test. Jim went to London, came back with a contract to read over and that was his ticket out of the car factory. However before he left, they would send him up songs to learn which

he would rehearse with me on my acoustic in our bedroom. He had a big voice like Tom Jones and didn't hold back when he sang. At times I used to cringe, waiting for someone banging on my door but the neighbours must have liked him as it never happened. When he went to London to record the songs the backing would already have been put down. It used to amaze me how they worked out the most suitable key for Jim to sing in, as he never had any problems when it came to recording. It wasn't long before Jim and Maureen moved to London. He had his singing career until that type of song became unfashionable.

A great memory for me was working in the yard at the time of the U.C.S. crisis. I remember my shop steward Adam telling me I would be better leaving as I hadn't been there two years and would be made redundant. Two of my colleagues, Tommy Bolam, George Kerr and I went to see the head of our department George Troup and asked for his advice. He promised us that if we stayed our jobs would be secure as long as the yard remained open. George Kerr was Helen's uncle. The U.C.S. had the financial and moral support from workers all over the country. Our motto was, 'We'll fight for the right to work'. We had lunch time concerts in the canteen with folk artists like Matt McGinn, demonstrations, and marches to the city centre from the yard. I went on one demonstration to lobby the Tory conference at Brighton. We travelled down by train overnight. "Can you imagine a train full of shipyard workers with their carry outs of booze to help them get through the night? I wouldn't like to have been a cleaner on that one"! We marched down from the railway station and along the front to where the conference was being held. Ted Heath and his cronies were verbally abused as they made their way inside. We broke up at 11am and our time was our own until 11pm. I had noticed a windmill along the coast at Rottingdean and walked there to sketch it as I had taken a small oil sketchbook with me. I drew the windmill and wrote in the colours so that I could paint it when I got home. I took the bus back in to Brighton and then another to Arundel to draw the castle as Constable had painted it. When I arrived it was starting to get dark. I tried to find the spot where Constable did his painting but before long it was black and I had no chance but I'm glad I went there, as it was a lovely place. By the time I returned to Brighton it was nearly time to leave for Glasgow. Everyone else had spent the day in the pubs but my visit was cultural. The three yards involved in the Upper Clyde Shipbuilders were John Browns, Clydebank, J.R. Connel & Son,

Scotstoun, and Fairfields, Govan.   Leaders of the negotiating committee were Jimmy Reid, Clydebank, Sammy Barr, Scotstoun, and Jimmy Airlie, Govan. At mass meetings a worker known as 'The Pig' entertained us. He was a caulker-burner from Fairfields called Jimmy McCrindle. Jimmy said, "What else could you call me with a face like this". He used to go to Douglas in the Isle of Man every Glasgow Fair and by entertaining the holidaymakers, his vacation didn't cost him anything. Tony Benn used to be a regular visitor at meetings and demonstrations. The crisis was resolved in 1972 when the Tory government was brought down. Labour formed British Shipbuilders with us being a subsidiary, and we were given a new name, 'Govan Shipbuilders Ltd'.

I am proud to have been involved in an important part of Glasgow's social history. One thing many others and I could not understand was "Why was the receiver brought in when we had a full order book?"

One evening my sister Gladys brought her friends' mother to

see my paintings as she had been interested in purchasing one. As she looked around my collection I sat at my easel working on a painting. As I said before, our walls were like an art gallery but out of all the work on display, she offered me five pounds for the painting I was working on. I, being the temperamental artist, told her to get out of the house as I had been working on that particular painting for weeks.

In 1971 we moved from Govan to Pinmore Street, Nitshill. Across from our ground floor flat were fields where I used to go sketching. Before I had left I sold my acoustic guitar to Brian Corr's brother John. Most of our weekends and summer holidays were spent in Helen's parents' caravan at Inveraray. I used to wander the surrounding countryside sketching and in the evenings at home I would do paintings from the material in my sketchbook. I would get scrap pieces of calico from the yard's insulators to use as canvas. At times my Argyleshire paintings would be production line work, as my colleagues at work would all want the same picture. The money earned from these sales was spent on materials to continue my hobby. There was a hotel not far from the caravan site called the Dalchenna. Arthur the proprietor used to hang my work for sale on the dining room walls, and when I went to the caravan for the weekend I often had money to collect. Arthur had bought the building as a shell and built it up over the years. He was a real character and always wore a kilt. I have seen him up to his neck in dirt and he would appear at the ceilidh that night in the same kilt. We would take our own drink until he eventually got a license. In the summer on warm days we would see many basking sharks. Now and then one would jump out of the water which I believe was to get the lice from their backs. That was a great sight! Helen's dad had a cabin cruiser and we had got friendly with a crowd of Germans from Hamburg. There were two brothers Peter and Klaus Dieter Braasch who were seven feet or over in height. Bert took them out in his boat to see the basking sharks at close range and we have a video of that trip.

Because of the weight of these two guys you can see the boat keeling over when they went to the one side. They had a great time and returned the following year with some more of their friends. They invited us over to Hamburg but we declined. Helen's youngest brother Raymond would go to the caravan for the whole of the school break in the summer. He was an enterprising youngster as he would hire out his father's dinghy. He would also go out in the dinghy and catch loads of mackerel which he would then sell to other caravan owners. On a nice day we would go out on the loch in the cabin cruiser and drop anchor to make dinner before moving on. I don't remember ever staying the night on the boat even though it had bunks but we used to go away all day. One time we went out to shoot duck. Raymond rowed the dinghy into the shore and chased the ducks out to where we were waiting in the cabin cruiser. Helen's older brother Jim got one with his dad's shotgun. When we returned to the caravan Jim plucked the feathers and put it in the oven. Hours

later when he opened it the smell was terrible, he hadn't taken out its innards so nobody would taste the duck. Another time when our children were small we went a run down to Lochgilphead in the minibus. On our return we saw a basking shark on the beach. It had a rope tied round its snout and the other end to a tree. It seemed massive out of the water. We couldn't resist pulling on the rope to open its mouth, revealing no teeth and just a big channel of white blubber.

Brian Corr, his brother John, Cousin Ronnie Young, and Frank Donnelly had a band when The Five Interns was on the go. By 1971 Stuart Brown replaced John on lead guitar, George Nimmo replaced Frank on bass, and Frank became the driver. Ronnie was the drummer and also lead singer. They were called Nevada. I went to see them playing at The Vega in Union Street Glasgow one Saturday afternoon and afterwards helped them to load then unload their gear at Brian's house at Calfhill in Pollok. Brian's brother John loaned me the guitar I had sold him and I wrote some songs before returning it. When the band heard my songs they asked me if they could feature one and would I come to their practise. The night I went Stuart hadn't arrived so I was playing his Fender Telecaster and enjoying it. Frank told me he and Ronnie used to come to see The Five Interns at Barnbeth hall. He said when they walked in to the hall they were

impressed with the set up before we even struck a note. Our three Vox AC30's sat on chrome tubular stands with our Fenders strapped on to them. The sad thing is that none of us have photographs of the band at that time as you are not nostalgic when you are young. They also liked our harmonies as we used to switch them during a song. Before the summer holidays of 1972 Ronnie George Frank and Brian asked me if I would join the band. Brian and Stuart were leaving and Frank would replace Brian on rhythm guitar if I came in on lead. I asked Helen and she said, "Yes".

Chapter 5

They all went to the Isle of Man at the Glasgow Fair and we went to the caravan. When we returned the band began to rehearse. I didn't even own a guitar and could not afford to buy one until we were earning so Brian loaned me his  Telecaster and combo amp. He had to sell the Telecaster before we started working and I bought one myself as we were about ready. I had to sell my Abu fishing rod and reel to get the deposit. Our first gig was at the Vega in December 1972 and we had called ourselves Freckles. It was a great feeling to be playing music once again and getting a response from all the Nevada fans. I got through that first night drinking only one sweet stout. We used to rehearse in my bedroom. Tracey and Pauline would come in full of beans and Tracey would always jump on George's back while he was playing, after all she was only four years old but that became a routine. Now that we were making money I returned my Telecaster to Biggars where I had bought it and traded it for a sunburst Fender Stratocaster. This was January 1973 and in the evening of the day I got it we played at the Mushroom in East Kilbride. The Bier Keller, which was just up the street from the Vega poached us for a couple of pounds extra. We were to play there three nights a week for the next two years apart from a spell in the Charing Cross Hotel. We shared the week with another band, Raintree County. Sometimes they played Monday Tuesday Wednesday and we did Thursday Friday Saturday and vice versa. We also did the odd Saturday lunchtime and Helen could bring the kids as they were serving food. The Bier Keller was in a basement and used to be queued all the way up the stairs on to the street on a Friday and Saturday when we were playing there. We kept our gear in a storeroom except for our guitars which we would take home every night, and we travelled there on the bus as there was no need for a van. We changed our name slightly to 'Frekels'. On Sunday afternoons we would go to the Watermill hotel in Paisley to see bands like Tear Gas, The Sleaze Band, and Nickelson, then go back to my place to rehearse. Tear Gas joined up with Alex Harvey to form 'The Sensational Alex Harvey Band' and we were fortunate to see their debut at the Watermill. East Kilbride's Davie Nicholson formed the band 'Nickelson'. Junior Campbell left the Marmalade to go solo and was replaced by Hugh Nicholson. Hugh left Marmalade in 1973 to form the band 'Blue' with Ian MacMillan and Timi Donald. They had a hit with a song called 'Little Jody'. Drummer Raymond Duffy left 'Marmalade' before they had a hit with The Beatles' 'Obladi Oblada'. Dougie Henderson replaced Alan Whitehead when he was sacked by 'Marmalade in 1971. When Hugh left in 1973 Mike Jaap replaced him.

In the shipyard at that time I would work on a ship in the stocks until her launch, then go with her to Stephen's wharf for fitting out. My foreman was Bob Jamieson and charge hand Davie Thompson. Every Friday when we were at Stephen's they would give me a pass to get me out of there and into Fairfields but I never went there. Armed with a sack I would go to the pub and get them half dozen cans of beer, put them in the sack and return to their hut. Each Monday Davie would get money from me and pay me back on the Friday. It saved him from going to the pawnshop. The pipe coverers in the engine room used what we called "Monkey dung". We used to throw it at each other not knowing that it was asbestos. At that time we were ignorant of the dangers. In the winter we would build a canopy out from the stationary mobile crane, put seating under the canopy and site a salamander heater out from it. Anyone waiting for a lift from the crane would sit under the canopy to get a heat until it came to their turn. A crowd of us used to gather there and the patter was wonderful. There was an engineer's helper called Bobby Starret who was a painter and decorator to trade. Bobby was brilliant at doing cartoons and I remember him doing one of his squad sitting round the salamander. The last I heard of Bobby he was painting film sets and I'm sure his name will have appeared in the credits. Bobby was a friend of Roy Fitzsimmons who was an electrician in Fairfields. Roy and I used to get together when I lived in Govan, as he was interested in painting and carving. The only painting I did between 1972 and 1980 was a second copy of 'The Haywain', which I still have today.

In July 1973 Helen and I went to the Isle of Man for a week with George and his girlfriend Anne Marie. We took the Fair Friday overnight boat from Ardrossan. Ronnie and his girlfriend Irene had got an earlier boat and we were to meet up in Douglas the next day. Everyone boarding the ship had a carryout, it was one big all night party where you just fell asleep wherever you were sitting, or standing. In the morning I was still drunk and Helen had stayed awake all night with her contact lenses in. We disembarked and got a taxi to our accommodation. When it came to pay I discovered that I had lost my wallet or should I say, Helen had taken it out of my denim jacket pocket. We left our luggage at the bed and breakfast until we could get in at eleven a.m. By that time Helen was in agony with her eyes, they were streaming with tears and we had to call the doctor. As it was Saturday the doctor said we would have to search to find a chemist open so off I went never having been to Douglas before. Eventually I found one and got the eye drops but on my return I met Ronnie and Irene and we had a pint before I went back to Helen. Anne Marie stayed with Helen while I had been away and George went for a sleep. The proprietor gave us dinner in our room that evening to save Helen from embarrassment and we stayed in all night. For days Helen wore dark glasses and held on to the back pocket of my denims when we went out. The live music scene in Douglas was brilliant at that time with Witticome Fair at the Villiers, The Mimics at the Lido, and bands at many other venues. When Helen's eyes were better we all hired bikes and while on our way to Laxey Anne Marie was being buzzed by a wasp, so she just jumped off her bike and let it go along the road without her. Luckily it didn't cause any damage. We enjoyed the Isle of Man so much that we returned the following year with the children and Helen's young brother Raymond, staying at the same accommodation. George and Anne Marie got married on the sixth of October 1973. I was best man, Helen was best maid and Tracey and Pauline were flower girls. Most of our first time in the Isle of Man was spent in pubs but on the second with the children we spent a lot of time on the beach enjoying the fine weather. One evening while being served dinner the proprietor noticed my legs were badly blistered with sunburn so he took me to the hospital for treatment. I had to walk around for the rest of our holiday bandaged from my groin to my toes. We were walking along the prom one day when one leg's bandage must have worked loose, as there was a long trail behind me. Tracey and Pauline bought laughing bags and drove us up the wall but it was a great family holiday and a complete contrast to the previous year.

The kids went to St. Bernard's primary school. Tracey was good at athletics and was always bringing home certificates. I took Tracey and Pauline to violin lessons every Saturday morning at

Bellarmine secondary school. Tracey didn't play, she just came with me, and after two years Pauline told me she wanted to stop. I do not believe in pushing a child into something they don't want to do. Some years later she started playing the violin again and berated me, saying that I should never have let her stop. "You can't win!"

'Frekels' entered a talent competition ran by Tennent Caledonian and the Evening Times in 1975. On reaching the quarter finals we had white suits made and my sister Gladys made us silk shirts, each one a different colour. The suits were delivered to my home just before we were due to leave for the competition and after all that we didn't get through to the semis. We were also advised to join the musician's union as the semi finals were in the Glasgow Pavilion and finals were to be shown on S.T.V. Although we got nowhere with 'Starmaker 75' I'm sure our new stage suits were significant in getting us many of the jobs that were to follow. I had been writing songs since joining up with Frekels. The best one out of the bunch was called 'Dear Madeline' written in 1974.

Dear Madeline

Dear Madeline, I still love you do not keep us apart
Where have you been, please come on home as you're breaking my heart
Oh how I cried, I aint got no reason to live anymore
I've tried and I've tried, but things can't go on like they used to before

I'm so alone since you left me, give me a chance to reform
Please do not try to forget me, without you I just can't go on

Dear Madeline, I know that I hurt you I've been so untrue
I didn't mean, all of those things that I said about you

I can't stop thinking about you, bring back the kids come on home

Can't go on living without you, don't leave me here all alone

Another song written at that period.

Springtime's Here

Pretty flower of the spring, golden daffodil
When the birds come out to sing, on your windowsill
Springtime is here again, summertime is near
Everybody's happy when, springtime's here, springtime's here.

Melting snow on mountain slopes, sliding to the glen
Summer climbers check their ropes, venture once again
Springtime is here again, summertime is near
Everybody's happy when, springtime's here, springtime's here.

Helen has always enjoyed her bingo. One evening in early 1978 she was going to the Bedford while I was going out to do a gig. I knew that there was going to be a special game played that night for a holiday to America. While carrying the band gear into the house after the gig Helen said, "You haven't asked me how I got on"? When I replied she told me she had won the holiday. I didn't believe her and just carried on bringing the gear in. When the van was unloaded she showed me the letter stating that she had won a holiday for one to Seattle, Washington State. The manageress of the Bedford told her that the alternative to the holiday was one hundred pounds. She also said that Helen should write to Mecca stating that we have never had a holiday since having the kids and never been apart since we were married. It worked, as we were soon to get a reply giving me a place on the trip which was to be at the end of May. My dad had a sore on his ear which was not healing at the time Helen won the holiday. He also got dermatitis on his hands and was taken into hospital where he was given a blood transfusion and let out. He had been working nightshift for years shunting corporation buses from one garage to another and also driving during the day for Tweedie's Coaches. I thought he was just run down. He returned to the hospital to have bone marrow extracted and I remember him telling me that it was the most painful experience of his life. They let him out and he went back in once again for another transfusion. Every Tuesday Helen and the kids would go to my parents straight from school and I would follow them after work. I went to see my dad on Sunday the twentieth of March and he said, "What are you doing here, I'll see you on Tuesday"? He never did! When I arrived on Tuesday the twenty second at 5pm he had passed away at four, I had missed him by an hour". Helen had been there and said she heard footsteps coming down the stairs when he died. I really miss my dad and I suppose I never really got to know him until after I was married as he was always working and I was never around my own home.

Mecca sent us return rail tickets to Gatwick and an Itinerary of our trip to America. None of us had flown before so we were quite excited. On Friday the twenty sixth of May we travelled down to Gatwick where we were to spend the night in the Europa hotel. After

settling in we played bingo that evening for bottles of spirits as there was no license to play for money. We were up early the next morning for our flight. The aircraft was a DC8 and only had a central passage. I was seated at the passage when two lovely girls came by and the blonde one gave me a big smile. During the flight there was a bar at the front, which I duly visited. While there I got talking to Archie McCulloch and told him about me being in the band that won his Costa Clyde competition fourteen years earlier. He introduced me to Andy Ross who was the conductor of the Come Dancing orchestra. Andy was Scottish and told me he used to play in bands around Glasgow in the sixties. I asked Andy who the two girls were and he told me the blonde was Miss World, Mary Stavin. The other was Miss UK, Elizabeth Ann Jones. Then I realised why I had got the smile from Mary as she was knocking about with Graeme Souness at the time and I had on a Scotland T-shirt. While we were in America, Scotland were playing in The World Cup in Argentina and Graeme was in the team. We were seated at the port wing which was full of patches, not a pleasant sight for first time fliers. The aircraft refuelled at Goose Bay Labrador, and as we were flying in we could see cars driving towards the airport. They were taxi drivers that saw the plane coming and were hoping for business as Goose Bay is in the middle of nowhere; unfortunately for them no one was disembarking. I got my photograph taken with the two girls on my own camera at Goose Bay. At that time no one knew who they were. Arriving in Seattle, I wasted no time in using up the rest of my film in order to have it developed in a twenty- four hour service. When I went to retrieve my photos I was given a free film and told that my film was destroyed during processing. We stayed at the Washington Plaza hotel which was near the monorail terminal that took you to the Seattle Center where the World's Fair was held in 1962. We had quite a bit of time to ourselves during our eight-day visit and spent some of it in the Center. One day we went in to Center house where there was a dance going on and the dancers were dressed in various world national costumes. In the evening we went to a laser rock show in the Pacific Science Center. The ceiling was a dome and the floor concave so the first people in lay down at the bottom of the cone with the next row putting their feet at the former's heads and so on. Wherever you were lying you could see the whole show and contemporary rock music was playing at ten thousand watts. What an experience! When we came out we were deaf and blind but that didn't stop us from going up the external lift to the top of the Space Needle which does a complete three hundred and sixty degree revolution in an hour. Every time you looked out, you got a different view of the city without moving.

Another day in the park I had taken my shirt off to sunbathe and was told by the police to put it back on as I was breaking the law. America has different laws for each state which would be really confusing if you were touring. We were taken on a trip to a restaurant near Mount Rainier which is fourteen thousand feet above sea level. The snow was fifteen feet thick at the side of the road and it was around eighty degrees at the end of May. We were told that it would be July before the snow was gone. As Vancouver was only three hours away by Greyhound bus Helen and I caught the first one of the day with another couple who had won the holiday at the Flamingo in Glasgow. That city has it all, including mountains and beaches. We spent a wonderful day there but the customs at the American border were a pain as they wanted to know why we were only in Canada for the day. They searched our bags and gave the four of us a right grilling. When we returned to the hotel we met another couple who were in our party and we invited them in to our room for a drink as we had brought over a couple of litres of spirits. We had no soft drinks so I went back out to get some and didn't feel too safe walking the streets on my own. I had to go farther than I thought and got a taxi back. We also saw the film, "Thank God it's Friday" and the sound system was far superior to any I had ever heard. Before I left Scotland a friend in the shipyard had given me a hundred pounds to get him ice hockey gear as it would be much cheaper there than in Scotland. Washington State has a mild winter climate similar to ours and was told I would have to go to a place out of town to get it. After making many inquiries how to get there I finally got a guy with a pickup truck to take me. He had a couple of stops before we got there and when we arrived I asked him if he would have a beer with me. Because of my accent I did not have to put my hand in my pocket. Every time I took my wallet out someone else would pay for the beers and join in on the conversation. I left the bar slightly tipsy with umpteen addresses from people inviting Helen and I over for another holiday. I got my mate's hockey gear and waited for a bus back to Seattle. Lucky for me a lady started talking to me, and when she found out where I was going, she told me I was on the wrong side of the road. If I had got on a bus it would have taken me to Canada, the opposite way to where I wanted to go. While I was there Helen stayed in Seattle shopping for gifts. I had purchased a Polaroid camera while we were in Seattle and tried to get Miss World and Miss

UK together at the airport but by then everyone knew who they were and it was impossible. However I managed to get one of me with Mary Stavin who was later to be a 'Bond Girl'. I will never forget our return trip as we left Seattle at twelve thirty on the third of June travelling through the night, landing at Keflavik airport Iceland to refuel and never saw darkness. We left Iceland for Gatwick flying over Glasgow where we had to return by train. Unfortunately I couldn't tell my dad about our trip!

On the twentieth of November 1978 while playing at a twenty first-birthday party our van was stolen from outside the Rolls Royce foremen's club next to the Bellahouston hotel. We only had it three months and two of our white suits were in it at the time so that was the end of them. I got Frekels barred from Rothesay when we were playing on the pier sometime in the seventies. We took the van over, set up and then went to see the digs. I think our friend Jimmy Murray was with us and Frank was going to sleep in the van. Jimmy Frank and I set off up the serpentine and the van kept skidding as it was raining. We completed our journey on foot and when we found the B&B we were knackered. A woman answered the door and said, "Follow me and I'll show you your room". Frank and Jimmy let me go upstairs and the lady showed me a room with a double and two single beds. I said, "That'll do fine". I asked her how much and she said "A pound a head". She had told me that they were having problems with fire doors. On the way downstairs when the guys came into view, I shouted to Frank that it was £1 a head so he said, "Count me in". We went back upstairs to be shown another room with a room off it. We got a carryout for after the gig and headed up to the B&B when we finished. The lady said, "You must be hungry boys". Aye, so we tanned a plain loaf and half pound o butter with half a pig of bacon. Then we went up to the room and tanned our carryout, deciding that we wouldn't have breakfast in the morning. Next morning I went to the hatch at the kitchen and told the guy that we were just going to catch the first boat and not bother with breakfast so I handed him a fiver. I couldn't contain myself when he said, "Who's next"? We had no money between us as it was paid to our agent. Nae mair gigs for us on Rothesay!

Our holiday in 1979 was to Looe in Cornwall where we stayed with my sister Chris and her partner Kit. They had a small flat above a shop on the east side of the harbour and it was almost directly opposite the 'Shark Angling Club Of Great Britain' on the west side. In the early evenings if we were in the flat we would watch the angling club's boats coming up the river. We could tell by the number and colour of triangular flags they were flying if they had caught any sharks and what size they were. If they had anything big we would watch them hoist the shark from the boat for weighing. We had fine weather during our two-week stay and I did things I would never have done. As Kit was a local lad he took me out to the surrounding fields dressed in camouflage to try my hand at shooting rabbits. We didn't get any but it was fun. One day at low tide Kit and I walked up the river and he showed me how to catch flounders by hand. When you spotted one you would approach it from the front with your hand open, palm facing the riverbed and as it swam under your hand you just clamped it with your fingers. On the same walk I found an old stone beer jar buried in the silt. When it was cleaned up we showed it to an elderly local man who reckoned it to be about a hundred years old. On an evening stroll we picked bay leaf and ate wild strawberries. Kit and his dad arranged to take me out fishing on their boat. I had a couple of pints of cider before we left, and as it was raining we put on oilskins. We were about three miles out from the harbour and catching fish; the rain had stopped when suddenly, I started to feel funny. I removed my jacket then I became violently ill and remained so all the way back to Looe. They said that as I removed my jacket my face had turned green and it was intentional as I had caught the largest fish. One day Helen, Tracey, Pauline and I went to Polperro and decided to take the four-mile cliff walk back to Looe. Before leaving Polperro I purchased a half-gallon of scrumpy cider. It was scorching all the way back and much to my irritation; I had to give the girls some as there was nowhere in between the two towns where they could have a drink. At one point Helen was walking backwards when she fell. She thought she was going over the cliff and I was laughing as I could see she was only falling into fern. You should have seen the look on her face! We enjoyed a trip to Bodmin Moor and went to see the Cheese Wring. It was a misty day, which made it eerie, like in a horror film with wild horses appearing out of the mist. That holiday in Cornwall really inspired me and made me think about painting again. I stretched canvases before we returned to Looe the following year.

The band was playing up to six nights a week around 1978-79. We played in 'Fergies' at Paisley Road Toll when Alex Ferguson was the proprietor. At our break we would cross the road to have a drink with Jim Baxter and his wife Jean. When we returned to 'Fergies' to do our second set, Jim would come over, have a chat with Alex and send us a drink up. While backing cabaret singer Beau Brummel at Maryhill Juniors social club on March the second 1979 he turned on a strobe light. He must have looked good from the front but we couldn't see the music as the strobe was facing us but our experience saw us through a funny situation. The social convener of the club was Willie McNamara. Willie was a painter's gaffer with the council based in the Pollok area. He was always apologizing for the low fee the club was paying and said if we needed any paint that he would see us all right.

There was a welder in the shipyard that was known as Mr Wonderful. His name was Willie Adamson. He told some crazy stories and said his son played drums with The Searchers. We got a booking to support them at Condorrat club on the fifth of May 1979 so I told Willie and he said he would be there. When we arrived at the gig their gear was already set up on the stage so we had to set up on the dance floor in front of them. They arrived as we were doing our set but we didn't see them come in so as soon as we finished I headed straight for their dressing room. When the door opened there was no doubt Billy was a younger version of Willie Wonderful. He said "You must be Jim!" and when I asked him where his dad was he told me he had too much to drink during the day and they left him at home. They were brilliant and left right after their set leaving us to play on. We claimed their fame as we ended the night with 'Needles n' Pins'. Willie was quite happy when I returned to work to confirm his story.

A good mate of mine from the shipyard was Jamie McGettrick. Jamie was an apprentice sheet ironworker and played with St. Mirren when Fergie was their manager. When Sir Alex left to go to Aberdeen Jamie got a free transfer to Clyde. Our band played at Jamie and Joan's wedding on Saturday the twelfth of July 1980 at the Glynhill hotel, Paisley. At that time he was playing with Kilbirnie Ladeside. The following day they were going on their honeymoon to Torquay and we were going back to my sister's at Looe. They came through to Looe later in the week with Jamie's mate Tam and his girlfriend and we all went to Mevagissey for the day. We went to Paignton zoo one day and a seagull shat on my sister. Tracey and Pauline thought it was hilarious. We also went to Newquay for the day. The weather hadn't been great that year and neither had my sister's relationship. She told us just before we left that she had fallen for her boss who was older than me. We had met him during our stay; he was a dentist, married with two kids. Chris told us his marriage had broken down before they began their relationship.

The sheet iron shop manager at work, Alfie Blunt, lived along the road from me. Alfie used to pick me up for work every morning and his horn was my alarm. He used to have a problem getting his son James out of bed and then would have to wait for me. James was a joiner in the yard. I said to Alfie one day that he was crazy waiting for me every morning and he told me that my manager John Young told him to get me in. If it were not for Alfie I would have been paid off for bad time keeping. We played at James' wedding to Cathy who was his second wife at the Crookston hotel on the fourth of October 1980. I was invited back to Alfie's after the wedding and not long after I got there, James also appeared for the party. His brother John sent him packing back to the hotel, and his new wife.

Helen's mum and dad had moved to Irvine in 1974 and her youngest brother Raymond finished his schooling at Greenwood Academy. When he left school he used to stay with us a lot, some times for months and he would come with the band and do his roadie. On Wednesday the eighth of October we did Blantyre Celtic's player of the year dance. Jimmy Johnston was playing with them at the time and was at the dance. Wee Jinky even bought the band a drink. Ronnie won a half bottle of vodka at the raffle and gave it to me as that was my tipple. I had booked the next day off work as I knew it would be a late night and I would be under the weather. When Raymond and I got home I poured myself a vodka and said to him that it was good him staying with us as it would keep him out of trouble. The next evening at tea time, Frank phoned me to tell me that when we left the club the previous night we were chased as far as Rutherglen by someone from the club before they lost us. The night's takings from the bar were supposed to have been in a briefcase which had gone missing and we were being accused of taking it. Frank asked if Raymond and I would be willing to go to the police station to sort it out. Ronnie lived in Craigie Street next to a police station so we all went in and explained the situation. They knew nothing of our story and phoned Blantyre who then asked us if we would be willing to go through there to be interviewed. When we got there we were taken one at a time and asked," If it wasn't you who took the briefcase, who do you think took it?" We didn't have a clue and I'm sure the police knew we were innocent as we didn't get too much of a grilling. When we were allowed to go they warned us not to go near the club, but we ignored them and went there to show our disappointment at being accused of a crime. We had played there regularly a couple of years beforehand and built up their Saturday nights but we would never play there again. We heard through the grapevine that it was the bar manager who took the cash but heard no more about it officially.

My Aunt Peggy was seventy-five when she died from cancer on the first of December 1980.

One morning in 1981 Helen asked me if I remembered urinating outside the back of our close during the night. As I couldn't, she reminded me that I had two daughters of twelve and thirteen and couldn't remember what I was doing so I stopped drinking for five months and took us to France Austria and Italy. I haven't touched vodka since then. Tracey had been on a school trip to France just before we went and I thought I would surprise them with this holiday so I hadn't said anything about it. We were to leave for Paris by coach from London 's Victoria at 9am, so we got the overnight train from Glasgow Central to London Euston arriving at 7am. This would give us two hours to relax before our coach journey to Paris. As we were approaching London I threw down our travel documents and when the kids saw where we were going they said, "We knew where we were going because you've been singing 'Just one cornetto' for months". The train was delayed at various times through the night and did not arrive in London until eight thirty giving us half an hour to get our coach. We made it with two minutes to spare and the courier allowed us to get something to eat before leaving. We arrived at a campsite on the outskirts of Paris late afternoon and after dinner we were taken on a tour of the city before retiring for the night. The next day's journey was a long one and quite boring as that part of France was very flat so there was nothing to look at. We crossed into Switzerland at Basle, then the Arlberg Tunnel to Austria. I will never forget coming out of the tunnel; it was like coming into another world. We were in the Alps with a raging river running beside the road and snow-capped peaks all around us. We camped in a small village called Kolsass Weer which was near Innsbruck. The next morning after breakfast the sun came out and it was scorching so I donned my shorts for our trip to Innsbruck. First they took us to the Olympic ski jump. We were told that as the skier leaves the ramp he or she is looking directly at the graveyard in Innsbruck a couple of thousand feet below. It started to rain just as we left, then we were dropped off in Innsbruck for three hours at our leisure. I was absolutely frozen and spent most of that time in a bar. The following morning we were up at 5am to leave at six, as our drivers were to bring a party from our destination in Italy back to Kolsass Weer. As we climbed up the mountains leaving a wet Innsbruck behind we came through the clouds to blue skies. Looking back we could see the band of cloud covering the Inn valley with the alpine peaks protruding through. It was a brilliant journey over the Brenner Pass, The Dolomites, and finally to Lido De Jesolo where we were to spend eight nights. Flying is great, but that coach trip was one experience I will always treasure. On arriving at our campsite we immediately got our kit off and hit the beach. The kids headed straight into the sea while Helen and I lay on the beach. After a while I was heading for a beach kiosk to get soft drinks when but felt dizzy before I got there and had to return to the tent as I had sunstroke. We booked a day trip to Venice, going by boat and returning by coach. It's well known that it is expensive to hire a gondola in Venice. Through our courier we got a special deal and the four of us with another couple in our party hired one. As we waited in the queue I loaded my thirty-five-millimetre Canon AV1 camera and photographed all the sights including Marco Polo's house and the gondolier. I had just bought the camera before we went on holiday and hadn't loaded it properly so the trip through the canals is just a memory. I had plenty of film with me so I still managed to capture other parts of Venice. Before going on holiday I had been mentioning to a colleague at work where I was going, and that I intended to take a trip to Venice. He and his wife were going to Yugoslavia and were also intending to visit Venice. While we were having a coffee in St. Marks Square among thousands of people, my colleague and his wife appeared out of the masses and sat next to us. We couldn't believe that we went on the same day and actually managed to meet up. On another trip to a market I bought a leather jacket for forty pounds after a bit of haggling. On our last day in Jesolo another Scottish guy and I went to a drinks supermarket which was about a mile away. It was a 'Scotsman's Paradise' so we borrowed a shopping trolley and loaded it up with booze for our return journey. We were to leave Jesolo around lunchtime and I remember having to drag Tracey and Pauline out of a place where they were watching Charles and Diana's wedding on television in Italian. We returned to Kolsass for a night, and then on the return trip to Paris went via Munich and the Black Forest area. The return journey from Italy was just one big party with singing and dancing as the drink was passed around. We had got friendly with a couple from Birchington in Kent as their daughter went around with our kids, so we left the coach at Canterbury where they had arranged transport to take us to their home. We stayed with them for two nights and as we still had money left and the time, I thought we should take the opportunity to visit Constable Country. It was a pleasant journey from Birchington to London as the train hugged the Kent coast, then the Thames estuary. We took another train from London to Colchester and booked into a bed and breakfast for two nights. Helen couldn't be bothered going to Constable Country the next day so she just stayed with the girls in Colchester while I took a bus which dropped me off near East Bergholt where Constable was born in 1776. It was a beautiful morning as I approached the village so I went into a field and changed into my shorts. I bought a footpath map of the area and with my knowledge of Constable's work began to trace the spots where his major works were inspired. Although he was buried in Hampstead London in 1837, his father was buried in the churchyard in East Bergholt. I saw his grave before going to Flatford to see Willy Lott's cottage, (the one in 'The Haywain'). I had purchased a bottle of Riesling

at Dedham and was drinking from it while strolling along the road in my shorts and sandals. I could see an old man who was approaching me on the opposite side of the road stop and fold his arms. As I drew level with him he unfolded his arms and gave me the thumbs up sign. In other words "That's the way to live son," but he never said anything, he only gave a big smile. He was a large man with a long grey beard whom I was later to see on the television, being the artist and forger, Tom Keating. I had a great day in Suffolk and walked for miles so when I got to the B & B around ten p.m. I fell into bed exhausted. After breakfast the following day we headed back to London to catch the Glasgow train.

Chapter 6

Inspired by my two trips to Cornwall, I began painting again in 1980. I noticed the steady decline of traffic on the Clyde during the late seventies. To me shipbuilding was on the way out and here I was, working in a shipyard with many years knowledge behind me, knowing of no other artists painting shipyard scenes since Muirhead Bone and Stanley Spencer. I became more observant of what was going on around me although I had always asked questions in the past. A shipyard is not a pleasant place to work especially in the winter. Before I began painting shipyard scenes there was many a day I hated going in to work. One evening while working late I was on the deck at the hatch guiding ventilation into the engine room. The engine room hatch is up level with the funnel and it had started to snow. There was only one way to signal the crane driver which meant my outstretched arm had snow blowing right up it. I have seen us having to dig jobs out of the snow in the morning to rig them up for a crane lift and having to stand in the cold all day before getting a lift. My two best workmates were Helen's cousin Ian Morrison and John Gray. John's father George was the boilermaker's convener during the UCS crisis, and Ian's dad Jim was a liner off for the sheet iron department. John, Ian and I were known as the 'A' team as we were always together. While working on a ship we used railway wagons as departmental offices cum changing rooms and canteen. We had a helper working with us who was nicknamed 'Superchicken'. He used to regularly fall asleep on the job. One day while he was sleeping during the tea break, someone poured salt on his tongue as he slept with his mouth open and he never even stirred. The characters were the one thing that kept you sane. There was 'Wullie the dug' who used to creep up behind you, bark and grab your ankle, and it didn't matter how many times he did it to you, you always jumped. Then there was 'The Doonhamer' who's trade was a shipwright. He always walked about with his maul over his shoulder and when no one was looking he would smash things up with it. While a ship is on the slipways it doesn't sit directly on them. There is a centre keel and on each side of the ways are bilge keel blocks. These keels are topped with jacks and the ship rests on them until her launch. There is also timber between the ship and the ways. They are known as oaks and are numbered and wired together as they go with the ship when she is launched and have to be retrieved later. The dismantling of shores and keelblocks begins days prior to the launch. All the shores are numbered and removed in a calculated order by four teams of eight men with a ram, two on the port side, and two starboard. The shores and keels all have a removal time marked on them. When all the shores and keels have been removed and the ship rests on the ways, she is prevented from moving by electro magnets that hold the sliding ways to the standing ways. As well as the magnets the apparatus has a safety pin and is supported by a light pole. Just before the honoured guest pushes the button to release the Champagne and electro magnets, two shipyard apprentices will have removed the safety pins and poles to present them in front of the launch platform. This display lets the shipyard management know that it is safe to launch the ship. The ways are laid out in a curve fore to aft so that the ship moves slowly before gaining momentum. The distance she travels is calculated and checked by tonnes of drag chains. After the launch small boats retrieve any flotsam and tie it next to the vacant slipways. The Doonhamer's job was to go out on the river and undo the wire connecting any timber and bring it ashore. He was sculling in a clinker type boat, which means using one oar through a rowlock at the centre of the stern. While I was working on a ship in the next slipway to one where a ship had just been launched I went up on the deck for a smoke. There was The Doonhamer, standing on his boat in the middle of the river waving his bunnet and shouting for help as he had lost his oar. There was a plater known as 'The Paratrooper' who told the story of flying over the desert during the Second World War and spotted a woodbine cigarette on the sand so he landed to get it. Our department had a sheet ironworker called 'Monty' who always wore a red beret and kept his money in a handkerchief. When he got his pay on a Friday he would sort out his cut and put it in his hankie.

We were under threat of closure again in 1979 when the team of Chief Executive Eric Mackie and Production Director Bill Gallagher were appointed to the board in December. These two Ulstermen had previously worked as a team at James Brown & Hamer in South Africa. On his arrival at Govan one of the first things Eric Mackie did was get the yard convener Sammy Gilmore to introduce him to the yard's characters, probably because he was one himself. The first contract they got for us were two engine conversions from steam turbine to diesel. The ships Discovery Bay and Moreton Bay were sister ships of the Jervis Bay which I worked on in 1969. Our next order was for the ships Pacific Peace and Pacific Patriot. I did a small oil painting of one of these ships and it was purchased by Eric Mackie who had it hung in his secretary Christine's office as he thought it would have a larger audience in there. Bill Gallagher was a hard man feared by the management as he would lose his head with them, swear, and fire them. The next day he would apologize for his outburst. He also had a kind streak as I have heard of him giving cigarettes and sending out for food to let workers carry on working on a job, which had a deadline. Bill has been a facebook friend of mine in recent years. Another character was a plater called John Mitchell who was known as 'The talking horse.' John was also a keen beekeeper and used to sell honey in the yard. Whenever there was a mass meeting John would plan his bombardment of the shop stewarts, as he would call them. No matter what the meeting was about John would have something to say?

At every mass meeting he's there
To shout abuse at the chair,
You hear the lads cheer
When they see him appear,
With a speech the last week
he's prepared.

I mustn't forget "The Hambone." This guy was special, as he was never known to refuse a challenge. Hammy was double jointed and used to get into some crazy positions. I have seen him standing on his hands with his legs behind his head, also hanging from a deck head pipe by his hands with his legs behind his head. I have also seen him packed into a drawer measuring 24" X 24" X 12." His contest manager Mick Giblin who was also a welder assisted in all these feats. Mick used to arrange contests for "The Bone" at lunchtimes. I remember one that was a race across the Elderpark pond in the kiddie's paddleboats. His opponent was a caulker that they called "The Trogg" who was nearly always Hammy's challenger. When they were half way over, Hammy jumped into the water followed by The Trogg, and to the cheers of the workforce, they pushed their boats to the finish. Word of these contests spread like wildfire in the morning and most of the yard turned out to see them. I have also seen Hammy descend from a ship in the stocks climbing down welding cables. He had no fear! Helen's cousin's husband, Sam Mooney, was a crane driver in the yard. One day while I was waiting for a lift he shouted down to me, "Jim, are you still shagging my cousin?" Everyone looked at me with surprise not knowing that Sam was talking about my wife.

On Monday the twenty second of November 1982 'Frekels' hired the Plaza ballroom to hold our tenth anniversary dance. We booked a disco and bought new clothes and gifts for a free raffle. As the Plaza is such a large venue we upgraded our PA and bought a pair of Cerwin Vega speaker cabinets. We chose them because we had seen The Fortunes and Magic use them, and as we were also a harmony band, what we heard was the sound for us. We began selling tickets six weeks before the gig and also at the door on the night. The place was absolutely jumping and well worth all the effort. We played regularly at the American naval base at the Holy Loch, Dunoon. We always went across by ferry from Gourock and drove home via the 'Rest and be thankful'. They got us to do all the big formal occasions like Sea Bees', Marine, and Chief Petty Officer's Balls which were nearly always held in the Queens Hall where The Interns had won the beat contest many years before. When we performed there the food and drink would be free all night and we always came home with a giant carryout. The base itself had three clubs, the Enlisted Men, Chief Petty Officers, and Officers. On arriving at the base in the early evening in summertime there would be a barbecue on and we would get a couple of rolls and steak each before unloading the van. Although we played all three clubs we were mainly in the C.P.O. where they always laid on a buffet so we always had food for the journey home. You could only use dollars at the bar so we had to change our money at the office before we began playing. If our audience was kind, any dollars we had left were kept until our next gig there. One winter evening it started to snow as we began playing at 9pm and by 1am when we finished it was a foot thick and after phoning the AA, we were advised not to attempt the drive home. One of the officers put us up for the night. We played in the C.P.O. club at Hogmanay 1982 where they had a champagne fountain running and no one bothered to use it as the drink was also free at the bar. At the end of the night we asked if we could take some champagne with us as the empty bottles were still there. We just taped up the necks to seal them and drank some on the way home.

Nitshill had steadily declined since we moved there and Helen and I decided we had to get our kids away from that environment. The local glue sniffers were using our close regularly. In May 1983 we took a new Lawrence built flat at 10 Fochabers Drive, Cardonald. It was shared ownership where we had a mortgage for 25 per cent of the price and also paid a rent. It was quite expensive to stay there but it was a nice area and only a twenty minute walk to the yard and a little longer to Helen's work at McGill School in Pollok. The kids were at Bellarmine secondary school and as they were aproaching fourteen and fifteen we let them continue there so that their education would not be disrupted. We went on another camping trip to Blanes in Spain for our holiday that year, leaving once again by coach from London. We decided to travel down to London the day before and spend the night in a hotel that we booked through our travel company so that it would be near our departure point. We spent a nice evening in London visiting the sights but it was so hot through the night that none of us slept. In the morning when we boarded the coach we were all told that there was a small lounge at the rear just below us, which we could take our turn to visit and stretch our legs. I went down before we reached Dover and there was a couple sitting whom I hadn't seen going down as we were sitting right at the stairway to the lounge. It turned out that they had booked at the last minute and the company had overbooked the coach so they were told to stay in the lounge. When I asked their names, they were Jim and Helen from Paisley and Jim worked in the yard beside me although I didn't know him. It was another boring journey through France arriving in Blanes the following morning. I spent most of the night sitting next to the driver to keep him company. We didn't see much of Tracey and Pauline on this trip as they made friends and went their own way most of the time. I had mates from the  yard who were staying at Lloret De Mar which was the next resort up the coast. Pat Currie, his wife Sadie, son Duncan, and his girlfriend Caroline came through from Lloret to see us at our campsite. Pat was the groundsman for the big crane in Fairfields and his son Dunky was a red leader. They were both great characters. Pat and Sadie would book their annual holiday and Dunky and Caroline would get a flight only and sleep on the floor of their self-catering apartment. Like me they used to go where the locals drink, as it is always cheaper. The day they came to us we spent the afternoon on the beach and in the evening we were joined by Jim and Helen and an Irish couple. First we went to a small bar at an open-air carnival and ordered ten glasses of wine at seven and half pesetas. It was like vinegar so we got another round at fifteen pesetas and so on until it was suitable to drink. Pat discovered an outdoor hockey game with a bar so we piled in there and changed our drink to Bacardi and coke. Pat and Sadie went back to Lloret, the Irish couple said they would look after our girls as they were camped facing us, and Jim and Helen returned to the campsite. Dunky, Caroline, Helen and I carried on drinking and on our way back to the campsite there was a bar pulling down their shutters. We shouted to the hombre asking if we could have something to eat. He waved us over and locked us in as the place was full of Spaniards. After we had eaten I noticed a guitar lying in the corner and asked if I could play it. I sung a couple of songs before they requested The Beatles. I didn't know the words to many of the songs although I knew the chords so I just made them up and they thought it was great. Helen tells me there was a girl there mesmerized by my playing but I hadn't noticed as I was too busy making up words. Every evening when we went out we had to pass a bar which had a rodeo type bucking bison, and one night we sat down to watch people being thrown off it. Soon a Belgian couple joined us at our table. His English was poor so his wife interpreted for him. He said that he had been on the bison and after a few drinks said to me, "You go on, I go on". I wasted no time going up on the beast and remember the strain of the first forward movement. I was determined to beat this guy and held on like grim death digging my knees in to its body. It twisted and turned until it finally threw me off. My right forefinger was bleeding and both my legs were grazed on the insides as I had shorts on. He was hardly on the thing when it threw him off. When he returned to the table he said, "You win my friend". Somehow I don't think my win was worth it and when he saw the state of me when I came off, he probably thought the same. The following day we had booked to go to a market and a visit to a bodega with wine tasting. My finger was huge and I felt miserable throughout the trip. When we returned to Blanes I visited a local clinic and was pleased to know that heat only caused the swelling and my wound only needed dressing. We went through to Lloret one day to meet up with Pat, Sadie, Dunky and Caroline and got a street artist to do a portrait of Tracey and Pauline. I didn't' like it and wasn't' going to pay him until Helen eventually talked me into it.

In the yard that year we completed three Lakers for Misener Transportation of Toronto Canada. The ships were Selkirk Settler, Canada Marquis, and Saskatchewan Pioneer. These three ships were specially built to go to sea in the winter when the Great Lakes froze over. I did a painting of the first ship and the chief officer Bob Hull purchased it. Bob was a giant of a man, over seven feet tall. The officers who came for the first ship said they would be returning to crew the other two and some of them commissioned me to do paintings of these ships. The third ship had different colours from the other two as Misener was only managing it. When the Canada Marquis had been doing her trials at the Clyde estuary I got the yard's official photographer David Miller to take me to Gourock where we caught a small boat out to her. During our return from the ship Scott Misener, president of Misener Holdings introduced himself to me saying, "I hear you've been doing paintings of our ships for my officers, would you do one for me?" I told him that I had been working on a panorama of the yard with the three ships in it and he said that it sounded fine and when it was finished I had to tell his overseer Graham Mitchell the price and he would deal with it. I had invited Bob Hull for dinner at my home and he had returned the favour by inviting Helen and I on the last ship that was in Govan dry dock, on the night before she was due to leave for Canada. We were to be on the ship for 8pm and I finished Scott's painting at seven thirty. We got a taxi to the ship and I had to hold the wet painting all the way to the dry dock. You have to remember my position in the yard as a helper and here I was socialising with the chief officer and captain of the ship. As I was carrying the painting through the stairwells of the ship I bumped into Bill Gallagher who was showing guests and his wife Janet around and they all admired it. Bob and Graham Mitchell were with the party and Graham asked me what the price was. I said "Five hundred pounds" and Bob said, "Did you not tell me six Jim?" so I got my six hundred. For me that was a real achievement for an amateur painter. Bob wrote to me in 1985, he had gained his master's certificate and was sailing on the Selkirk Settler at the time. He told me that the crew on her says, "She is the original and the others are copies." He also said, "Tell Harry the boss at the joiners that his beds aren't too good, this one just collapsed. The one on the Pioneer did the same. In case he asks, I was alone on both occasions."

We had begun to build prefabricated cabins at the yard and I had a painting in each of the three samples. One day while I was waiting for a lift from the crane Eric Mackie approached me to let me know that many visitors to the sample cabins admired my work.

In 1984 Bert and Nellie had put another caravan at Kircaldy, Fife. The sun shone every day for our two-week holiday at Kircaldy that year. Every morning after breakfast I would go for a walk. The caravan site was at the top of a hill beyond the ice rink. I would stroll down to Dysart, along the beach to Kircaldy Castle and back up the hill to the site. One day from Dysart, I walked all the way along the beach to Buckhaven and Methil. I had played there in the sixties with The Five Interns. There was a small club in the caravan site and surprisingly I won fifteen pounds in the talent contest. The weather had been so good that as I had another week off work, we decided to stay on. I had a gig to do at the US base at Dunoon on the Saturday at the end of the second week so I had to take the train home and return the next day. I had to change trains at Edinburgh so I thought I would visit the Royal Scottish Academy's summer exhibition. To be quite honest I was not impressed with some of the work and as it is an open show. I made my mind up to submit something the following year. I took the train to Glasgow to be picked up by our van for the ferry crossing from Gourock to Dunoon, did the gig, came home, and returned to Kircaldy on the Sunday. We had another great week there and returned the following year.

Our next contract in the yard was three colliers for the Central Electricity Generating Board. The ships were Sir Charles Parsons, Lord Citrine, and Lord Hinton. I always kept my loaded camera in my locker at the yard so that I could capture events and

anything special that happened within my place of work. I had a free hand as the yard's directors, drawing room staff, management, and workers encouraged me. I have been up on most of the cranes and roofs of buildings to photograph the launching of ships. This activity did not interfere with my job as I always asked permission from my manager John Young before taking my camera out. To me, the plater's shed was like a sculpture workshop with all these wonderful shapes.

'The process of building a ship provides the onlooker with an ever changing display of sculpture. Each piece when complete being lost in the sheer mass of the final exhibit'.

107

My mate John Gray used to say to me when I was excited about a certain shape that it was only a piece of steel. I was delighted when we received the order for the roll on roll off ferry from P&O. She was to be the largest passenger ship to be built in the UK since John Brown's QE2. She was for North Sea Ferries and would operate from Hull to Rotterdam in Holland. At the same time we got the order for the Norsea, Japan received one for her sister ship, Norsun. One Tuesday in April 1985 while working in the engine room of a ship, my shop steward came aboard to ask me if I had a passport and would I like to go to Holland on Friday with my wife. I told him I would have to contact my wife and the band before giving him an answer as I had commitments. Helen and I decided to go and she took the Friday off work. P&O had given sixty couples a free trip so that we could see the standard of work required in building a ferry. Because of this the yard had invited the press to see us off. When we returned there was a photograph of us all in the Evening Times and Helen was worried in case her boss saw it. A coach took us to Hull where we boarded the Norland for Rotterdam. The ship left Hull at 6.30pm and although she arrived at Rotterdam earlier than the disembarking time of 8.30am the following morning, passengers are not allowed to disembark until then. We had a great night on the ship and were in the disco until the early hours. NSF public relations manager Tony Farrell was looking after us. Our personnel director Bob McCann and his wife were also in our party. We had a nice outside en suite cabin with a window and bunk beds. On returning from the disco Helen claimed the bottom bunk and I climbed into the top and fell asleep. The next thing I awoke as I landed on the deck. I remember having a pee over the side of the ship dressed only in my underpants and I was freezing. Tony Farrell ushered me back into my cabin. My nose was sore and when I looked in the mirror my face was covered in blood, I must have hit it off of the bedside cabinet. There was no way I was going back up top and it took some persuading to get Helen to let me in beside her. She couldn't stop laughing in the

morning when she saw my face. It was embarrassing at breakfast
with my mates and at passport control, but the crew sympathised as
it had happened to most of them. Some of my mates said that they
heard a bang, and then oohhh. On the Saturday we visited the Royal
Delftware factory, model village at Maduradam and The Hague. We
had a typical Dutch lunch and for me, the highlight of the trip was
Panorama Mesdag in The Hague. You entered by a long dark passage
before ascending a spiral staircase which leads you on to a platform.
This disrupts your senses and makes you believe what you see to be
real. From the viewing platform you are surrounded by a huge
canvas painting of a typical Dutch landscape, cumulous clouds and
flat land surrounds you with villages dotted here and there. Sand was
laid from the platform all the way down to the bottom of the canvas
so that you couldn't see the edge. There were objects laid on the
sand, some of which were the same, but varying in size to give you
the feeling of perspective. Above your head was a large disc which
obscured your vision of the top of the canvas. In the centre of the

platform was a tubular glass with the scene drawn on it. Mesdag put his head inside the tube and directed his assistants at the canvas where to put certain points in order to reproduce the scene drawn on the tube. I took it easy with the alcohol on the return trip to Hull as I didn't want to fall out my bunk again. The band had played without me on the Friday and Saturday but I made it back in time to do the Sunday night gig at the Pollok Inn.

In 1985 I did a painting of Sir Charles Parsons under construction in the stocks. It was a small oil of about sixteen inches by twelve and entitled 'The Art of Shipbuilding.' I submitted it to The Royal Scottish Academy and on being accepted; I received my free entry pass for the duration of the exhibition. I went to the RSA on varnishing day with my kit and while touching up my painting I was approached by another exhibiting artist. He told me that he had been exhibiting there for years and had never seen anyone doing what I was. My embarrassment didn't last long as a Canadian buyer purchased the painting three days after the exhibition opened to the public. When I told Bob McCann about my achievement he arranged a liaison with the press and presented me with a company tie. The Scotsman and Evening Times used the story and I was famous within the shipyard. Helen's brother Raymond got married on the twenty eighth of June 1985. He had met his wife Catherine in the Caravan Park at Kircaldy.

We had began construction of the Norsea and considering my sale to Misener and the RSA painting, I felt confident to approach North Sea Ferries to see if there was any possibility of me doing work for the ship. I was informed that Albert Taconis was coming to the yard and he would be responsible for both our ship and Japan's. I organised an exhibition of my work in an office and met with him to discuss the possibility of doing paintings for the ship. It took some time before I got an answer and my first commission was for three oils of the ship under construction for NSF technical offices in Rotterdam. Following that I was commissioned to portray thirty

Scottish landscapes that would be reproduced to hang in every inside cabin on the red and blue decks of the ship. If the cabin had a window it didn't require a picture. There were a hundred and fifty three inside cabins on the two decks. This task gave me a problem as I would have to find thirty images of Scotland without infringing copyright. In the spring and summer of 1986 when the roads were quiet I would go with my niece Doreen and her partner David on trips up north in their car. It's amazing the distance you can travel in a day when you are not held up by traffic. David was also a keen photographer so we would stop at anything that looked interesting. By leaving Glasgow at 7.30am we timed it to catch the morning mist on Loch Lomond then head up through Glencoe, Fort William and on to Plockton before Hamish Macbeth made it famous. We returned via Appin to catch Castle Stalker at sunset before carrying on to Oban for something to eat. By then it was dark but we still managed to photograph Inveraray by using our tripods as it was fairly well lit up by the streetlights. On another trip we went to Castle Urquhart at Loch Ness. While we were taking photographs of the castle there was a huge black cloud approaching from the north. The next thing it began snowing which followed us for miles as we headed south. As well as images that I gathered on my trips, I borrowed photographs from workmates who were into photography.

It was hard working on the Norsea as many jobs had to be carried much further than any other ship I had worked on. Ventilation was much heavier in the car decks and everywhere else, more compact. I enjoyed watching the ship taking shape and photographed every stage of its completion. Engine room ventilation went through a shaft and there was little room to work. The shaft also had an offset, which meant transferring each vent from the crane on to chain blocks before lowering it down. I worked many nights until eight o' clock and after a late dinner, I painted sometimes until 3am and rose at seven for another day's work. I don't know how I managed it but I completed the thirty landscapes and when they were accepted I was asked to do another four oils for the de-luxe cabins. Nearing completion of the ship I wrote a poem titled Govan-Built. There were a couple of Dutch subcontractors working on the ship and I asked them if they could translate it for me. It was inspired by the Norsea but could relate to any ship built in the yard.

Govan – Built

Men of steel at Govan create
A ship from many tonnes of plate
Put together on the ways
Until her launch, there she stays.

Patiently waiting the tide on the turn
Her back to the water, she faces the sun
There to protect her, the tugs are in gear
Come to your mother the river is clear.

"I name this ship" the lady cries
"Hip hip hooray" the crowd replies

A bottle breaks upon her bow
Down she glides to water's plough.

Now she's docked for fitting out
By men who know what they're about
Dougie, Jock, Tam and Bill,
Many trades have shown their skill
As she heads towards the sea,
Never to return to you or me,
Away to show the World with pride,
That she was built, upon the Clyde.

One of these workers was Peter De Kwant. I painstakingly laid out Peter's translation using Letraset and photographs on a sheet of card, which I then had mounted and framed, with the intention of giving it to Albert Taconis. Peter had left the yard and I received a letter from him on the eighteenth of February 1987.

Mocambique – Guilimane – 18-2-87

Hello Jim
I found your adres in my book of friends and disided to wriht. Please do not mistake my mis-spelling of your language for a lack of interest. I am a man of spoken words, preferably on rhym. By the way; try to get hold of a record sung by the Dutch singer "Nady" – she's a perfect and beautiful expression of thoughts. Your image of Scheveningen has a rather prominent place in my house and I am very anxious to learn what has become of the amateur translation that made me the owner of it.

As you have guesed by the start of the letter; I am trying to become an African; never will be black; but trying to be beautifull "in vaine?"

ROTATION

At my feet the moon touches the sea
The star sinks in the tree.
My surprise and me are falling.
Backwards.
Greetings Peter

While temperatures reach 36 degrees I still remember the yard. You could not imagine the world of difference between Scotland and Mocambique. I feel though; a strengthening of mind, a step back in civilization is healthy, at least to me it is. If and when you receive this letter, allong with my regards to your family and friends, please put a note to the following 2 (two) addresses. My wive, Hanny, and Jacqueline de Kwant (my rebel daughter) 25 year And Jim – keep using your imagination, the world needs us
Hou je faai P.

Another artist visited the yard during the construction of the Norsea and I spent most of my lunch breaks keeping him company

and making him yard wise. His name was Iain Robinson. He was a freelance artist and a great architect. I admired his drawing skills and he admired my artistic achievements. I remember him telling me that someone had said to him when he first began sketching in the yard. "What are you doing, we already have an artist in here". Iain had an exhibition at Irvine's Harbour Arts Centre some months after his departure from the yard. I went along to the preview and was amazed to see how he had twisted and distorted images that originally had been drawn so precise.

When the Norsea was doing her trials in the spring of 1987 we travelled from Govan to Greenock every day for weeks. She would leave her berth every morning to do her trials off the coast of Arran while everyone carried on with their work. There was no guarantee what time you would return to Greenock, it just depended on how the trials were going. My reproductions and paintings were held in the yard's stores until she was ready to leave for Hull. The owners wanted me around so Bill Gallagher put me in charge of carpet cleaning. There had been a large spillage of oil in the engine room and it was carried in to many of the cabins. I was given plans of the accommodation areas and had to decide and mark on the plans, carpets that required industrial cleaning. A company from Greenock was hired and I took charge of them. I was also asked to go with the ship to Hull to carry on the same job with a local cleaning firm. The owners also wanted me to hang my four originals and hundred and fifty-three reproductions. When we left Greenock I had all the pictures put into my cabin and began hanging them as soon as we departed for Hull. Each reproduction had two security fittings, which meant putting screws in to the light steel bulkhead of each cabin, pressing the picture on to the screws and pulling it downwards. This action locked the work and it could not be removed without destroying it. While going through the Minch I was violently ill and had to get seasickness pills from the ambulance man. I was fine after that and enjoyed the unusual scenery as we went round the north of Scotland. The sail took forty-eight hours. As we approached North Sea Ferries terminal at Hull I presented Albert Taconis with my framed translated poem Govan Built wrapped in tartan paper. It was a grand sight as we sailed into the harbour as there were many people gathered to see the fine new ship. Many workers sailed with the ship so at Hull we were split into different hotels. The one I was in had a restaurant that was a Berni Inn so I had steak, wine, and a knickerbocker glory nearly every night. I was to work there for a week and received a little help from the yard's joiners in hanging my work as well as seeing to the industrial carpet cleaners. I had to work all night myself on the night before leaving. It was pure hell and by the morning there were still ten prints to be hung so I gave them to the purser who would see that they got done. I got a taxi to the hotel and collected my belongings for the coach trip home. I was absolutely shattered. We had beaten the Japanese as our ship went into service before the Norsun. Some weeks later I bumped into Bill Gallagher in the yard and he told me off for not hanging all the pictures.

When I returned from Hull, Helen and I went over to Arran for a few days. This was the first time there for us both and we enjoyed it. We hired bikes on the first day and cycled to Lamlash. It was hilly there and back and when we returned the bikes the owner said we should have went in the opposite direction to Corrie, as it was flat all the way. The following day we got the bikes again and cycled to Glen Rosa before going on to Corrie, parking our bikes and walking through South Glen Sannox. It was a beautiful hazy day in May and the mountains looked striking. In the summer of 1987 I

booked return flights for Helen and I to Rimini in Italy. Before going I had purchased the Berlitz travel guide for the Italian Adriatic and decided that Rimini was too big a resort so we thought Cattolica looked about right. The flight was booked through Thompsons so when we cleared customs at Rimini we headed for their desk to see if there were seats on their bus. We were told that as we had only booked flights we would have to make our own way by taking the local bus. We boarded a bus for Rimini and noticed people punching their tickets after it had left the terminal. I asked if anyone spoke English and found out that tickets should have been purchased before boarding the bus. We left the bus at Rimini rail station where we caught the train to Cattolica which cost us fifty pence each. Days later we met a couple with a small child whom we recognised from being on the same flight as us. They were in the same position and took a taxi from the airport which cost them twenty-five pounds. We said they should have come with us as we made our journey for a pound. On arriving at Cattolica we went directly to the tourist information centre and were taken to view an apartment by the owner. A price was agreed for twelve nights and we gave her a deposit before she left leaving us her address. During our evening out we priced pensiones, which would have worked out cheaper and included continental breakfasts. The next day I went to the owner's house and got the price knocked down by two hundred pounds. Most days we would go to the public beach at Gabicce Mare. Before leaving Glasgow I made my mind up to visit Gradara. One day after leaving the beach at Gabicce Mare and walking to the top of town I noticed where we were heading but said nothing to Helen. It took us hours to get there walking in the mid-day sun and Helen kept asking where we were going. Eventually we arrived at Gradara where we had a late lunch and a few drinks before discovering the town. It was dark before long and when it came to making inquiries how to get back to Cattolica my Italian was tested to the full. There is never a problem in the main tourist areas but once you leave them few people speak English. We had time for dinner before leaving on the last bus to Cattolica. It cost us about forty pence and Helen said I was miserable for making her walk for hours to get there. I had been playing regularly in the Cedarwood pub in Glasgow and one of the waitresses and bar steward came to Cattolica on our second week and we arranged to meet them as I knew the name of the hotel they were staying in. We hired bikes with them one day and cycled to Gradara, which only took twenty minutes. We used to go to the same bar every night to eat and drink. We met an Italian couple that we told to be there on our last night as I had asked the owner to get me a guitar. They came with all their family, inlaws, outlaws, children and grandparents, and no guitar, but I managed to entertain them throughout the evening. We went on our own to Florence by taking the high-speed train up to Bologna then down through Tuscany. You would be enjoying the beautiful scenery which would disappear as you entered a tunnel, and that happened throughout the whole journey as the trains go straight from A to B cutting through the landscape. Florence was very humid and busy and although we had a good day you would have to spend at least a week to appreciate this wonderful city. The four of us also took a trip to San Marino to gather up our duty free booze. One thing I will never forget about that holiday was the night there was a thunderstorm and it became freezing. It was a lesson learned that if we were ever to return to northern Italy at any time of the year, we should take warm clothing for that sort of emergency. That was our second visit to Italy and I could live there quite happily as the food, architecture, scenery and people, were all pleasant to the senses.

Just before our Easter holiday of 1988 the directors of the yard sent for me as NSF general manager Bill McCarthy had contacted them regarding the purchase of a painting. Their technical superintendent Albert Taconis was retiring and they remembered him talking about one of my paintings of the Norsea under construction which fortunately I still had in my possession. The yard faxed a photo of the painting to NSF and I received a phone call at home from NSF general manager telling me they would like to purchase it as a retirement gift for Mr Taconis. He also invited my wife and I to come down to Hull for the presentation which was to be held on the ship the following

Monday. I told him that I would have to speak to our directors first as this was during our Easter break and I should be returning to work on that day. I phoned the yard and spoke to Bill Gallagher who told me to go down and I would be paid for my time as I would be representing Govan. They put me up in the Post House hotel on the evening before the presentation and gave me my cheque on the ship. Helen couldn't go as she had her work. I returned to work on the Tuesday and reported to Bill who made sure I was paid for my day. Following the departure of the Norsea we were laid off every alternate week for around nine months. This gave me time to concentrate on my painting and when we went back to full time work my heart wasn't in it as the yard had been taken over by the Norwegian company Kvaerner who didn't want unskilled labour. I decided to take advantage of the opportunity of voluntary redundancy. I could have stayed if I wanted, but after talking it over with Helen we decided that I should leave on the sixteenth of June 1989 to try and make a living as an artist. In my last year at the yard I had really given up. I spent most of the time sweeping the floor in the blacksmith's shop and helping the tradesmen. P&O gave every worker in the yard and their partner the opportunity of a free three-day trip to Holland on the Norsea. Helen and I took advantage of the offer and went to Amsterdam this time. We didn't have a lot of time there but we managed to visit the Rijksmuseum where I enjoyed seeing Rembrandt's Night Watch and the Vermeers. I have always had long hair and on our return to Hull Helen and I were singled out by customs. It didn't bother me as we only had our allowance and nothing illegal. As we were standing waiting to be searched I wondered who else from our party would be pulled but we were the only ones. However, the husband of one of the yard's cleaners decided he had to go to the toilet and jumped the barrier, so they were both taken away and strip-searched. We were held up by this episode and the poor woman was in tears when she returned to our coach.

In 1988 we went on holiday for a week to Helen's dad's cousin, Tom Morrison, who lived in Peterlee, County Durham. I enjoyed a trip to Durham Town where I took loads of photographs. One day we drove down to Hull to show Helen's mum and dad the Norsea and all my paintings in the cabins. I phoned before we went to make sure she would be there and not the Norsun, and also to get permission to board her. Helen's brother Raymond, his wife Catherine, and her mum and dad were going on holiday to Bridlington so we had arranged to meet up with them at their accommodation as they had given us the address and it wasn't far from Hull. We got there shortly before they arrived. We had a couple of drinks with them before we left for Scarborourgh where we booked into a hotel for the night. We were awakened in the early hours of the morning by the squawking of seagulls and couldn't get back to sleep for them. We spent the morning discovering Scarborough before we left for Peterlee stopping off at Robin Hood's

Bay and Whitby. While we were down that way we also visited the Open Air Museum at Beamish and on a trip to Whitley Bay, tasted the

best mulligatawny soup I've ever had in an Indian restaurant. On the way there we spotted a car with Scottish champion darts player Jocky Wilson on the side of the vehicle, so Bert used his charm for a photo opportunity. Tom's girlfriend had a longhaired Chihuahua dog she no longer wanted so Bert phoned his son Robert who asked us to bring it home for his wife Rita. We were going straight from Peterlee to spend our second week at the caravan, which was now at Drumlochart near Stranraer. On our way there the small dog was getting in the way of Bert's driving and we had to stop to buy a lead for it at Annan. The dog was a little pest during that week and Robert and Rita didn't keep it for long. While at Stranraer we visited Portpatrick and the lighthouse at Mull of Galloway. We bumped into my friend from the sixties Joe Short and his wife Isabel in Stranraer and they told us they had a caravan at Portpatrick.

1988 was to see the demise of the band Frekels after 16 years together. We played at a wedding on the Carrick on 31 May. At that time she was moored in the Clyde at Glasgow across from the Maritime College. It was a bit of a struggle getting our gear on board as we had to carry it down a narrow gangway and in through the hull. This meant lifting heavy speakers and drums above the safety rails of the gangway. Then we had to negotiate a spiral staircase to get to our destination. It was worth the effort for while we played, our eyes were focused on the illuminated Glasgow's suspension bridge. Ronnie had been singing in pub talent competitions and winning them on midweek evenings. He had always wanted to leave the band to do cabaret and it looked like the time had come. The first Saturday he didn't play with us was the 18 June and by October he had left completely. He had told us that Dougie Henderson was available, as his Dead Loss Band had broken up. I went to see him as he had been staying in Meikle Road Pollok at the time and he agreed to stand in for the gigs that Ronnie couldn't do over the summer months. I was delighted that when Ronnie eventually left, Dougie came in full time. We changed our name to Deliverance. We were support band to

Ronnie at the Royal British Legion Club, East Kilbride on 28 October 1988. Bert came along and videotaped the gig. George left some months later and we got Ian (Busby) McCallum in on bass. Helen's mum had a heart attack in early April 1989. We visited her on Saturday the fifteenth and Helen didn't go the next day so that the rest of the family could visit their mum in intensive care. The hospital only allowed two visitors at a time. She seemed to be doing fine and was let out on the Monday. I answered the phone at seven o'clock the following morning to be told by a distraught Raymond that his mother had passed away. That was one of the worst moments of my life having to tell Helen and I knew then that part of Helen died that

day. Her mum was cremated at Craigton and everyone came back to our house as it was only two minutes from the crematorium. I had done a painting of Glasgow Cathedral, which was quite large and lay against a wall at home. I asked one of our neighbours to look after it on the day of the funeral in case it got damaged as I knew our house was going to be busy. When I went to retrieve the painting my neighbour said that her brother Tommy who lived round the corner from us at Ladykirk Drive would like to speak to me about purchasing it. I went to see him a couple of days later. His house was like an antique shop as he was a collector of various artifacts. Soon after pouring me a very large whisky and coke in a half-pint glass, he offered me £1000 for my painting. I didn't give him an immediate answer. Halfway through my second large whisky my brain was cluttered with all those pounds and I accepted his offer. The following night I took the painting round to him and came home with £1000 cash in a polythene bag. I bought a small Yamaha mini keyboard at £199, as I had always wanted one.

Chapter 7

Two years later, the opening of Pauline's degree show was on Friday 21 June 1991 in the Macintosh building of the Glasgow School of Art. The place was buzzing and the wine flowing so we had a great night. I was a proud dad at her graduation in the following week. Helen, Tracey, Pauline, Martin, Bert and I all went for a curry after a couple of drinks in the Vic. Pauline's graduation certificate has got a nice stain as a result of this celebration feast.  The second of Kvaerner's liquid gas tankers was due to be launched at some time through the night of Monday 15 July. This was supposed to be the last conventional launch at the Govan shipyard so I went there at 7pm to photograph the shipwrights ramming out. I left the yard at 3am and went over to Meadowside Granary to await the launch. She went down the slipways at 4.35am just as it was getting light, and it was raining, so you had all these reflections from the lights that were still on. I spent the day at Tom McKendrick's home studio on Friday 9 August 1991 and he showed me certain techniques that I would use in my future work. Just listening to him that day would make me think about what I was doing and where my work was going. That one day, made me change my direction and begin to experiment with mixed media, and that experimentation period helped me in later years. Local Pharmacist George Watson commissioned me to do a small oil of his wife's lingerie shop "Dangerous Liaisons" which was situated next to the Burns Tavern, Irvine. Vinnie Walker and I moved back into the empty shop at Bridgegate on Wednesday 14 August 1991 to set up the entries for a kid's art competition which would be a part of Marymass. This time it would be used as an information centre for the festival and Vinnie put his Marymass photo's up once again. During our ten days there I did a montage with portraits of the previous three queens in pastel and an acrylic of Jim Williamson, who was Captain of the Carters during that period. I mounted them beneath four windows in a mount board and painted the Carter's and Incorporated Trades crests on the board with acrylics. Helen and I went to the Leith Open Exhibition on Friday 23 August as I had two paintings on show. This was held in Citizen's Studios who were situated in Assembly Street, Leith, and were managed and leased by WASPS. (Workshop and Artist's Studio Provision Scotland). We met the actors Phil McCall and Jackie Farrell on the train from Edinburgh's Waverly Station as they were appearing at the Edinburgh Festival. I had another exhibition titled "Influences" at the Pearce Institute Govan, which opened on Saturday 31 August and ran until 13 September. I travelled through to Govan every day excluding Sundays for the next two weeks and sold four paintings so it was a worthwhile exercise. The 1991 Cunninghame Arts Council Roadshow was on Sunday 29 September at Saltcoats town hall. As well as exhibiting I performed an acoustic set during the course of the day.

I signed on as unemployed in October to get my National Insurance Stamp paid as I had reached my maximum overdraft and was finding it hard to repay it. On 13 October Helen and I went to Cardiff as my sister Chris, Paul, Jonathan and Bryony would be at their house in Llandaff. We would spend a couple of days with them before their return to Anguilla. We spent most of the rest of the week floating about the Valleys and paid a visit to the Welsh Agricultural Museum. My next exhibition that year was at Greenock Arts Guild. I took the paintings there on Sunday 3 November and hung them as the preview was on the following night. When we arrived on the Monday night I was pleased to hear that I had sold one of my larger

paintings **Guardians**. I had always wanted to use this feature at the yard's main entrance and although Mr. Draegebo didn't like the painting, I was happy that someone else did. This was a good start, and I was to sell another two on the night, one of which was purchased by Irvine collector Tommy Harkness. Tommy was a supporter of local artists. He has a room at home that is like an art gallery with a rocking chair so that he could relax and enjoy his paintings. He has so many that he changes his exhibition every now and then. Mae Beattie invited me along to her art club at Kilmaurs on Thursday 7 November to talk about my work, for a fee of course. I received a phone call from Steinar Draegebo at 6.30pm on Monday 2

December 1991. He told me that the ship Havfrost was to be commissioned the following day and would I have something suitable that the yard could purchase as a gift for the owners. I told him that all my work was presently at Greenock Arts Guild but if he wished, I could meet him there later in the evening. He came to Greenock with his wife and Bert drove me up from Irvine to meet him. After some time he decided on what he thought would be suitable. It was an oil titled "Made from Girders" and measured 24" x 12". The Arts Guild allowed me to take it from the wall as the show was only on for a few more days so Mr. Draegebo went away quite happy. The price was £300 but when I received the cheque, it was made out for £400. I would think that the extra was because I had gone to the trouble of accommodating him.

I decided that the painting I had done during Marymass should be given to the Incorporated Trades of Irvine to auction it for charity. I was told to take it to their next meeting in Irvine's Burns Club. I had arrived early and went into The Turf for a wee half. Proprietor Iain Murray came in while I was there and asked to see my painting. When I told him where I was going, and why, He asked how much I would hope to raise. I told him £300 and he said that he would have it. I then had to go to the meeting and explain my intentions and the result of my conversation with Iain. They were quite happy with Iain's offer and it was decided that the money would go to Irvine Cancer Care.

At Pauline's degree show I had met a couple of guys who were hairdressers. They were known as wee Billy and big Billy. The latter was the owner of Scrimshaw's hair salon in the merchant city. Wee Billy's brother had just graduated with Pauline and that was the reason they were there. Anyone who has known me will know that I have never been a lover of hairdressers but they told me to drop in and they would give me a free haircut. I took them up on the offer and big Billy said that I should bring some work in and hang it before the Christmas period. I had been working on some strange mixed media paintings that were small so I had them mounted and framed all in black to go with the décor of the salon. Pauline and Martin had been living in Possilpark and they moved into a rented flat at Nursery Street in Govanhill on 4 December.

On the 14 of December 1991 my mate Doug Whitton and I went to the preview of Peter Howson's exhibition, "The Blind Leading the Blind" at the McLaurin Gallery, Ayr. This was an amazing show. I noticed there were no strong primary colours in his work. The colour had been neutralized in some way. Doug and I managed to speak to Peter and when I asked him how he achieved that effect, he told me that it was down to priming the canvas with Vandyke brown. From that day I became addicted to this fugitive colour. I found Peter easy to talk to and was glad that I attended this preview as I got something important out of it. Steinar Draegebo sent me a copy of a letter he received dated 8 December 1991 from the Master of the ship Havfrost. It begins with, "At sea bound Houston". Thanking him for the magnificent decanter and glasses he sent on board at the initial departure cruise. He goes on by thanking him for the gift of the Jim Collins painting, which he presented to Mr. Pal Caspersen. "Mr. Caspersen decided that the most apt place for this work of art was on the finished product, namely the LPG Havfrost. For those of us who were based at Govan for the latter stages of the building, this painting brings back many memories, and we are very grateful." Mr. Draegebo says in his accompanying letter, "As you will see, at least one of your paintings is now travelling world wide, and bringing pleasure to the crew of that fine ship."

Our drummer Dougie Henderson played in the Scotia bar with The Blues Poets every Sunday afternoon and I went along to see them on 5 January 1992 as I had been at the framers in Glasgow. The singer was George Gallagher who was with the original Poets back in the sixties. I also knew the lead guitarist Fraser Watson who played with Dave Hunter and the Arrows before joining the Poets, then White Trash. Big hairy Jack, (Jackson Clarkin), the bass player, stood in with us every now and then. I was standing at the bar listening to them when I turned round and found Billy Connolly and Danny Kyle standing along the bar from me. I thought this was an opportune moment so I introduced myself to Billy and he replied immediately, "He was talking about you today" referring to the now seated Danny Kyle. I was to have the good fortune of spending around twenty minutes speaking to Billy before he left. He told me early in the conversation that someone would give him abuse and sure enough after a while a guy came up to him and said, "You're a big eejit". When he left the pub I shared some time with Danny who was rather annoyed at the reception Billy got since he returned to his old haunts, which he didn't need to do and all he got was an earful of abuse from some jealous idiot.

I was to meet another great Scot, John Byrne, the following month. Dr Anne Lorne Gillies had replaced John Mathews as Community Arts Development Officer at Govan Initiative Ltd and she had planned a three-day exhibition and one day arts forum for Thursday 16 January. "Arts is for Everybody" was an opportunity for the people of Govan to discuss what the arts meant to them. It would also give them the chance to see and hear about local arts activities in other communities as participants in the arts were well represented. The day began with an introduction from councillor Iain Davidson who was chairman of both Govan Initiative Ltd and Strathclyde Regional Council's Education Committee. The first speakers were Alison

Cutforth, curator of Springburn Museum, and the Museum's Outreach Worker, Eileen Gordon. Next came John Murtagh, Artistic Director of Borderline Theatre Company, Ayr. Helen Crummie told us the successful story of the Craigmillar Festival, Edinburgh. John Byrne and I were asked to join the top table for questions along with two Springburn mothers, Jan McKay and Betty MacKee. The first two questions from the floor were aimed at me, the ex shipyard worker who declined to be a speaker. I couldn't believe that with all those intellectual people around me, they wanted to hear from me. I suppose it was because of the subject of my work, and in reality, I was one of them. Ron Culley, Director of Govan Initiative opened the next session followed by Anne Lorne Gillies who told the community about what was going on in the arts in Greater Govan. We then broke in to discussion groups to talk about the problems with funding etc. We were entertained by The Red Road Young Yins during lunch, and had more discussions in the afternoon where we would try to find answers to any problems and make recommendations to the organizers, Govan Initiative Ltd. I was to meet with John Byrne many times throughout the day as we vacated the premises at every opportunity for a cigarette. At that time John had been working in the Glasgow Print Studio and he told me to come and visit him there.

My next solo show was to be at Citizen's Studios Leith in February. My cousin Irene's husband Billy Tees worked as a typesetter in a printer's so he got the posters designed and arranged the printing for me. I collected my 300 posters from Glasgow on 30th January and took them by train to Edinburgh. I arrived at Waverly Station then got a bus to the bottom of Leith Walk. I had arranged to have them put in to appropriate venues in Edinburgh through an arts distribution service whose premises was situated in Leith. When I left the bus I realised that I did not have my posters, I must have left them on the train. Luckily I had some in a polythene bag so I made my way to the distribution service. I explained my predicament and arranged to have monochrome photocopies done from my original blue in the event of them not turning up. The rest of the day was spent at Waverley Station trying to find my posters to no avail. They turned up at Inverness and were returned to lost luggage at Waverley where I picked them up at a later date, but in time to have them distributed in place of my photocopies.

I spent an hour with John Byrne at the Glasgow Print Studio on Saturday 1st February. Speaking about the downside of being an artist, and waiting for money to come in. I was surprised to find that a man as successful as John had once ran up credit of £800 for a food bill at his local grocer's. I found him to be a really nice laid back honest person and am honoured to have spent some time with him.

My Leith exhibition opened on Friday evening 14 February 1992. Helen and I took the train from Irvine to Edinburgh via Glasgow and had dinner in Leith before arriving at the Citizen's Studios. Some young people interviewed me on video before the opening. I had to go round the show talking about my work and answer questions. I would never find out who these people were, or get to see the video. Irvine proprietor Iain Murray had given me a case of white wine and I had purchased a half a dozen boxes of both red and white. I think that every artist in Edinburgh turned up as the place was packed all night. My work was well received and this was the first solo show in the venue from a non-residential artist. They would look after the exhibition from Monday to Friday and the middle Saturday, but I had to go there the following morning and the last Saturday of the two-week run. It would have been ideal if we stayed in Edinburgh that night but as I sold nothing at the opening that was out. We had to return to Irvine that night and I had to make the journey early the following morning to open up for 10am. There was plenty of wine left from the previous night and when a young lady came in, I offered her a glass. She accepted and introduced herself as Lorna Waite an art critic from The Scotsman newspaper.

Well I did say in 1990 when asked by The Scotsman to explain my work that I was waiting to suffer the critics. I was quite happy with the article she wrote as it at least made me aware that my work was important as social documentation. That was my aim but I felt then that I had done enough on the subject and it was time to move on. My old school mate Frank Cusack also came along on that first Saturday as he lived in Leith and at the time was the manager of one of Edinburgh's Safeway's stores. He had also contributed to the previous night's refreshments. The show closed on 29 February and on 19 March I received a letter from Brian Gill QC saying he was sorry to have missed my exhibition as he was working away at that period. He asked if I had any unsold paintings would I send him a list with details so that we could make arrangements for him to see them. I don't think I admitted to him that I had sold nothing, however, after some communication I went through to his home in Edinburgh and he purchased two paintings.. Mr Gill went on to become Lord Gill and is now retired. He was Lord President and Lord Justice General from June 2012 until May 2015. He previously served as Lord Justice Clerk from 2001 to 2012.

I brought a welding helmet into the house on 10 March, and drew it in various positions. The result was my painting "The Dimming Light of Life" which took me 28 hours to paint. I was invited

to St Constantine's primary school in Govan on Tuesday 31 March to talk to the children about my shipyard paintings and answer all their questions about them. I attended the launch of Kvaerner Govan's third liquid gas tank carrier Helios on Friday 3 April.

Pauline went off to work in one of the hotels at Disneyland Paris from March to September 1992.

From 30th April until 10th May 1992 I was really unwell with sickness and diarrhoea. During this illness I had to take my work to Roselle House, Ayr for my exhibition titled "Recent Work". The opening was on Friday 8 May and fortunately the gallery hung the show for me. I attended the opening feeling very weak and I had lost a stone in weight. Our old neighbours from Fochabers Drive, Ian and Rosemary McLellan had come along and we invited them back to our house for a drink after the opening. I got an Indian curry carryout for them and took a little myself. I'm sure that's what cured me as I felt much better the following day. I was invited to attend the launch of Jimmy Miller's book of short stories, "Tenements as Tall as Ships" at the Renfrew Ferry on Wednesday 13 May. Jimmy had died on 8 October 1989. Govan Workspace published the book. Jimmy had worked there prior to his death after taking early retirement in 1996 from British Shipbuilders where he was Training Manager. I was feeling better now after my illness and hoped that the glass or two of wine I was to take would not affect me. Glasgow Herald columnist Jack McLean launched the book. I was astounded when he told the bar staff that he didn't want any of their rubbish wine, so they sent out for whisky to please him. It was a pleasant afternoon and I enjoyed conversing with Martin Baillie and his wife. Martin was a painter and lectured in the History of Art at Glasgow University. When I returned home there was a card from environmental health informing me that they wanted to discuss my salmonella poisoning. I was furious that I should receive this information from them before I heard it from my own doctor. The doctor's surgery said that they received the result from the laboratory at the same time as environmental health, so I let it go. The main thing was that I was fine now and no repercussions from my wine.

    As I was on the WASPS waiting list for a studio in Irvine, I had sent an invitation for our forthcoming exhibition, "Ayrshire Artists at the Vennel" to David Cook who was Property Manager of the organization at that time. I also sent him an invitation to pass on to Peter Howson as he was working in a WASPS studio in Glasgow. He sent me a letter apologizing for not being able to attend and also letting me know that Peter had been out of the country at the time of the opening. He also said that the Irvine project was looking good and he would know by mid June if the funding was in place. He asked me if I would assist him in contacting local artists as Sarah Proudler of Cunninghame District Council had recommended me as a responsible contact. Sue Selwyn from Strathkelvin Museum at Kirkintilloch came to my house on 20 May 1992 and picked 30 paintings for an exhibition which would be December/ January 1993. Ayrshire Artists at the Vennel was an exhibition put on to coincide with the 1992 Cunninghame Arts Festival. The exhibiting artists were Louise Turmine, Margaret Skelton, Susan Porteous, Lucy Baird, Hugh Loney, Pamela A. Beattie and myself. The exhibition ran from 22 May until 27 June. Lucy was the current Artist in Residence for the New Town.

Our band Deliverance played support to Freddie and the Dreamers on 29 May 1992 at Dalbeattie town hall. Jack McGenily who was our agent at the time picked me up in his car. We went down the Sanquar Road while the rest of the band travelled in the van down the M74. Freddie didn't go down well and we stole the glory.

Vinnie Walker and I occupied another vacant shop in the middle of the Rivergate Shopping Centre, Irvine, from 25 May-6 June for the two week Arts Festival. This time I was to work in inks, dropping them on to various types of clear or coloured polythene bags and moving the wet droplets around giving them time to dry before continuing. This was a slow process and the members of the public who had seen me work representationally in oils at the previous year's venue, thought that I had gone mad. I took 4 paintings to the Pearce Institute on 8 June to be included in an exhibition titled "Made in Govan". I had an idea that I had been thinking about for a while. It was to construct an installation that would represent the double bottoms of a ship and would be called "The Keel." My idea was to give the public the opportunity to experience how uncomfortable it is to a shipyard worker working in that environment. There would be a central passage with compartments off to each side. Each compartment would represent a different trade with murals on the bulkheads (walls) and objects relating to that particular trade lying around the space. Every compartment would be viewed from the central passage as the viewer negotiated 9" girders on the deck (floor) every 18." They would also have to crouch down as they made their way through, just as the shipyard worker has to do. I had meetings with the Council's Environmental Health Officer and Bob Thaw, manager of Caberboard, Irvine. I thought that my structure should be built from MDF and Bob agreed to supply this free of charge. I also wanted to site it permanently at Irvine's Maritime Museum. I had a meeting with Director Jim Tildesley, who said that I could construct it in the

Linthouse Building, but they were having the floor concreted and I may have had to move it. Caberboard closed and I went off the notion but I believe that it could still be a successful project if I were to pursue it in the future. Once again Vinnie and I set up our information Centre in the same shop within the Rivergate Centre for Marymass. This was beginning to be a real asset to both the annual Arts Festival and Marymass. We hung the children's entries for the Marymass art competition on Wednesday 12 August and that year Irvinites loaned Vinnie their Murmass photo's from the past so that they could be seen. This time I had to leave Vinnie on his own as I had been offered the chance to go to Edinburgh's Festival-Fringe Summer School. Every year Cunninghame District Council would send someone along with another lucky person funded by WEA. (Workers Educational Association)

I arrived at Edinburgh University's Pollock Halls on the afternoon of Saturday 15 August to check into the room where I would be staying for the next week. All 44 participants had to register at Riddle's Court in the Lawnmarket at 4.30pm. Following our introductions we went to the fringe club for dinner at 7pm, then on to the Pleasance to see Borderline Theatre's "Waiting for Tommy". While we were waiting in the queue I spotted Eddie Jackson who was producer at Borderline. He told me to stay behind after the performance, as there was a party. I met a few faces from "The Ship" such as John Murtagh, and members of the production crew, as well as big Iain MacColl. Breakfast the next morning was something to be remembered as you could eat as much as you wanted. There was cereal, a guid Scottish fry up, toast, rolls, orange juice, tea and coffee. Some people actually made up rolls to keep them going throughout the day as the breakfast didn't cost us anything. You had to be up early to catch breakfast, as it was quite a walk to Riddle's Court every morning for 10am. On reflection I felt that my outlook on theatre had been broadened, especially as I hadn't been an ardent patron in the past. My insight to the theatre through my week at summer school would be beneficial to my position as an active member of Cunninghame Arts Council and Festival Committee.

I arranged to exhibit in two Govan venues at the same time, the Pearce Institute and Elderpark Library. The exhibition was titled **'Look Here-See There'** and opened on Saturday 7 September. This was a smaller show in the Pearce than on the previous two years and included my recent work with mixed media. Anne Lorne Gillies kindly spent an hour at the opening talking to my guests. She also purchased one of my new works before the end of the show. She couldn't make her mind up between two paintings and eventually bought one of them. Two friends I had made from the Edinburgh visit, Hilary Scott, and Stephen Fleming came to the show and were impressed with what they saw. Stephen from Castlemilk was only around eighteen or nineteen at the time and played guitar. He was a really nice guy and I am pleased to say that nine years later I was to hear of his success with the Glasgow band **'Cosmic Rough Riders'**.

Our silver wedding was coming up in October and we all think we could never be taken by surprise. Although the 28 October 1992 was a Wednesday, we were taken in on the Saturday before. Frank phoned me on the Friday telling me that the gig in the Sou' Wester Club the following night had been cancelled. The next thing I got a call from my mate Doug Whitton asking me what Helen and I were doing the following night as his wife Carly had won money at her work and they wanted us to join them in an evening out. I said that it was funny as I had just had my gig cancelled and we would be happy to come out for a meal, and then, supposedly to a disco in Saltcoats which had a sixties night on. They picked us up at 7pm and Doug asked if we would like to go for a drink somewhere as they had booked a table for eight o'clock. He asked if the Stanecastle Hotel was ok, knowing that I am easily pleased, and, it was only minutes away from where we live. When we arrived at the car park Doug distracted us by making us look at something in the car as he had seen someone we knew and didn't want the game to be given away. When we approached the bar entrance and walked by it to the main one I wondered why, but carried on nevertheless. We were hardly through the door when we were pushed through another door to our right. As we went through, the lights went on, and there was our nephew George and two of his mates from his pipe band playing away, and all these people, some of which we hadn't seen for years standing in front of us. It was sometime before we got seated after going round everyone. We both had been off the fags for five months and when we sat down, we looked at each other with the same thought, we need a smoke! So that was the end of our attempt to stop smoking. Someone actually got us a box of polo mints as a gift. We had a brilliant night and we were surprised when we found out that Tracey and the rest of our close relatives were sneaking in and out of their homes which were right next door to us carrying food all that day. They were also surprised that they had got away with it. Tracey, who was pregnant at the time and still living at home with us gave birth to a lovely daughter ten days later. She went into Ayrshire Central Hospital at 1am on the morning of Tuesday 3 November and Louise Paula was born at 9. 47am weighing 7lbs 8oz. Helen went with her and was present at the birth. She phoned Bert and we were at the hospital an hour after Louise was born. I was amazed at how her eyes were everywhere at only one hour old.

Glasgow's Museum of Transport had put together a touring exhibition called **Voices from the Yards**. They had taped shipyard workers stories and had them printed on to large panels with photographs of shipyard scenes. I exhibited along with this exhibition at the Auld Kirk Museum Kirkintilloch from Saturday 5 December 1992 until Saturday 9 January 1993.

Also at the end of 1992 our bass player Ian said that he wanted to leave the band. He didn't like playing outside Glasgow and the rest of us didn't mind travelling to a gig anywhere. He had wanted to leave a year earlier and we talked him out of it but he was insistent this time. Frank had said to me that we should give it a go as a two-piece and we bought a disk recorder. I had to do the backing for songs on my baby Yamaha keyboard which I played one-finger chords at the time. Our first gig was at the Harmsworth bar in Partick on the 22 January 1993. The Manageress said that our music was all distorted but it seemed all right to us. It took some time to sort out our problems as it was distorted and also I didn't have the bass working with the bass drum which was something I had never had to think about in previous bands. It was also sad to leave Dougie behind, as he was an excellent drummer and a good friend. He always used to surprise me by slipping in something neat which I had never heard before in a particular song.

Chapter 8

I signed on as unemployed in October 1992 as I had hardly any income from sales of my artwork. Helen was working at the time therfore I received no benefits. Every gig I did had to be written down on a form, and if I had a sale then it also had to be recorded. All I got was my insurance stamp credited. I wrote a nice little song at this period. It was formed from a bass run and told of my present position.

A Song for Me

All alone on a Saturday night
I sat down and I started to write
A song, just for me
To take away the misery of being on the dole
Stuck in a hole
It's not so funny when they don't give you no money
Too many thoughts going round my head
Confused and tired I went to bed

I awoke with the morning light
Beautiful sunrise I thought I might
Take a walk around the block
Music in my head I may just write my song instead

Four chords and a bass line nice little rhythm it sounds fine.

At that time I was self employed
Making no money I was quite annoyed
Now I'm retired, no stamp required
I'm a happy man, Making music while I can.

I wrote that last verse in 2019.

I was back in the Pearce Institute in April 1993 for the Govan Festival. This event was sponsored by Govan Housing Association and ran for a week. It was put on as a celebration of their 21st birthday. I showed a small number of shipyard paintings as I was in a room with the Govan Reminiscence group. I worked on a small painting daily and someone came in with a video recorder every day to record the development of this work. The great welder in the sky gives guidance through his right eye to the welder on the bottom left who passes this on to the one in the centre. He relays it to the one in the bottom centre, who then passes it to the one at the top left. The result of this is the ship at the bottom right. Parts of the ship are constructed in the plater's shed where the great welder is giving his guidance to all the welders through his left eye. A painting of Helios

just after her launch was purchased by the South Side Business Club to present to Glasgow City Council. I had known their Director Bob McCann when he was personnel Director at Govan Shipbuilders. The presentation took place at Lord Provost Bob Innes' private chambers on Thursday 3 June.

As part of the Cunninghame Festival for 1993 I exhibited in Brodick Library on the Isle of Arran. I had gone over a couple of times before the show to distribute invitations for the opening, which was on Saturday 5 June at 2pm. I couldn't believe it that no one from Arran turned up except an old couple who lived next to where Helen and I were staying at the Anchor Hotel. The secretary of Cunninghame Arts Council Marie Blackwood from Beith came over with her kids along with my mates Tam Gardener and Doug Whitton with his wife Carly Smith. I had brought loads of wine with me and there were only a few friends to share it with so I tried to put away as much as I could before going to bed depressed at 6 o'clock. It had been a beautiful sunny afternoon and I was in and out of the library looking to see if anyone would come. I remember seeing one person from the folk festival committee I had personally given an invite to walking across the street and he didn't even bother to attend. I had taken my guitar and amp across as I had played at the Anchor hotel before to pay for my keep. Proprietors Tony and Dylis were friends of my mate Johnny Beattie from Irvine. Old Tam Gardener played the accordion, so he did the Scottish material and I did my thing which kept all of the audience happy. We always had some of the locals joining in such as Tam Dolan and Danny on bowran and Gavin on accordion. Danny's wife Ina was a white witch. I always enjoyed being in auld Tam Gardener's company as he had led an interesting life and always had a different story to tell. He had worked on building the railway system in Canada. I wish that I had recorded the many stories of his life which would have made very interesting reading. I wrote this song the following year about my Arran adventures, some of it fact, and some fiction.

Isle of Arran

Took a ferry from Ardrossan to the Arran Isle
Disembarked at Brodick Bay, stay there for a while
Strolled along at leisure to the Anchor hotel
At night with friends I made we played some music as well
Isle of Arran, Isle of Arran

Got outa bed one day the rain was pouring down
Stepped out in the fresh air, had to leave the town
Walked in to Glen Rosa like an Indian reservation
Tents beside a winding river like a little nation
Isle of Arran, Isle of Arran

Cycled round to Corrie, went through the Sannox Glen
Onward to Lochranza back to Brodick again
Climbing up Goatfell I saw an eagle flying low
Red deer were on the hillside, look at them go
Isle of Arran, Isle of Arran

Her mystical magnetic power draws you back again
A highland lowland Island I give ten out of ten
Her beauty and her friendliness cannot be surpassed
The first time that you visit her will never be your last
Isle of Arran, Isle of Arran

Pauline was off on her adventures once again in August. She had been working at the Rockware glass factory in Irvine since she came back from Paris. She had paid for a short course of Teaching English as a Foreign Language and the college got her a job in Pforzheim, Germany. Pauline, Tracey, Louise, Helen and I went over to the Anchor hotel for a couple of days before she left for Germany.

I had made my mind up that my exhibition of 1993 would be the last one on the shipbuilding theme. Dr Anne Lorne Gillies had left Govan Initiative and left me her home number so I asked her if she would open the show to which she agreed. Jessie Scott from the Glasgow Vennel where the show was on took Anne, Helen and I for lunch at the Ship Inn before the official opening on Saturday 18 September. The show actually opened to the public on the previous Monday. I had set my gear up in the gallery and did some songs before Anne opened the show. I had said over dinner that I felt like giving up being an artist as I felt I wasn't getting much out of it financially for all the work I was putting in. The preview was well attended and after Anne left, I did some more songs for the hardy drinkers who were still there. Before she left I presented her with the other painting that she liked from the Pearce Institute exhibition the previous year.

Frank and I did a wedding with big Jack and Dougie at the Post House Hotel, Erskine on Saturday 9 October. I had this wedding booked from the previous year and had asked them if they would play at this particular gig. Frank and I were doing fine on our own by now.

Since leaving the shipyard in 1989 I had grown a ponytail and as the exhibition at the Vennel was to be the last one on shipbuilding, it was time to sever that connection by having my hair chopped. My mate Doug Whitton was the west of Scotland organiser for Save the Children so we thought that we could make some money for them from my haircut. I managed to raise £413 which went to their Children Under Fire Appeal.

I was invited to the opening of John McLaughlin's (The Govan Chairman) gallery at Skylight International Ltd on 20 October. John had turned part of his workshop into a gallery with a huge carved table in the centre and magnificent carved chairs surrounding it. All around the walls were more chairs and other carved objects. Most of the work was done from wood found by the banks of the river Clyde and were done by John specifically for a celebrity. It was here that I was introduced to a man who would give me a reason to carry on painting. Ben Donnelly took Bert and I back to his workshop at Clifford Lane, Ibrox, and baffled us for two hours with the science of photo luminescence. He had clothes, paper, and various other objects, all of which glowed in the dark. Ron Culley at Govan Initiative had previously showed me a telephone that glowed in the dark and told me about Benny. He was a real character and as I was to find out later, a kind and genuine person. I left that day with a little bag of pigment really excited. Benny told me to play around with it and return to show him the results of my efforts. I tried various effects with mixed media, mainly inks and acrylics as a watercolour technique and returned to Benny after a couple of weeks not knowing what to expect. He placed my work around his dark room, put the fluorescent lights off and turned on an ultra violet black light. Very slowly all these wonderful colours emerged from my work, getting stronger as the light penetrated them. After ten minutes he turned the black light off and my work was glowing in the dark, but the colour had gone. I was to find out later that you have to use fluorescent colours to achieve colour in darkness. Benny sent me away once again with more luminous pigment and a supply of red blue and yellow fluorescent pigment, along with an ultra violet light so that I could see the results of what I had done immediately. I tied the light up in my attic studio at home and got to work. Benny advised me to make up a colour chart and take note of the measurements of luminous and fluorescent mixtures. The main aim was to achieve colour in darkness. The luminous pigment absorbs frequencies of light and emits it in the dark. The fluorescent colour is activated by ultra violet light and will not be seen in the dark unless mixed with the luminous pigment. The problem is getting the right mixture of luminous and fluorescent pigments as one will drown out the other. If there is too much fluorescent then the image will not emit light for long. The binder used for this type of paint was acrylic polymer emulsion. I would be like a mad scientist from then on possessed by this newfound inspiration. I had been telling Sam Stellard, a friend from the local Arts Council about this exciting new media and said that I would like to exhibit the work with accompanying music. He told me his friend Bill Kerr from Dreghorn would be the ideal man to produce a piece of music for a project like that. Bill taught music from his home and was interested in getting involved when Sam told him about me. I had pleaded with Jessie Scott at the Vennel to try and fit me in with an exhibition as soon as possible, even if only for a couple of weeks. She managed to slot me in from 18 February until 5 March 1994. Bill came to my attic in November 1993 and was inspired by what he saw. This would be the beginning of a lifelong creative relationship. I decided the exhibition would be titled **New Beginnings**, as it was, and all the paintings would have titles based on musical directions. Paintings I had completed and titled before I met Bill were translated into Italian. He inspired me with his musical sketches just as my work gave him inspiration to compose. Bill was educated at Dalmellington High School and Ayr Academy. He studied pianoforte and theory of music under renowned music teacher Hubert Cresswell (O.B.E.). In 1971 he gained an associatship with the Trinity College of Music, London, and in 1976 he graduated with a Batchelor of Art honours degree from Newcastle Polytechnic. He started as a self-employed teacher of music in 1977 teaching pianoforte, theory of music, piano accordion, organ and electronic keyboards. I exhibited work at the end of 93 at two venues, Contemporary 93 at the Dick Institute Kilmarnock, and the Harbour Arts Centre Christmas show, Irvine. Sarah Proudler had left the Council as she was moving to Malta. Kim Jameson replaced her in December as Community Arts Officer.

Can you imagine the pleasure I was getting from my experimental work as I was creating images in a media I had never heard of before. I was surprised at the changes to each image as I hit them with UV light and then let them shine on their own in darkness. I found that by using traditional acrylics, some colours would show as tones under UV light and others would go black. I used this effect in some of the work for my show. Inks would appear dark under UV light and if water was added you could achieve tones depending on the amount of water. I used PVA glue and dropped pigment on to it. The glue would dry clear leaving the pigment scattered. Bill's piece of music was brilliant and was in three parts to co-inside with the light changes. As he knew when the changes were in the music, he operated the lights on the opening night, which was Friday 18 February 1994. Jessie had given me the heckling shop at the Vennel and I blacked out all the windows. The room was not very large so we could only allow a certain amount of people through at a time. There was a lot of people there and my local Councillor Stewart Dewar officially opened it. The door was closed as the audience viewed the work for ten minutes. I had erected fluorescent and ultra violet lights that were plugged in separately to a switchbox situated next to the sound system. Then the fluorescent lights were switched off as the ultra violet ones went on. The music lifted and the gallery was filled with an explosion of colour. Ten minutes later the ultra violet lights went off as the music went into a soft droning phase and out of the darkness shone my 19 images. Benny came along with his wife Kit, and at one performance everyone clapped when they saw the effect of photo luminescence. No one that evening except Benny, Bill and myself had ever seen, or experienced anything like what they did that night. Bill and I were elated with the effect our innovative collaboration had on our visitors

Polly Hamilton had recently been employed at the Harbour Arts Centre as the Outreach Worker and her partner Ian Cooper was the new Artist in Residence for Irvine New Town. They both came to the opening and Polly wrote a poem for me that would be published in the next Cunninghame Arts Council's Focus magazine. It was not intended as an interpretation of the works, but rather a third dimension to what could already be described as an exhibition of audio visual poetry.

New Beginnings

When all's said and done, it seems the best is yet to come.

Ghost busting was never enough and now I'm taking more from this than spectral exorcisms to ship it back to life.

So from sheet to sheet I've travelled, welding light and steel and sound.
My flight from clocked-off dockyards has broken unfamiliar ground.

This wild fluorescence thrills until it's all I can do to keep myself from spilling   beyond these frames.
My luminosity hits you right between the eyes.
They frighten me, these singing stars, this wicked trick of the light.

I'll fight but still you'll come and search by face for secret lines, which count the months and speak of steel in measured tones.
It burns.

I turned myself inside out for you and now it's your turn to turn for me.
So feel the changing seasons, and let the cadences of colour crescendo in your ears

© Polly Hamilton 1994

When Ian Cooper arrived in Irvine, Polly introduced me to him at the Harbour Arts Centre. We were to have our artist's studios at last in Irvine. Irvine Development Corporation, Cunninghame District Council, and Enterprise Ayrshire had pulled together and transformed the former stables next to the Ship Inn into purpose built studios. They wouldn't be ready until March so Ian had to work from the workshops at Montgomery Street at the top of Irvine harbour. I went down to see him a couple of times to get to know him. It had been decided by North Ayrshire Arts Council that they would take a studio and give three artists the opportunity to develop their work at low cost. Cunninghame District Council would equally finance this. I was elected to be one of these artists and manage the studio on their behalf.

Me and Dougie Henderson

Chapter 9

I collected the keys of studio H/I on Tuesday 8 March 1994 on behalf of Cunninghame Arts Council. This was one of the two Largest studios, the other being K/L. Studios A, B, C, D, and E all had windows to the front looking across the harbourside to Kilwinning. F, G, H/I, J, K/L, and M were perpendicular to the former and they all had sliding doors opening on to a large courtyard except studios D and E which opened into a passage at the kitchen-toilets area. D and E also had doors that opened on to Harbour Street. Colin Mackay, musical instrument repairer and music teacher had studio A, while Jimmy Trainor who made glass ornaments had B. John Bass who decorated ceramic tiles occupied C. Margaret Carslaw who would graduate from Glasgow School of Art in the summer took D. Painter Morag Lindsey occupied E while F was reserved for sculptor Ian Cooper. Photographer Charlie Gilmour and painter David Reid shared G. North Ayrshire Arts Council had H/I while J was shared by painters Hugh Loney and Kirsty McTaggart, jeweller Suzin McDonald, and writer David McMillan. Graphic designer John McLaughlin occupied K/L. Painters James O'Dea and Brian Craig shared studio M. The studios landlord was WASPS who would manage them on behalf of the owners. The first thing I did was mark the floor out in equal areas and chose mine as we had not yet found another two occupants. Bert and I began building a small dark room in one of the corners, as I needed it to pursue the development of my light reactive media. It would be a few weeks before Ian moved in from his workshop at Montgomery Street as his studio had to have an office built inside it. Ian was born and grew up in Sheffield and followed a mechanical engineering apprenticeship before studying art. He graduated with a first class honours degree in visual arts from Bretton Hall College of Further Education of Leeds University. I was impressed with the small amount of work that he brought with him in both wood and stone. Ian would prove to be a great asset to the studios and also a good friend to me. There were some minor problems to be rectified such as security locks, window grills etc. before some artists and craftworkers could move in. Morag Lindsay had been travelling from Kilmarnock every day to find that the grill had not been fitted on her window so I offered her a part of my studio to erect a couple of racks and store them until she felt confident to move them. She took me up on the offer and began building her racks until one day I jokingly commented on her leaving early. She stormed out, returning later to take her racks away.

I had been working in my dark room during this time trying to produce work relating to Lord of the Rings as I had an appointment with Lord Glasgow at Kelburn Country Park. He had been looking for artists to provide work for his recently constructed Secret Forest. My appointment was at 2 o'clock, he arrived at 3 and said that was the time we had arranged, after checking his diary he said I was right but didn't apologise. He then dragged me round his Secret Forest showing me where he wanted work done and didn't bother to look at the work I had brought with me. I made my mind up there and then that I wanted no more to do with him. Then I found out what was bothering Morag. She said that I was copying her work. I couldn't believe what I was hearing so I told her to stay out of my way. I had been trying to help her out and all I got back was a grief. This life is so different from shipbuilding. We decided to call the place of our work Courtyard Studios because of the layout. Sculptor George Wyllie officially opened the studios on Saturday 4 June 1994 and we were all taken for dinner into the Ship Inn next door. I was fortunate to have sold a painting to Irvine Development Corporation's Vice Chairperson Jeanette Mason. The official opening ended at teatime and then we had our own opening party that went on until the early hours of Sunday morning. I had set my music gear up in the studio and played for most of the night, while Hugh Loney had all the children who were there chalk drawing in the courtyard. Bill Kerr came along with his wife Jill and their three daughters Elaine, Alison and Mairi.

The first time I took Louise to the studio she had got out of the straps in her buggy and when I went to cross the road near the studios she fell out and bumped her head on the ground. She was  crying uncontrollably until I produced marshmallows from her bag. When I popped one in her mouth she began laughing. I used to change her nappies in the studio, as she was only one and a half. Polly Hamilton had arranged a visit by primary 7 pupils from St John Ogilvie's school one day in May. They liked my work so much that they sent a letter asking if I would come and do a workshop. I went along and had them all covered in inks and luminous dotted shoes. I was half expecting complaints from parents but at least the kids enjoyed themselves. I had taken along a cardboard box and cut a small hole at the top so that they could see their work glow in the dark. The first occupants of our studio apart from me were Jean Andrews who knitted dolls and painter Caitlin Foy who had recently graduated from Duncan of Jordanstone College of Art & Design. I had been on a Community Industry Arts programme through the DHSS, which gave me £10 on top of my unemployment benefit which was £0 as I was unemployed self-employed. As well as that I got £20 materials allowance every month which came in handy.

Tracey had been working day and night to pay for Helen and I to go with her and Louise to visit Pauline and Martin in Germany. We flew to Frankfurt via Birmingham on 19 July and Tracey picked up a

155

hired car from the airport. The car was much larger than the mini she had been driving in the UK and I was worried all the way to Pforzheim as I was in the front passenger seat. When we arrived at Pforzheim I phoned Martin to arrange for him to meet us and direct us to Pauline's flat. We clipped a car's wing mirror with ours and Martin said, "Turn round here." He told us to stop when we were hardly round the corner. We had arrived! Our mirror was easily straightened out but later on when we went out for a walk, the other car's would have to be renewed. We didn't report it as it would have been too much of a hassle going by what Pauline and Martin said about Germany and their ways. After we had eaten, Martin took Helen and I round to his flat where we would be staying for the next week. The thing that struck me right away was the size of the bed. You could have let the whole family sleep on this it was so wide. There was a pub in between their flats so I said to Helen that we would meet them there as she was going back to Pauline's. Martin and I had a few drinks and he was talking to the barman in German. The next thing, he came over with three glasses of schnapps and joined us. The rest of our team arrived and every now and then the bar man would come with another tray of schnapps and join us. My favourite place on that trip was Heidelberg. It was quite a long drive to get there, but worthwhile. There were many Americans around as they had a base during the Second World War. Seemingly many of them who were there at that time returned either for a visit or to open up a business. Americans owned many of the bars and restaurants. We spent a day in a park near Pforzheim that had many swimming pools, including an Olympic sized one for the professional swimmers. You paid to get in and there was a restaurant and bar but you could take in your own food if you prefer. One evening we went to a bar in Pforzheim to meet some of Pauline and Martin's friends. There were hundreds of people all around us and when it came to closing time, everyone had dispersed without a sound. Not like here in Scotland where there is always a lot of shouting such as "Goodnight," and "See you later." We also went to a party in the middle of the Black Forest where the scenery was beautiful. We returned home on the 26 July and Pauline and Martin were to follow us in August as they had both applied for teacher training. Martin got accepted and Pauline didn't, but she decided to return anyway.

I was given a week's residency at Loudon Hall Ayr, where I exhibited and worked every day in the gallery, so that I was able to discuss my work with visitors. There were six residencies during the summer months and I was lucky to be one of the artists. It was decided that I would show my light reactive work and since I was exhibiting with the Community Industry Arts project at Intermedia Gallery in Glasgow the following week, I decided that I would build a light box before going into Loudon Hall. When I was there I decorated the interior of the box. I cut a hole in the bottom to which I fixed a fan. It was actually a small heater with three speeds that could also blow cold air. I made a Perspex tube the same diameter as the hole and glued it inside. I glued cloth that I had already spattered with Luminous and fluorescent paint on the inside walls and fixed string so that it would move when the fan was switched on. Small pieces of polystyrene were painted, some fluorescent and some luminous, and placed on the bottom of the box. I fixed a three-way switch to the front and cut out another hole where I fixed a diving mask so that the viewer could look inside without any light getting in. The top of the box, which was removable, had small fluorescent and UV lights fitted. There was also an on-off power switch on the front. Ensuring the three-way switch was at position 1, power was switched on lighting up the inside of the box with the fluorescent light. When the switch was moved to position 2, it switched off the fluorescent, and on the UV and fan. The polystyrene was blown around the box and the string moved. At position 3, only the fan was on and you saw the moving parts within the box. With help from Ian and his brother Steve, they did the electrics before I went to Loudon Hall and by the end of my week there, I was able to show visitors the finished product. I enjoyed my time there and I'm sure the same went

157

for my visitors. There was a small balcony off from the room I was in and a group of actors performed a kind of Romeo and Juliet thing every day so I had to vacate the premises while this went on. It only lasted about twenty minutes so it didn't bother me too much.

When I returned to the studio with my finished box I had to make a plinth with an open top as the fan protruded from the bottom. Ian being the craftsman made it in no time from MDF. I then covered the box and plinth with woodchip paper and painted them both white. Then it was off to the Intermedia Gallery Glasgow for the opening on Friday 19 August. Roy Fitzsimmons turned up at the opening and it was nice to see him again as I hadn't seen him since the day he arrived at The Ship in 1990. I was the granddaddy of all the artists exhibiting and they were queuing to have a look inside my box, which was so intriguing and titled, **Behind the Mask**. This exhibition marked the end of my six Month Community Action project. I felt that things were looking better for the future and decided to become self-employed again. Polly Hamilton invited me to contribute to a mixed media event that explored the decline of heavy industry in Britain at the Harbour Arts Centre from 4-19 September. It was titled **Paradise Lost and Foundry** and included a play called *Dead Fish*, which was performed by the Hull Truck Theatre Company. Jean and Caitlin had left the studio by October as they did not have the time to spend there and were possibly keeping out someone who needed this easily affordable space to develop their work My work was changing due to my experimentation. My image of Gandalf from Lord of the rings was painted on a sheet of clear polythene. The mixed media of inks and luminous acrylics was not applied by brush; only the finishing touches were, to make it more representational. The media was poured on, spattered, and moved around until I could see an image that I could bring out for others to see.

Having no response to our advertising for artists to share the studio I contacted David Cook at WASPS and he gave me the name of a local girl who was on their list. Clare Hamilton came in to work in the studio on 1 January 1995. Clare was a Primary School supply teacher and was very talented. She had failed to get into Art School and had recently graduated as a teacher from Craigie

Campus in Ayr. Her artistic work was mainly glass and silk painting. She compiled a report for the North Ayrshire Arts Council's AGM in April.1995. In it she says, "My first love will always be art and to be offered sponsorship has been a second chance for me to experiment, learn and develop my arts/craft work. My sponsorship began on 1 January 1995. Three months on my experience has grown, my work developed and my style progressed. Although I am involved in many arts/crafts I have mainly been working on techniques, colour studies and designs for my glass painting. I also silk paint and hope to use the studio to teach this skill to a small group of silk enthusiasts during the summer months. On my pre-visit to the studios I was very apprehensive about sharing the space with a painter. There can often be conflict between artists and crafters. However this has not been the case at all. Jim Collins and I get on very well together and Jim has become a good friend as well as a teacher. Watching him paint and organise his time to meet commission deadlines has been a learning experience for me. Jim's work has encouraged me to dig deeper into myself and explore my feelings for design techniques and colour combinations resulting in my taking up fabric painting on canvas and combining this with embroidery, resulting in a compatible, expressive combination of media. Working in the studio alongside Jim has allowed me to meet other artists and art enthusiasts. In February, I saw Ian Cooper, our artist in residence, prepare, panic and participate in an exhibition of his work. This in itself was a worthwhile experience for me to view. Jim has encouraged me to become actively involved with the Arts Council and in the last few weeks I have become the craft representative to the roadshow committee. I look forward to working with the Roadshow team and I hope to take part in any other future events the studios may take part in. I intend to enjoy my forthcoming year at Courtyard Studios and look forward to what may lie ahead for me in the arts".

Unfortunately for her art, Clare got a full time job teaching after the summer that year and did not have the time to spend in the studio. She gave up her space in November. I am happy to say that she is back studying art in 2021 and producing some fine work.

I began a four painting commission from Govan Initiative Ltd in December 1994 for the Festival Business Centre at Brand Street Ibrox. I stretched and spattered 140lb Bockingford paper with watered down acrylics until I was happy with it as this would be the background colour for each work. Before it was dry I sprinkled on some ground sandstone that Ian Cooper had given me. The polymer emulsion in the acrylics would hold this to the paper. I then used soft pastel and pencil to create the representational images relating to shipbuilding and the Glasgow Garden Festival from 1988, since the building they were going into was on the site of the festival. I only created the images in the centre of the paper and left the outsides to fuse into the mount that would frame each work. I was introduced to Doctor Maria Fitzpatrick at the launch of Govan Initiative's 1995 calendar. She was the Director of Skillshops in Anderston and said that they were opening a new office space that could do with a large painting. I met with her in January 1995 and we agreed on the content, price, and size of the work.

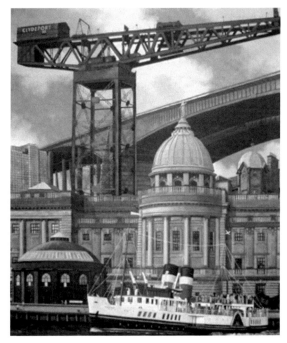

The six-foot by five **Anderston** painting had The Finnieston Crane dominating in front of the Kingston Bridge. The Moathouse Hotel was on the left with a former TSB building which was situated at Argyle Street. The Mitchell Library had the North Rotunda building in front of it with the Waverley paddle steamer at the bottom. I didn't want to make it too cluttered and think that I achieved this with the finished work.

Cunninghame District Council's Director of Leisure Mick Gallagher had asked me if I could create an installation with my light reactive media in the main hall of the Valley Arc Glengarnock for the forthcoming Cunninghame Arts Festival in June. He wanted the Council's parks Department to be involved. This would be something

I had never done before and the prospect of getting a fee for the job rather than doing a painting and waiting for someone to purchase it made it more inviting. Kim Jameson, Cunninghame District Council's Community Arts Officer employed an assistant to help me with administration and planning the installation. His name was James Mair BA from Saltcoats, a nephew of poet Henry, and whose specialist subject was photography. Jim built a model of the hall and we decorated the inside as I wished it to look. There was a piano that had to

Photo by John Keachie

162

remain, so we created an island with the piano in the centre, surrounded by plants and palm trees. The entrance door to the hall came from a passage, and as there should be no light getting in. We had to create a foyer in which the visitors would enter before coming into another world. A room upstairs had a window that looked into the hall making it ideal for someone to operate the music and lights. This room had also to be blacked out. Once again I asked Bill to compose a piece of music and we decided to call the installation **Music and Mystery.** It took some months of planning and I had fun at the studios covering hundreds of feet of eight-foot wide calico with inks, fluorescent and luminous paint. I hung up a washing line across the courtyard, soaked the calico in water, and then hung it up. I threw red, blue, and yellow inks at it, then more water. As the inks ran I would take the bottom of the cloth at various points and hold it up so that the inks ran in a different direction. Then I took it down and scrunched it up, leaving it to release most of the water before hanging it up once again to dry. Under UV light this would produce tones as the calico itself fluoresced. When the cloth was dry I laid it on the ground and spattered it with fluorescent and luminous paint which I had made up. This cloth would go all the way round the hall from the floor up to eight feet. The end where the window was had another strip on top to conceal it. I tore a small hole in the cloth where it was in front of the window so that the music and lights operator could see into the hall. Jim Mair had worked out the area that would require plants as the parks department would have to order them. The first thing we did was to cover the wooden floor with black polythene as this was going to be a messy project. Next, my father in law Bert built the foyer. We hung up four UV lights and four speakers. The wires from these had to be ran out of the door, along the passage and into the office before going up the stairs to our operating room where the music system and light switches were. We then put up all the calico as the parks laid out plants in front of it round the walls. A fan was placed on the top of the foyer. The string that hung from above was dyed fluorescent and dotted luminous so that you would see full lines under UV light and broken lines moving in darkness. I made two batches of lava from wallpaper paste, one red, and one orange. Two basins were set up one behind the other, at different heights among the plants. Black polythene was draped into the top basin and then down into the bottom one. Each batch of lava was placed into the two cavities and the top one made to run over the sides into the bottom colour. Two small buckets were cut down and placed upside down into each batch of lava. A fish tank pump with two outlets was placed underneath where it couldn't be seen, and each outlet tube placed into the bucket so that it built up air before escaping making a large bubble. Once again, Bill's new age music was a magical complement to this creation. I had told him about the lava and he had this popping sound within the piece that sounded just like bubbles bursting. I was fortunate to have Martin Polonis and Ian Cooper loan me a sculpture each. Martin gave me a large steel head that he allowed me to paint luminous. I laid Ian's plaster cast of a head on top of a sheet of luminous paper situated on the top of the piano. When there was no light, the paper reflected its stored light onto the head to let it be seen in the dark. Ian showed me another side to his talents by making him and I suits for the opening. I decorated them just the same way as I had done the calico. This time we used the theatre lights as well as fluorescent and UV. I went round all the plants except the three hired palm trees, sprinkling them with luminous pigment and testing them by switching the lights off to make sure they would be seen in the dark. Then I made up batches in various colours of fluorescent pigment and sprinkled it higgelty piggelty on the plants so that they would stand out under the UV light.

Although the Cunninghame Festival opened on Saturday 3 June, the official opening of **Music and Mystery** by Mick Gallagher was at 2pm on Monday 5 June. Cunninghame District Council had laid on a buffet, which we had before entering the hall. I had borrowed a smoke machine from the band Vein. Before letting the people in I told them to wait in the foyer. I released the smoke to give the place atmosphere and when I was happy, signalled up to Jim Mair to start the music. When they came in, the place was lit by UV light. I had luminous tape on my fingers so that I could point to the light or lights I wanted on next. There was a period in Bill's music where thunder was heard. At that time the UV lights were switched on and off from a rocker switch giving the impression of lightning. Once again Bill and I were on a winner. I thought that it would be fine to let the audience see what the room would look like in normal lighting after what they had just experienced. We had the good fortune of giving people, including ourselves, a new audiovisual experience. I really enjoyed going to the Valley Arc every day to be on hand to receive some very positive comments. The best one was when a guy came in with a

migraine headache and went out cured. Can you imagine the joy of giving people a new experience, creating something that they had never seen before! Bill and I were on a new trip that would take us into other venues over the next couple of years.

Artist Suzanne Le Blanc had come in to the Studio with Clare and I. Suzanne was a graduate from the Slade School of Art in London and was head of graphics at The Scottish Maritime Museum in Irvine at that time. She was involved in the setting up of Cunninghame Arts Council and was an executive committee member. While I was preparing for **Music and Mystery** Courtyard Studios had their first exhibition. It opened at the Harbour Arts Centre on Sunday 21 May and ran until 9 June. I had also met with the Convener and Director of

Finance of Cunninghame district
Council on 27 April, to discuss the commissioning of four paintings which would eventually hang in the Council Chambers when they were renovated. Each painting would represent a particular area of Cunninghame District. I met with all the Councillors from Irvine New Town first and asked them what they would like to be included in the montage of buildings and other points of interest. Then I went out and photographed what they had suggested and worked up a drawing, eliminating some of the suggestions. I submitted the drawing at another meeting and talked them round to accepting my

proposal. I finished the first painting and delivered it to Cunninghame House by the beginning of July. I went through the same system of meeting Councillors from the next area, taking photographs, submitting a drawing, until I completed the last one by 23 November 1994.

As I had money in the bank for a change after my hard work, it was time to try to book a late deal holiday. At such short notice, all we could get was a week in Majorca leaving from Manchester and checking in at 6.30am. We booked the last British Airways shuttle flight from Glasgow to Manchester on the evening before our departure for Majorca. This meant spending the night in the airport. Daughter Pauline had told us that there was a pub at the end of the runway where you can have a drink and watch the planes take off and land. We found it but it closed at 11pm and we had to sit around the desolate airport terminal for the rest of the night. We didn't know where in Majorca we were going until we got there. After meeting the holiday rep we were told we were going to the Lagoon Center Apartments in Alcudia. On arriving in Alcudia, we were dropped off last and  Helen was getting worried that we were going to the jungle. However, the accommodation was excellent and Alcudia was just a nice size for strolling around, and also not too noisy for us auld yins. Talking of the jungle, the picture above was the view from our balcony and the animal on the wall is a cougar. It was chained up, but I would not like to have been walking along the street and be surprised by its appearance on the wall. We spoke to the owner out

167

of curiosity and she told us that the cougar was just a big pussycat. We became friendly with a family from Cowdenbeath in Fife. Drew and Lorna Lindsay were there with their son Andrew and daughter Michelle for two weeks and we met up with them during their first week. Andrew 16, was disabled but was a champion swimmer. He was first selected to represent Scotland at the European school games in Lisbon in 1994. Then when he was 16, he represented Great Britain at the Paralympics in Atlanta in 1996, then again in 2000 in Sydney and Athens in 2004. He got silver in Atlanta and gold in the other two. Andrew held the world record for 10 years in the s7 class

in 100 metres backstroke. The girls all loved him! We spent some time with them and have met a couple of times back in Scotland since then. We took a trip to Puerto Pollensa, but I thought that it was just too quiet to spend a holiday there. I was impressed with the Old Town of Alcudia and would certainly return to this resort. As we touched down on the tarmac at Manchester, the aircraft dipped left, then right, and I thought my time was up. Although I had booked our return flight to Glasgow for hours later in case of any delays, I managed to get us on an earlier flight. Instead of our in-flight snack, I asked for another bacardi to calm me down after the incident on the last landing.

I completed the third painting for the council on 7 September and went to Arran with Johnny Beattie and auld Tam on Monday18 for a couple of days. Following the success of **New Beginnings** and **Music and Mystery**, Bill and I agreed to do workshops at the Cunninghame Arts Council's seventh annual Arts and Crafts Roadshow that was to be held in the Ardrossan Civic Centre on Saturday 4 and Sunday 5 November 1995. We both occupied separate rooms in the building as I had to black out the room I was in to give pupils the opportunity of producing a luminous painting. Both workshops were well attended and enjoyed by the participants. I received the following letter from Largs dated 22 November 1995. "Thank you very much, Jim, for sending my masterpiece along with Miss McCreadie's. I am sorry I am late in writing. I wasn't sure of your address – but Clare says this should find you! I really enjoyed your workshop and wish I could have been there longer. It was fun! The effects of the different lights on the two types of paint have raised astonished "Oohs" and "Wows! It's fascinating! Thanks again, Enid"

1996 was to be the tenth anniversary of Govan Initiative Ltd, and since they liked the painting of Anderston that I did for Skillshops, I said that they should have a painting done to commemorate the occasion. Ron Culley had sent me a letter on 9 November asking me to work up some rough sketches of my proposal so that no significant time was allocated to the project until his Chairman gave his approval. He had already discussed the matter with him following a letter I sent to Mr Culley, and they agreed on the value of commissioning a painting of the kind described in my letter.

I had a busy time ahead of me as I had been commissioned by the Glasgow Vennel Museum to produce The Lion, The Witch, and The Wardrobe to run over the Christmas period. The Council also commissioned me to create another installation for the 1996 Arts Festival. They had commissioned renowned Spanish writer Medardo Fraille to write a story, which

169

would then be scripted and dramatised by Largs school kids with music once again by Bill Kerr. Glasgow Vennel Curator Jessie Scott was very polite and asked me if I required anything to be ordered for the **Kingdom of Narnia**. When I called her on the phone and told her I needed a lion, she had a fit! I must give her full marks for getting a loan of paisley Museum's lion. I had said to her that even the head would be sufficient, as I could have disguised the background. I went into the Vennel on Sunday 3 December and worked all week as the opening was on the following Saturday. Once again, I was in the Heckling shop, which was ideal for an installation with its stone floor and overhead beams. Ian and Polly had given me an old wardrobe, so we had the door to the heckling shop taken off and placed the wardrobe in front of the opening. I left the wardrobe doors open and hung a double-layered blackout cloth from the top of it. I also placed mothballs on the top of the wardrobe. There is a kind of foyer between the heckling shop and Gallery, so I was able to keep the lights off in the foyer. Visitors could still see where they were going as there was some light coming from the Gallery. When you entered through the wardrobe you were entering a forest at night in winter as I had placed Christmas trees in that area. Jessie had dressed a mannequin in a long white dress, fur stole and longhaired blonde wig and I made a crown from luminous paper and painted her lips red fluorescent. At her feet lay a tin of turkish delight. Not many of the children who were to visit tried my turkish delight as they were scared of falling under the witches spell. Jessie had also borrowed a lamppost from one of the Largs amateur theatre groups. On leaving the forest, you went along a small tunnel to Mr Tumnus's room. I had placed Ian Coopers sculpture of a minataur as feature at the end of the tunnel and did up the room just as it is explained in The Lion, The Witch, and The Wardrobe. I had baked cakes, adding fluorescent pigment to the flour and laid them on a small table. Cunninghame District Council's libraries had given me old books which had not sold at their previous book sale and it took me ages to cover the bookends with luminous paper and Letraset them with new titles. I built a

fireplace and hung a painting above it which I had done of Mr Tumnus's grandfather. I also made a clock that sat on top of the fireplace. The books that I had covered were placed in a bookcase and on the table beside the cakes I laid another book that lay open at a page where I wrote a little ditty. As you left Mr Tumnus's room through an opening in the cloth that you pushed aside, you were faced immediately with the head of Aslan the lion. Some of the young kids were scared when they saw him but most of them loved him. He was a harmless soul as most of his teeth were through an opening in the cloth that you pushed aside, you were faced immediately with the head of Aslan the lion. Some of the young kids were scared when they saw him but most of them loved him. He was a harmless soul as most of his teeth were missing. I had made him a crown and covered his plinth with bracken to hide it. Ian loaned me another couple of his sculptures to place in the same room as Aslan. When you left Aslan's room, you came back into the first room you were in which was now lit by UV light. On one of the backdrops that were in front of you when you entered Narnia there appeared the castle of Cair Paravell that I had painted in inks with fluorescent highlights. It was there all the time but couldn't be seen when entering in darkness. Bill's music was once again wonderful and atmospheric. There were bells in it and birdsong for spring when you entered Aslan's domain. There is no doubt that Bill's compositions were as important as my artwork in making these installations a wonderful experience for the people who came along to see them. It was very well attended and many schools paid a visit while it was on from 12 December 1995 until 13 January 1996. It made the headlines of the Irvine Times on December 15 and also the Irvine Herald on January 12. Jessie told me that it was advertised in *The* **Guide** of the Guardian newspaper for three weeks and that this was the first time that they had advertised anything from the Glasgow Vennel. I had placed bark around the forest area and while sprinkling the trees with luminous pigment; the excess fell onto the bark making it look like snow. It was a really cold period over Christmas that year and the Vennel flooded. There must have been six inches of water in the building because my backdrops were bleached at the bottom and the bark was soaking and smelly after that. Luckily it didn't really destroy anything or interfere with the running of the Installation. After dismantling the Kingdom of Narnia my work was to remain at the Vennel, as Courtyard Studios were the next exhibition. I had taken many photos of the greasy pole at the previous Marymass Festival and had done a couple of paintings of it which I showed at the exhibition.

I got the go ahead for the Govan painting and spent the first few months of 1996 researching, preparing, and developing it for completion at the beginning of April. This painting was to be a real challenge, but most rewarding as my roots lay in Govan and I could identify with it. I decided to build the composition around Govan's coat of arms and show how the community had developed since it was a village. At the bottom left are the cottages of Water Row, and bottom right, the old horse ferry. The parish of Govan used to include Partick and Whiteinch on the north side of the river and the ferries connected the community. Govan's motto Nihil Sine Labore means nothing without work. The explanation of the shield in the coat of arms says "Within the shield, a modern ship in the stocks." I changed what was an old timber built ship to a modern one. The two supporters to the left and right of the shield are John Elder on the left, and Sir William Pearce on the right. John Elder was the the founder of the former Fairfield shipyard built on the grounds of the Fairfield farm. Sir William Pearce, his successor, was the first MP for Govan. His idea of the Atlantic Blue Riband has lasted until the present day. There was a need for fast crossing of the Atlantic at that time. Sir

William financed and built the first ship to hold the record for the fastest crossing. There were many shipyards in Govan in the late nineteenth century and they built tenements to house the growing population. The tenement at the left was at Crossloan Place. On the bottom right, just above the ferry, is a modern housing development across from the Lyceum. The Old Kirk on the right, and St Anthony's tower at the top left represent the community's religious development. To the right of St Anthony's tower is the Angel Building which is situated at the junction of Paisley Road West and the Govan Road. It is also known as the Gateway to Govan. Above the Old Kirk, education is represented by Govan High School. This particular building burnt down in the seventies. I was told that business should be represented, so I included Ibrox Football Stadium just above the cottages on the bottom left, the Festival Business Centre above that, and Barr and Stroud's logo in front of the tenement. A well-known sight to old Govanites was the sea of bunnets coming down the Govan Road. I made the shipyard workers monochromatic within the coat of arms in order to make it stand out, and also to make them like ghosts from the past. They get stronger in colour as they proceed. I replaced a knight's helmet with a welder's in the coat of arms. The wheat sheaf and salmon remind us of Govan's past agricultural and salmon industry. Thankfully, the salmon has returned! The crane at the top right is not the Finnieston one, but the Fairfield. I titled the painting, **In the Shadow of the Fairfield Cran'**. The painting was to be unveiled at Govan Initiative Ltd's birthday bash at the Ranger's Club on Sunday14 April 1996. I set it up in the hall, placing it on two chairs and clamped at the top by my easel. A blue velvet cloth was draped over it and tucked in underneath at the bottom. Sir Alex Ferguson and I were to unveil it, one at each end. A slight tug and it would fall to the floor revealing the painting but not obstructing it. When Helen and I arrived we were taken into the hospitality room to meet Sir Alex. I said to him that I used to work for him when he had his pub, Fergies. I told him that I played there with Frekels and he said he remembered us. Then I said that one of my mates Jamie McGettrick played with St Mirren when he was Manager. His reply was, "He's dying from cancer," I said, "How do you know?" as I knew Jamie was in Perth Australia. He told me that Jamie's brother in law had contacted him. I was shocked as Jamie was such a nice guy and we had lost contact over the years. We unveiled the painting before our meal and I had to talk about it. During my explanation my mind went blank and I clammed up, it was so embarrassing! However, I had Ron behind me trying to spur me on and eventually I got back into the swing and managed to carry on without any more hesitancy. At the end of the evening Bert came to collect us. He didn't want to come in because he was dressed in his jeans but Sir Alex shouted him in and spoke to him about his dad, as Bert knew him from the shipyard. They had a good old chat and Sir Alex would not be interrupted while he spent his time with him. There is no doubt about it; this man has not forgotten his roots, as I watched him spend time with other people over the course of the evening.

Chapter 10

I had met Medardo Fraille and his wife Janet at the Glasgow Vennel while my **Kingdom of Narnia** was running. I wanted to let him see the effects achieved by the light reactive media before he began writing. The Council commissioned him to write the story because although he was Spanish and lived in Bishopbriggs Glasgow, he spent a lot of time in Largs because he liked it there. Medardo wrote his story **Out of the World and into Largs** in Spanish and it had to be translated. Freelance Drama worker John Welsh worked with local kids from Largs and I spent a long time planning the layout to suit the performance. Bill couldn't do much until he liaised with John. As well as composing, Bill had to put music to the words of a song that John had written to be sung by the children. Once again I had to use the courtyard at the studios to lay out the framework that would create different spaces within the Brisbane Centre. The story was about a little boy and his female cousin who came with his mum and dad to Largs from Glasgow. While they were having an ice cream at Nardini's, the parents told the children to go and play on the beach. The little boy finds a large boot and climbs into it. There are buttons on it so he presses them one by one until he is whisked up into the sky and lands on the only cloud in the sky. A ray appears in the sky and a little man slides down it towards him and takes him to what is like a large disc in the sky. It is full of funny little men who are joined at the back and are called tetramen. After some time he comes back to earth jumping from cloud to cloud until he finally arrives at the other side of Largs. He meets his cousin as he is walking back to the café and she doesn't believe his story. The hall had an emergency exit that opened onto the promenade. We used this door as the entrance. I created a passage from there to the café. The café area was small.

176

From there you carried on into the beach area. On the backdrops I painted Vikingar, the Pencil, and the sea in inks. On the wooden floor I laid black polythene. Between that, and a top layer of clear polythene, I poured blue fluorescent mixed with water. When you walked on it, it moved but your feet were still dry as the water was sandwiched between the two layers of polythene. I poured sand over a large area to represent the beach. On the beach lay rocks and shells which I had sprayed various colours of fluorescent. I made two jellyfish from wallpaper paste. Another room would be the dark area where the little boy is whisked to meet the tetramen. I laid sheets of

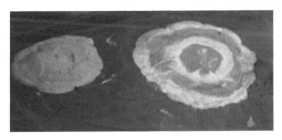

luminous painted cloth on the floor, which gave you a strange affect when the lights were out. I stuck planets and small stars on the walls so that you had the feeling of being up in another world. You returned to the beach area with the little boy and went out of the hall from what should have been the entrance. The installation was open to the public and performances were only on certain days. As an installation I felt that it was too empty because I had to leave plenty of room for the actors and audience. It was fine during a performance as the people filled up the spaces. This event was used as the opening of EXPO 96 with a Civic Reception next door in the Green Shutter Tearoom on Friday evening 31 May. My Manager from the shipyard John Young and his wife Laura came along that night. It was good to show him how far I had come along in the seven years since leaving the yard. There was a dress rehearsal the following day and performances on the Sunday from 2pm onwards. Nardini's sponsored ice cream for the event, so when the audience was in the café area, they were given a small tub of ice cream while they watched the performance. I went along on the

Sunday with Helen, Tracey, and Louise as that would be my only chance to see it.

Kim Jameson had left as Community Arts Officer in 1995 and with the restructure of local Government; Cunninghame was changed to North Ayrshire in 1996. Norma McCrone replaced Kim with the new position of Arts and Cultural Services Manager. That year North Ayrshire Council and Karmoy Kommune in Norway were having a cultural exchange to coincide with their annual Viking Festivals. Ian Cooper and I were nominated to go to Norway along with Garnock Academy's choir and brass band, and also Commotion, the youth theatre. Michael Durning had replaced Clare in our studio and Maree Meahan from Kilmarnock shared with Brian Craig and Jamie O'Dea. Sally Harkness took over from Jimmy Trainor in studio B and Graham McKean replaced Morag in studio E. Seven artists from the studios had work sent over to Norway for an exhibition, Michael, Suzanne, Ian, Graham, Maree, Jamie and me. I sent eight of my luminous paintings over as I was to do workshops and was told that they would be in the same venue as the exhibition. I sent over fifteen stretched watercolour papers on boards, UV lights, brushes, inks, and had made up batches of luminous and fluorescent paint. Ian lived five minutes walk from me. We were picked up by minibus from his house at 5.30 am on Wednesday 5 June as we were leaving by coach from Garnock Academy, Glengarnock, at 6.30 am. On the way there some of the youth theatre had to be picked up from their homes at Irvine, Kilwinning, and the three Towns. We drove up to Aberdeen where we got a Scandinavian Airways flight to Stavanger. We were met by coach and taken via a short ferry trip and roads that at times went under the sea, to our destination at Kopervik. There was a Civic reception at the Town Hall when we arrived. I'm not a great fish eater and all the food at the reception was fish based, but I managed to work my way through enough to keep me going, including caviar and salmon. We were given presents of a book and ceramic drinking vessel. From there we went to the Karmoy Hotel where we would be staying for four nights. After getting our rooms allocated, we went to the official opening of the Karmoy Viking Festival that took place just at the back of our hotel. We had a couple of drinks in the hotel after the opening before retiring early as I had to be taken to a primary school the next morning to do my workshops. After breakfast on the Thursday I was taken by car to Skudeneshavn to pick up my equipment from the Takelurfabrikken Gallery where our exhibition was held. I don't have a clue where the school was, or what it was called as I was in a strange place with names I have never encountered. After unloading my gear into a class I was told that I could do the workshop in the gymnasium as it had no windows. I was to find out that there were thirty pupils in the class but I had only prepared fifteen boards. I had sent a large sheet of polythene over which I spread out on the floor as it can be a very messy doing painting workshops with children. I laid out the boards in a circle and set up my lights. I had also brought three of my works from the exhibition to show the children what can be achieved from using this media. When I was set up the whole class came into the gym and their teacher explained to them that only fifteen could participate in the workshop so they decided who they would be. The first thing I did was to show the kids my work with the hall lights on; I don't think they were too impressed! When I had someone put the hall lights off and put on the UV's it was a different story, they were infatuated and I could hear them all gibbering in Norwegian. I hadn't a clue what they were saying but it didn't matter as I could tell by their faces that they liked what they saw. It was the same reaction when I put all the lights off and they saw my work change once again. I was cool! With their teacher interpreting, we began by firstly soaking their paper and laying a light wash of acrylic burnt sienna with the boards slightly tilted. Then laying the boards flat, the paper was spattered with acrylic Payne's grey, yellow ochre, cerulean blue, keeping the colours well diluted with water. Every now and then I would put the hall lights off and UV on to show them that they were building up a tonal background to their work. Some kids had not diluted the paint enough and the areas where that occurred had to be lifted off while the paint was still wet. I let them put on a small amount of fluorescent that day just to keep them interested as I was to return the following day to continue this necessary two session workshop to achieve the effects that would be seen in their finished work. What they had done on the first day would be dry by the next and the paper would be sealed by the acrylics. Then, PVA glue could be used on it without going through and sticking the paper to the board it was stretched on.

After the first day's workshop I was then taken to the gallery at Skudeneshavn to meet up with Ian who had been dropped off there earlier to be on hand to talk to visitors about his colleagues and their work. I also returned my three paintings that I had borrowed to show the schoolchildren. The gallery belonged to the Karmoy Kommune Council. The building stood on its own at the harbourside. On the ground floor was the gallery that consisted of two rooms; one of the rooms also had a franchised café area. There was talk that at future artist exchanges, the upstairs would be used as accommodation for the visiting artist, while the café area would be the studio, and his or her work shown in the gallery. When the gallery closed that first day Ian and I strolled through Skudeneshavn admiring the colourful wooden buildings of this beautiful harbourside town. We were shocked when it cost us twelve pounds for two omelettes and two half pints of beer. We noticed another gallery and went in to see the type of work that Norwegian artists were producing. There was no one there until a woman appeared, and when she heard my accent, she asked me if I was Scottish. I think her name was Elizabeth Mae and she was a real eccentric who got all excited at me being Scottish as she had lived near Oban for seven years. This was her gallery and all the work on show was hers. She made us coffee and we ate mars bars with it. We couldn't get away from her and we were supposed to be going out for dinner that night. We missed the bus to Kopervik and she had to run us back, meaning we also missed dinner. Later that evening we were all taken to an open air rock concert at Visnes. This is where the copper that was used for the Statue of Liberty came from. It was held in what was like a walled garden with a covered in stage at one end and wooden tables and benches laid throughout. We felt out of place as all the Norwegians were dressed as Vikings. We were at a Viking rock concert! It began raining and our pints were quickly getting refilled with water. Some of the Vikings had what looked like rhubarb leaves on their heads to keep them dry. At midnight everyone vacated the place and fires were lit along the shoreline, as that was how the Vikings of the past communicated. It really was a strange experience that night and we were soaked through.

On the Friday morning I was taken again to the school with Ian returning to the gallery. I let the children see their work under the UV light before they proceeded. Today they would not all use the same media so that their finished work would not be similar. Some would use inks to darken certain areas, and others would pour PVA glue with fluorescent pigment dropped into it. They would all use the luminous paint. This is when it all gets messy, you know what children are like, everything to excess! They were painting their trainers luminous because it was cool and the amounts of fluorescent pigment and luminous paint used was well over the top, but the main thing was that they were enjoying themselves. They loved their finished masterpieces which I left lying flat on the floor, and told the teacher to cut the paper from the boards when they were dry. It was a good feeling leaving the school that day as all the children were smiling and waving goodbye. I had done a painting myself to show the kids what to do and I left that one with the school. Once again I was taken to the gallery to meet up with Ian and leave my equipment there to be returned to my studio in Scotland. We watched our youth theatre do an open-air performance in Skudeneshavn before returning to Elizabeth Mae's gallery to say goodbye, as we would not be returning there. She took us into her home that was across from the gallery and gave us a glass of wine before her boyfriend appeared and ran us back to Kopervik. That evening we were to go for a posh noshup at a restaurant. The Mayor of Karmoy with members of his Council and Viking Committee were present along with our official delegation. We had crab soup for starter which I thought was really tasty, then we had Aberdeen Angus steak that was cooked to perfection. After dinner one of the Norwegian Council asked me if I would play guitar for them as we were going on to another venue. One of his colleagues had a guitar that I could borrow for the night so I was taken by car to collect it. On the return journey I was busy tuning the guitar and took no notice where we were going. We arrived outside this other place just as the rest of our group were approaching so I emerged from the car singing Flower of Scotland. They told me to carry on singing as I entered this place which was full of people. They were all there for an earlier historical conference and here was a mad Scotsman arriving to disrupt their quiet evening. As I entered singing I spotted a window ledge at the far end of the room and made my way there, sitting down until I finished the song. Ian and I got wine while everyone else had beer. After everyone was settled down and had refreshments I did some more songs. At the end of the evening as everyone was leaving someone asked me if I could sing Donovan's 'Catch the Wind.' By the time I had finished it, everyone from our hotel had vanished including Ian. I stepped outside and didn't have a clue where I was. I had to go back in and ask someone the way to our hotel. It was only five or ten minutes walk but when I got there the doors were locked. I banged on the doors to no avail, until

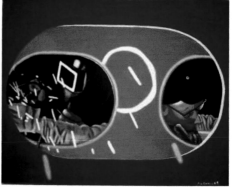

eventually I spotted Norma and managed to catch her attention. She came and opened the door to let me in.

You know the saying about leaving the best to last. Today, Saturday, would be our last day in Norway and I will never forget it. There was an open air Festival event in the morning, but it had to be cancelled due to the rain. I got soaked through once again and Norma, Ian and I were to be taken to meet Norwegian artist Bernhard Ostebo who lived on an island. I couldn't go as the only jacket I had with me was leather, wet, and very heavy. The Director of Education for Karmoy took me to a store where I bought a waterproof suit with my credit card. He then took Ian and I to his

home to show us his painting collection. His wife made us coffee, and we had chocolate ice-lollies with it, which I found strange, but different. He then took us to meet another artist at her home. Astri Vie Pollege was presently working in another country but had returned for the Viking Festival. On our return to Kopervik, we picked up Norma and made our way to Haugesund where we were taken by boat to the island of Feoy where Bernhard lived. You will see from the photo that it turned out a beautiful day and I didn't need to wear the suit I had just bought to protect me from the rain. It took us about a half an hour boat trip to Feoy where Bernhard met us at the pier. His wife Oloug was the primary school teacher on the island and they lived in the schoolhouse. They had two sons and one of them was at the school along with four other pupils. The schoolhouse was three tiered and Bernhard's studio was the bottom floor. We spent a couple of hours there and Oloug made wonderful lattice pancakes, which we had with syrup. We would meet Bernhard again as he was coming over to Scotland for the Largs Viking Festival later in the year. By the time we left, the boat that we came across in had stopped running but one of their friends took us back to the mainland in his boat where we were met by a taxi and taken to Avaldsnes. We were dropped off at St. Olav's Church. Leaning towards the church is the menhir called the "Virgin Mary's Needle". According to legend, the day the monument touches the church will be the end of the world. Hakon Hakonsen, the Viking leader we defeated at The Battle of Largs built this church around 1250. From there we were to make our way to the Saga evening, which would mark the end of the Viking Festival. Norma, Ian and I walked down through a field that seemed to go on forever, crossed a stream, and into a forest. It felt like we were little hobbits in The Lord of the Rings as we ventured though this dense woodland. All of a sudden we came to a clearing, in front of us were all these Vikings and a huge Longhouse sat on a hill. There were fires burning and a Viking Longboat was tied up at the shoreline. All your senses were stimulated with the sights, sounds, and smells that were around you. This was the highlight of our trip! We were late arriving there and all our delegation was already enjoying the Viking hospitality. The storytelling was funny, and we were in time to see a performance by our youth theatre and the beautiful singing of Garnock Academy's choir. Unfortunately because of where this event was situated, we had to leave before it got dark. We would be leaving Karmoy early the next morning.

As soon as we returned to Irvine I went straight to the studio to get my tools as I would be leaving by train to Largs in the morning to take down my installation at the Brisbane Centre. When I got there it was already ripped down. The community arts workers thought they were doing me a favour by dismantling it but I was furious. Everything I use in an installation could be used in a future one, saving a lot of time cutting wood and painting cloth. The cloth had been ripped down and the screwed joints in the two by two framework taken apart with a sledgehammer. The wood was lying in pieces, and what could be used in the future had bent screws sticking out of it that made them very hard to remove. The attitude was that the council had paid for it so I couldn't argue.

I had loaned some of my shipyard portraits to Govan Workspace in June for the "Right to Work" exhibition, which was put together to celebrate the twenty fifth anniversary of the UCS "Work In". My Govan painting was used as a CD cover for the compilation of Govan young bands album, "Stairway to Govan".

Since my return from Norway, I had spent my time on a painting to commemorate my visit to Norway. Ian and I were invited to the Civic reception for the 1996 Largs Viking Festival and I displayed this painting at the event. It was there we were to meet Bernhard once again, and also another artist from Galway Ireland. Padraic Reaney was to exhibit at Castlekirk in Lochranza on the Isle of Arran as part of the Viking Festival. His exhibition would then be moved to the Brisbane Centre in Largs. Although Bernhard was based at a hotel in Largs, Ian and I saw him for most of the two weeks he was here. His exhibition was held in Vikingar and he had brought his work over in a van via Stavanger-Newcastle. Ian had to drive down to Newcastle to meet him and direct him to Largs. Ian and I went over to Padraic's opening at Castlekirk that used to be a church, and at that time a Bed and Breakfast with a gallery cum music room. We met Tam Balloch there as he had arranged Padraic's exhibition.It was a

peaceful opening with a harpist playing and afterwards, we went
upstairs to bed.

We were to return a second time for an arts forum at
Castlekirk and I did a workshop in Arran High School as part of their
fiftieth birthday celebrations. Padraic Reaney was born in Carraroe,
County Galway in 1952. He is basically self-taught although he went
to Art College for a few years. Bernhard Ostebo was born in
Haugesund in 1961. He attended Bergen Art and Craft School from
1987-89 and Western Norway Art Academy 1989-90. Padraic's
exhibition "Images of the Tain" consisted of small bronze sculptures,
ceramics, watercolours, oils, monoprints, linocuts, and mixed media,
all on the Celtic theme. As Bernhard was a printmaker, his work was
more graphical than Padraic's who used many different techniques

186

and media. Padraic only stayed for the opening of the Viking Festival and his own exhibition before returning to Ireland. Ian and I took Bernhard through to Glasgow one day to show him the galleries. We took him to the Gallery of Modern Art first, then to the Glasgow Print Studio which highly impressed him. Then we went on to the Collins Gallery and introduced him to the Curator. Bernhard stayed with Helen and I one night and Bert and I took him up to the Towerlands Sports Club for a few drinks. I swapped him with my painting "The Dimming Light of Life" for one of his monoprints. It was sad when he left, as I didn't know if we would ever meet again, although we still keep in touch.

Chapter 11

My Govan painting was available as a limited edition print of 500 by the beginning of October and North Ayrshire Council offered me a Retrospective exhibition in 1997. This would be held in the recently refurbished Racquet Hall in Eglinton Country Park, Irvine. Norma had taken Ian, Bernhard and I to see the building which would make an excellent temporary exhibition space. Next to the hall was a cottage which the Country Park rents out. If the artist exchange were to develop, then the visiting artist could stay in the cottage, work from Courtyard studios, and exhibit his or her work in the Racquet Hall. Since this new space was made known to us, the present Chairman of North Ayrshire Arts Council Ron Smart had the idea to have an open art exhibition. A committee was formed to develop this project. North Ayrshire Council would fix a picture rail round three of the four walls and there was plenty of room in the hall to erect exhibition boards.

Helen and I took Louise to my Sister Chris's house at Peterston Super Ely near Cardiff during the October break from school. They had returned from living in the Caribbean and bought a large house there. Jonathan and Bryony were at school while we were there. We took Louise to Techniquest in Cardiff as Chris recommended it. There was a room in it that had a wall covered in luminous paper that you stood in front of, while a flash went off revealing your profiled shadow on the wall. The place was full of schoolchildren there on day trips as part of their education. There were many hands-on challenges in it for the kids.

Mick Gallagher was to leave at the end of November as he had a new post as Director of Leisure for Leicester City Council. I was sorry to see him go as he was very supportive of the arts and he and his wife Bev had become good friends to me over the years. I gave

Mick and Bev my Gandalf painting as a gift so that when they put the lights off at night to go to bed, he would remind them of me. Bev was expecting as Mick left for Leicester and she was due in December. Mick said that he wanted the child to be born in Scotland. If it was a boy, he would be able to play football for England, secondly Ireland,

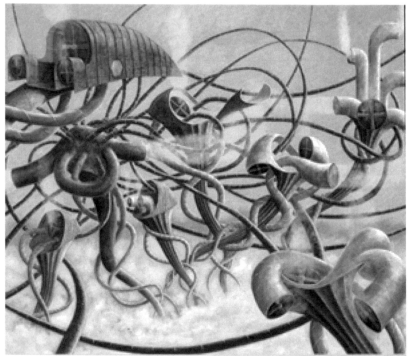

and thirdly Scotland because he was born there. Mick and Bev were born in Worksop England, and his father was Irish. Bev had a daughter on 27 December and they called her Caitlin. Over the winter I did a lot of drawing resulting in a composition that was to be my favourite painting, "The Purifier". I had a five by six foot canvas already stretched, ready to receive this image. It was composed to make you think about modern day air pollution. The objects in the painting were developed from ideas in sketchbooks, changing them as they were drawn on the finished study. They are bringing up the polluted air from below and sending it to the purifier at mid left, just below the controller above it at top left. The purifier, when it has done its job, sends the clean air back to them and they return it to earth. Off I went again on another tangent with a complete change in direction.

I had to decide what I was going to show in my retrospective. The gallery was large enough to take any size of painting, so I had no worries there. I gave North Ayrshire Council a list of previous customers so that they could write to them for permission to loan them the paintings for my show. Every Company and private owner co-operated except the owner of **Glasgow Cathedral**.

As Helen and I would be fifty that year, Bert paid for a week's holiday in Gran Canaria and Tracey and Pauline gave us our spending money. We left for Las Palmas on 28 April meaning we would be there on Helen's birthday which was the thirtieth. As we were told what coach we were going on and that we were all going to the same place at Maspalomas, I put our cases in to the coach last, so that we would be first to retrieve them. We were first at the reception of Venesol Bungalows and were given the key to bungalow No 50. At first I thought that it was a set up, but it was only co-incidence that we would be staying in number fifty for Helen's birthday. The complex was excellent with a large pool, restaurant, bar, and tennis court. The location was good, it was quiet, and on a hilltop overlooking Maspalomas. It was only about two pounds on a taxi to Playa Del Ingles if you wanted the nightlife. We went on a tour of the Island, stopping for lunch and dinner, and found that for a small Island, the climate was surprisingly different in the north than in the south. It was cold as we stopped in the mountains to take photographs of Mount Tiedi on Tenerife. Bananas are grown in the north of the Island in the winter, as they can't compete with other tropical countries in the summer. You will notice that all the holiday resorts of Gran Canaria are in the south of the Island where it is hotter. We spent a day in Puerto Rico and met people Helen knew from Irvine. I had taken a couple of Govan prints with me and sold one to the Caledonian bar in Puerto Rico. One day we walked down to the sand dunes at Maspalomas and as we tried to cross them, Helen's plastic shoes were nearly melting on her feet. I can well understand how people could perish in a desert! We walked to the beach from there and strolled at the edge of the water all the way round the naturist area to Playa Del Ingles. There were some sights there and none of them beautiful. We both agree that we would like to return to Maspalomas if we were to have another holiday at that time of the year.

Polly Hamilton moved to Poole as Community Arts Officer and Ian Cooper followed her around June 1997. I had worked alongside Ian for three and a half years and would miss him as he was like a leader in the studios. He was a good listener when you were down, gave constructive criticism when required, and was also very knowledgeable and helpful. As Irvine Development Corporation had been wound up in April; Ian would be the last Artist in Residence for the New Town. He has left his mark in the area by siting his sculptures such as renewing the Mercat Cross in Kilwinning, and carving into paving slabs that were placed in the pavement outside of the Kings Hotel Irvine. The slabs were removed while the town centre was being refurbished in later years and are now in the hands of Irvine's Burns Museum. Ian had work placed on various buildings of the newly built Gottries Road housing complex. Jamie O'Dea had moved to a house in Gottries Road and by co-incidence, he was allocated one that had one of Ian's relief's above the entrance. I wrote the following song for Ian and played it to him at his leaving party in the Harbour Arts Centre.

The Sculptor

To the sculptor, this I dedicate
For I've had the pleasure of watching, him create
Invisible to all, locked in stone
Seen by the eye of sculptor, alone

Artist in residence
Last of the line
In the new Town
He's a good friend of mine

Another chapter, completed and gone
In his book of life, it's time, to move on
I'm happy to say, I've shared a few laughs
In the Irvine chapter, more than a few, paragraphs

Jim Collins 1997

Photo by Charlie Gilmour

     I decided that I should show my luminous work in my retrospective exhibition as it had been an exciting part of my artistic development. As I said before, the Racquet Hall had picture rails on three walls. The wall that had no rail faced you as you entered the hall. Bert and I built another room at that end of the hall. It was sixteen feet wide by twelve deep with a four foot passage at the back which made sure no light got in as you would enter the room in darkness. On the face of it I had done a polyptic painting on four eight by four sheets upright, with another two eight by two feet on the top, horizontal. I had covered each panel with canvas and glued a framework on the back to stiffen them up. This painting acted as the front wall of the room and was a feature when you entered the main hall. I hung cloth used from previous installations on the inside walls of the dark room and also on the floor, covering it with clear polythene to keep it clean. In one corner I had a cluster of welding helmets that I had got from Yarrows, Kvaerner Govan Ltd, and the Ailsa shipyard at Troon. I used chicken wire to create an area below it where I placed a strobe light and smoke crystals. On top of the wire

I built up the helmets with a gloved arm holding a set of welding tongs sticking out of the middle of it. The scene resembled the welder's graveyard. I had sprayed the helmets with fluorescent paint and painted the rectangle luminous where the dark glass was fitted. I removed the glass on some of the helmets. Bill had composed another piece of music to suit the scene as I hung a couple of speakers inside the room connected to the music system that was accessible from a trapdoor on the outside. When the viewer entered in darkness, all they saw was a lot of rectangles at different angles in the corner. The music was like an echoed heartbeat so it was quite eerie walking in. When I put on the strobe light, the rays shot out between the helmets and out of the ones that I had removed the glass. It was just like a welder striking an arc! Then I switched the strobe off and put the UV on and the room was full of bright fluorescent colour. There was also smoke coming from the crystals and sometimes it was overdone like the time when one of my visitors told me he was a welder. I told him that he would love my room. As I operated the lights and music from the outside, I couldn't see what was going on inside the room. I popped my head in when this guy was inside to see what he thought of it and he was standing with his

195

inhaler. We had built the room so that there were emergency panels that were hinged and could be easily opened. I had to open them all to let the smoke out and felt sorry for the guy.

Norma McCrone took up a new post as Advisor in Arts for North Ayrshire Council's Education Department. Gillian Wall came in as the Council's Arts Development Officer. Ron Smart and I were elected Chair and Vice-Chair of North Ayrshire Arts Council for the second year in succession. We had our first Open Art Exhibition at the Racquet Hall in Eglinton Country Park from 9-24 August and it was very successful. We had no sponsorship and advertised it locally so it was mostly Ayrshire based artists who submitted work.

197

I did a painting called "The Slaying of Snilloc" which is a duel between Mij and Snilloc. In the next painting, Mij won and celebrated his victory by climbing to the top of a headland while Snilloc transformed into a monster. Finally, when Mij came back down from the headland, he was so tired that he fell asleep under a serpentreebird where he had a dream, that one day he would write a book.

On 14 August 1997, Frank and I played at the pre sashing of that year's Marymass Queen and her four Marys outside the Townhouse Irvine.

The opening of my retrospective was Friday 26 September and I had asked Tom McKendrick to officially open it. The Council took Tom and his wife Christine along with Helen and I for dinner at the Ship Inn prior to the opening. Tom thrives on public speaking as he is so good at it. He acknowledged the visually exciting atmosphere of the shipyards and said that it was a joy to see real physical evidence of this in my representational paintings. His speech, both humorous and serious, spoke at length about Scottish Art and the importance of Scottish working class traditions, values and culture. He said it was wonderful to see support for a local artist who paints the things he knows, telling not his own story, but also the peoples story. Tom also praised my courage for leaving the shipyard to enter the world of art. My sister Chris and her husband Paul, Jonathan and Bryony all came up from Cardiff. My Brother Fred and his wife Jayne came from Walsall in the Midlands and Ian and Polly came from Dorset. Drew, Lorna, Andrew and Michelle whom we had met in Majorca in 1995 came over from Fife. There must have been 150 to 200 people came along that night. I had fifty-seven paintings displayed at the show, including my polyptic **Destruction**, and a light box that I called **Echoes of the Attentive Viewer**. Earlier in the year the Gallery of Modern Art in Glasgow was looking for artist's proposals to decorate the inside of an old police box in Buchanan Street and this was my proposal but it was rejected. I drilled a hole at the front of the box for the viewer to look inside; the police box had a flap at the front. Inside, I placed mirrors on three interior walls and painted the floor with tiles. I put cloth on the top and a quarter face in one of the facing corners. Above the cloth I fixed a UV light connected to a switch on the front of the box. You switched on the UV light and looked inside the box, seeing the tiled floor and full faces mirrored to infinity. When you switched off the light you could see the same scene as I had painted the quarter face and alternate tiles luminous. . I thought I would show the painting I did from my window at Govan in 1969 to let my viewers see how far I had come on since then. I exhibited three of my Constable copies. I was on a new kick now! If you looked at some of my latest images through 3D glasses, they moved, because I used red next to green. I used this effect for other surreal paintings and had used it for previous installations. I handed out 3D glasses to visitors so that they could see the effects it had on some of the work displayed. I was at the Racquet Hall every day for the next two weeks working on a painting so that I didn't get bored if there was no one coming in. I caught two people out who said that they really enjoyed my show, not knowing that I was there all the time and knew that they were lying. Over a thousand people came to see and it was well received by those who did. Some people returned more than once which was satisfying.

Ian Cooper turned forty on Sunday 23 November and since he and Polly had come up for my show, I thought I would return the favour and arranged with Polly to meet them at Hot Rocks which had just opened at Bournemouth Pier. I flew down from Glasgow with a company called Euroscot who had not long operated flights to Bournemouth from Glasgow and Edinburgh. I took a taxi to the pier and when I stepped out of it, a girl came out of Hot Rocks and asked if I was Jim Collins. I had never been there before and I thought, "How does she know". Then it became obvious that Polly had informed them that I would arrive in a taxi carrying a suitcase as I would be staying until the following Friday. The girl said that they were upstairs. When we got to the top of the stairs, I sent the girl in with his card. I was looking through the glass door expecting Ian to turn round, and when he didn't, I walked in and stood behind him. I could tell by the look on his face when he eventually did turn round, that he was pleased to see me. We had a nice meal and a couple of drinks there, but it was some way to their house from where we were, so we left and went to a pub near them until closing time. They lived in a cottage at Mappowder, Sturminster Newton, right in the middle of the Dorset countryside. Ian had a studio at Stalbridge, which wasn't too far from the cottage, but Polly had about a thirty-mile drive to her office at Poole. Ian and I went to his studio on the Monday and he had produced more of the soapstone sculptures he had been making before he left North Ayrshire. Each piece of stone had a different colour, grain, and texture, making the pieces so different, although done in the same style. Ian said that there was nothing doing down there as far as selling went. After spending some hours in the studio, we went to Sherborne to have a look round the galleries. On another day, we took a trip to Shaftsbury which was only about twelve miles from the studio. We decided to go to Bath to look at the galleries and I persuaded Ian to put together slides and bring two of his soapstone works with us. We left the sculptures in the boot of his car, and if we found a gallery who was interested in his work, we would bring them out. Bath is such a beautiful city; I hope someday to visit it again. It

was a lovely day when we went there, and Ian did find a gallery that was interested in his work, but we forgot about the two sculptures we had brought along. We had a great time during that week and you needed a car to get around as public transport was nil. I would like to have seen the countryside in summer, as there were many thatched cottages in the little villages we passed through on our travels. I was glad to have made this trip as Ian seemed to be a bit down. Polly had been working late quite often and he was stuck in the middle of nowhere with no one to talk to.

After I left, Ian took two sculptures up to Beaux Arts in Bath to be displayed for sale.

Another challenge was to come my way when I received a call from Bev Gallagher saying that she and Mick would like to commission me to do a painting for them. She gave me the following information and asked  me if I could do anything with it. When she was in labour with Caitlin, she had a vision of three people walking away in a valley with high hills in front of them; they reminded her of the hills of Arran. The

three people apeared to be, her mother on the left, a three-year-old

202

female child in the middle, and Mick on the right and they were all holding hands. Caitlin Rowena was born in Scotland on 27 December 1996 and they moved down to Leicester on 12 January 1997. As they arrived, Bev's sister told them that their mother had passed away that day. Bev said her mother's name was Rose and she was small with a rose pink complexion. She said that the family grave had an angel sited on it at the beginning of the century that faced the wrong way, and that the family had to get permission to leave it in that position. She spoke of Caitlin's birth chart, so she was obviously interested in astrology. I began to build up a picture in my head as she spoke. I asked her to send me photographs of her mother, Caitlin, the statue of the angel, and Caitlin's birth chart. I worked up a sketch and phoned Bev to describe it before sending it to them. When I finished my description there was a silence, then she said, "That's wonderful Jim". It is a very personal subject and it was to be done for Caitlin's legacy, as she would never have met her grandmother. I thought the vision should be the lightest area in the painting and that Caitlin and her grandmother should be joined in some way. The connection would be that Caitlin would be a rosebud and her grandmother the rose, both on the same stem. I spent some time trying to paint Bev's mum within the rose and in the end we agreed to have her represented by just the rose. Rather than use the statue of the angel, I only used the wings with two arms painted representationally. The wings blended into the background, and while the right hand was laid on Caitlin's head, the left was beckoning to her grandmother. The praying hands added to the composition and subject of the painting. Caitlin's birth chart was painted lightly within the central area of the painting but did not detract from the scene. There were rays which would each represent a day of the seventeen days between Caitlin's birth and her grandmother passing away. I intertwined Bev and Mick's birth signs at the bottom left and Bev's mother's at the bottom right. There was a lot of communication between us, as I would send photos of the painting's progression, get feedback, and change things accordingly.

Frank and I were to play at Hill of Beath club on Saturday 24 and Sunday 25 January 1998. Helen came with us on the Saturday as we had arranged to stay overnight with Drew and Lorna that we had met in Mallorca in 1995 as they lived in Cowdenbeath. They came to the gig with their son Andrew. Frank drove home afterwards, returning on the Sunday night while we went back with Drew and Lorna and spent most of the night drinking and chatting. Helen got the bus from Dunfermline on the Sunday, as it would have been too late for her getting home if she had stayed for the gig. She had to work on the Monday morning. Drew and Andrew came along for a while at the Sunday night gig. We played with big Jack and Dougie at Jack's brother's wedding in the British Legion Club, East Kilbride, on 20 March 1998.

Helen and I received an invitation to attend Caitlin's christening at the Parish Church of St. Peter and St. Paul's, Syston, Leicester on 3 May 1998. Mick and Bev had booked us into the Millgate House Hotel at Newark for Saturday 2 and Sunday 3 May and I brought their painting with me. We arrived by train before Mick and Bev in the late afternoon and got settled into our room which allowed me to unwrap the painting. We had a lovely meal with them and their family before I brought out the painting. I had sent them a photo of the finished work, but it is always good to see the reaction of the commissioner's first viewing of your creation. Everyone there thought it was wonderful, and I could see Bev enjoyed telling people the story behind the work. They had brought along Mick's acoustic guitar for me to play so we had a singsong for the rest of the evening. The staff in the hotel wanted me to do the same thing on the following night but we had the Christening party to go to. It was a lovely morning the next day so Helen and I wandered round Newark. We boarded a coach at 3.15pm and travelled about thirty miles south to Syston for the Christening at 4pm. It was a lovely service in a fine old church. We boarded the coach once again and headed about sixty miles North to the Rose and Crown at Upton, Gainsborough This was Bev's sister's pub and it had a huge beer garden and as it was a beautiful evening , most of the people who were there enjoyed basking in the sun outside until it disappeared. There was a band booked and they were late in arriving so Mick asked me to start the evening off with his acoustic and my minidisks as I had brought my player with me. It was quite a large room so I just played the heavier songs until the band arrived. Later on I was able to calm it down a bit playing through their PA. I was surprised when Mick came up to join me; he seemed to know the words to a lot of songs. His brother also joined us with the rest of the band playing. We had quite a shindig! The Events Officer for North Ayrshire Council, Gary Hamilton, and his wife Leslie who also worked for the Council had also been invited, so there were a few people that I knew. The food we had when we arrived was excellent, all in all it was a brilliant night and I was the last one on the coach as we left for the hotel at Newark.

We returned home to Irvine on the Monday and it was sad to leave my painting behind. The thing about commissions is, most of them have to be completed for a certain date, so you work hard to meet the deadline. When the painting is finished you hand it over, never knowing if you will ever see it again.

At the North Ayrshire Arts Council's AGM 1998, I was elected Chair and Michael Durning Vice Chair. Ron Smart had resigned as he had become a member of Troon Art Club and had recently been elected President. Our second Open Art Exhibition was to be from 25 July - 8 August 1998 and we had secured sponsorship of £1750 from BNFL at Hunterston A. This money would be used to offer prizes of £1000, £500, and £250, and would hopefully attract a higher standard of work than the previous year. I couldn't make the opening on 24 July as Frank and I were playing at Helen's uncle Jim's seventieth birthday party at the Rangers Supporters Club, Ibrox. It seems to have been well attended and Ayrshire artists won all three prizes. Maree Meahan from Kilmarnock took the first prize, with Peter Fairweather from Beith taking second, and finally, Charles Craig from Ayr winning third.

On the 11 July 1998 Frank and I were going to do a gig at the Boilermaker's Club Clydebank. While sitting at the traffic lights at the junction of Crookston Road and Paisley Road, I looked out of the window at the three in one takeaway and there before my eyes was Jamie McGettrick. If you remember back to 1996 when Alex Ferguson told me Jamie was dying from cancer. I rolled down the window and shouted, "Jamie". He didn't turn round so I shouted again, "Jamie McGettrick". He turned round then and pointed at me just as Frank pulled away, so I shouted out my phone number and told him to phone me the next day. I never got the call so I looked up the phone book and there was only one McGettrick and it was a 01505 number which I knew was Glengarnock or Kilbirnie. I phoned and told my story to the recipient who sounded like a girl in her twenties. She said that they might be related and that she would ask her grandmother. It turned out that she lived in Paisley. She returned the call a couple of days later saying they were related then put her grandmother on. She gave me two numbers to contact Jamie. A young female with an Australian accent answered my first call. Assuming that she was Jamie's daughter,. I asked to speak to him. When he came to the phone, the first thing I asked him was how he was keeping. He was surprised that I knew he had been ill, and even more surprised when I told him how I found out. He told me that his illness was leukaemia and after a year's treatment of a new drug, he was completely cured. He said that during his treatment there would be times when his body was full of hair, and others when he had none. He had a business partnership with another guy back in Perth, Australia, and his partner kept the business going while Jamie was ill. On the day of the prize judging for the exhibition, Jamie and Joan turned up at Eglinton Country Park with their son and daughter and I am pleased to say that he was looking very well. It was great to see them after all these years and especially under the circumstances of his illness and recovery. To me, this was the perfect ending to a good story.

As well as BNFL sponsoring the three prizes, other sponsors were Caledonia Paper, North Ayrshire Council, and we received money from ABSA's pairing scheme because of our sponsorship by BNFL Brown Brothers of Irvine and Iain Crosbie Printers, Beith sponsored all our printing. Keith Bruce, Arts Editor with The Herald newspaper opened the exhibition and wrote an article on Thursday 30 July praising the exhibition. The show went down very well with the visitors as we were bringing a good mixture of art to North Ayrshire by artists from all over Scotland.

During 1998, Ashley Pringle had taken up the post of Director of Community Services for North Ayrshire Council, Marie Blackwood was appointed Centre Development Manager at the Harbour Arts Centre, and Karron Rae took over from Marie as secretary of North Ayrshire Arts Council. Linda Mallet was employed as Public Art Development Officer for North Ayrshire Council. As I was now chair of North Ayrshire Arts Council, Helen and I were invited by the Convener of North Ayrshire Council to attend the crowning of the Marymass Queen on 22 August 1998 at the Townhouse Irvine. From there the men walked with the parade to the moor while a coach took the ladies. As soon as we left the Townhouse I stood on horses droppings and there were thousands of people standing on each side of the road. I felt stupid and looked at the crowd to see if I knew anyone. From then on I kept my eyes on the road to make sure I didn't do that again. The publicans en route to the moor gave the official party a dram, and once you got there you received another dram from the Irvine Carters. At the moor we had a lovely meal in the Council's hospitality tent and as much drink as you could handle. We left around 5pm as I had to play at East Kilbride Bowling Club. I didn't have a drink all night, as I was drunk when I arrived, but managed to get through the night without too many mishaps.

Bill Kerr taught music seven days a week and took the same holidays as the schools, a week at Easter, six weeks at the Summer, a week in October, and two weeks at Christmas. Bill and I had a whisky tasting day at each break and would talk music all day. I had purchased another keyboard earlier in 1998 and Bill fitted me in for music lessons beginning in August. Since I had been playing music for nearly forty years now we thought it was about time that I understood more about it. As I was doing all the backing for the band on the keyboard, lessons would vastly improve my playing and make it easier for me to analyse and copy songs.

Brian Craig from the studios had a solo exhibition at the Glasgow Vennel Art Gallery and North Ayrshire Arts Council arranged an evening on 1 September for members to hear Brian talk about his work. We also booked some of the musicians from Irvine Folk Club to entertain us after Brian was finished.

Gillian Wall and I were invited by ABSA Scotland to attend the Pairing Scheme reception at The Scottish

Office, Victoria Quay, Edinburgh, on Tuesday 8 September 1998. Iain Kirk from BNFL was invited to represent our sponsors. This informal event was to be an opportunity for Sam Galbraith MP, Minister for Health and the Arts in Scotland, to congratulate Pairing Scheme Award winning businesses and arts organisations, and to present them with commemorative certificates. Our award was in recognition of our sponsorship by BNFL Magnox Generation Business, Hunterston A of North Ayrshire Arts Council. Gillian and I met Iain at the reception where we were treated to Pimm's before the handing out of certificates. When it came to our turn, it was Iain's name that was called out to receive the certificate on behalf of our sponsors and we got nothing. Then, it was a production line to shake hands with Sam Galbraith and have your photograph taken with him. Gillian and I were disappointed to have travelled all the way from Irvine to Edinburgh to receive nothing. I had expected to get to chat with Sam Galbraith as I remembered him coming to a mass meeting of the shipyard workers to thank us for supporting a nurses' strike. At that time he was a brain surgeon at the Southern General hospital and was obviously a Union Representative. Our photographs were posted to us so that we could send them out to our local press and get ABSA publicity for their sponsorship.

At the studios, John Bass moved from B into the larger K/L. Jamie O'Dea moved from M into B, and Susan Doyle took over Jamie's space in M. Chick McGeehan who was principal art teacher at Greenwood Academy Irvine took over studio E after Sally Harkness left. Stuart Lancaster had moved into studio J. We had an exhibition at Roselle House Galleries Ayr, from 24 October – 28 November 1998. I had a small room to myself and showed twelve paintings. When we arrived at the opening of the show on Friday 23 October, one of the gallery assistants was sweeping up broken glass in the room where my work was. At first I thought a painting had fallen from the wall, but it turned out that Stuarts friend Willie Wallace had sat on the glass shelf above a heater and it had collapsed. Louise was in her glory that night as I told her to give everyone who came into my room a pair of 3D specs and collect them as they left. I was fortunate to sell the painting **Industrial Plant** before the end of the show. My work was really vivid at this show and that was the reason for the 3D glasses. I had viewed the paintings through the glasses while working on them so that I knew how they would look to the viewer.

When I was doing the painting for Mick and Bev Gallagher I took photographs of my daughter Tracey's arms and hands to use as reference for the angel's. I took a photo of her head as she had her eyes closed and she didn't know anything about it until coming to the show at Roselle and where she saw her face in the painting, **Dreaming of Dad**. In a letter of thanks from Anne

Bontke at Roselle, she informed me that our exhibition had 1762 visitors.

The reason Ian Cooper and I were sent to Norway by the Council was supposed to be the beginning of artist exchanges. Nothing had happened in two years, so I approached Ashley Pringle and asked him if he had any objections to us developing the project under the umbrella of the North Ayrshire Arts Council. He said that if it didn't cost the local Council anything, then he would have no objections. I told him that I had already contacted Awards for All and they said that it would be possible to apply for funding regarding the visiting artist from Norway, but they would not consider funding for his or her fare. Ashley invited me to attend a conference at Vikingar Largs, as he knew that a delegation from Karmoy would be there and I would be able to speak to them about my proposal. They seemed all

for it but I wanted the exchange to happen in the year 2000, they wanted it for the next year.

My mother went into Darnley Court nursing home on 6 November 1998 as she had lost both her eyes and she was finding it hard to negotiate the stairs at home. As her sight deteriorated she had been sitting at home alone for years listening to the radio while

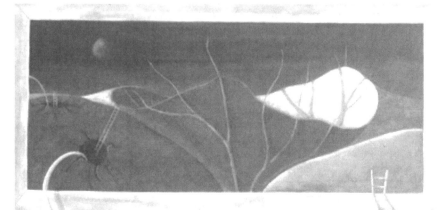

my sister Gladys was at work, so she went in to the nursing home for her own safety. I was commissioned by a local girl to do a painting for her boyfriend. It was all her own idea, I just created her vision. She wanted the planets in our solar system with the earth being a

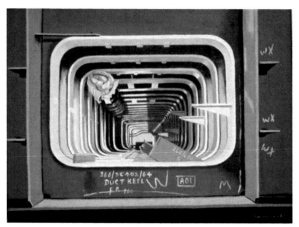

football. She was delighted with the finished painting Planet Football, and I enjoyed doing it. I thought that the type of background used would suit the type of surreal work I was producing so I started painting dark skies in some of my future work.

Chapter 12

In an article Jesse Garron wrote for the Irvine Times in 1997, he offered the use of his home recording studio at Dundonald which is only ten minutes on the bus from my house. I cut the article out and kept it until I wrote a song in 1998 which I thought was really good. I found out where Jesse lived and went to see him. After pleading my case for free studio time, Jesse recorded ten of my songs over the next couple of months. I went in for a couple of hours one day a week, sometimes two, until the tracks were all put down. Jesse's real name is Jim Campbell and I had played support to him many years earlier both as Jesse Garron and Beau Brummel. His wife Freda kept us going

with tea and coffee while we were recording. I had done most of the backing on my keyboard before I went to the recording studio. Jim had a nice electro acoustic guitar that I used to put down the rhythm tracks. I used my 72 strat for all other guitar work. The only thing that was added to my work was extra drum tracks put down by Jim. The song that gave me the inspiration to record was called "**We Were Free**".

We Were Free

Floating on a lonely cloud, drifting high above
Listening to the birdsong, with the one I love
Such a pleasant feeling, happy as can be
Just like the birds, we're free

See the colours changing, gently as we go
Looking down a rainbow, to the world below
Like a magic carpet ride, high above the sea
Just like the birds, we're free

Pushed along so slowly
As we move with ease
Lightly as a feather
Carried with the breeze
We're free

Gliding over deserts, through the zones of time
As we view the sunset, isn't it sublime
Welcome on this journey, with my love and me
Just like the birds, we're free

Now we're in the slipstream, colours so diffused
Are we in a daydream, dizzy and confused?
Time that we awakened, from our fantasy
Just like the birds, we were free
Just like the birds, we were free.

The other songs I recorded were, **The Trinidad Man, Dear Madeline, Achin' Head, Travelling on Life's Highway, The Sculptor, Frustration, A Song for Me, Isle of Arran, and Springtime's Here**. I really enjoyed recording, especially as some of the songs had been written many years earlier.

I exhibited at the Compass Gallery's Christmas show in 1998 and after some discussion with Lorraine Grant who was Arts and Cultural Development Officer with East Ayrshire Council; I would decorate Santa's Grotto in a vacant shop within the Burns Shopping Mall, Kilmarnock. This came about after I received a letter from Lorraine in my capacity as Chair of North Ayrshire Arts Council. She asked me if I could help with information about any artists in North Ayrshire who worked with light either in the form of projections, video work or light boxes. I didn't know of anyone except myself, and my light reactive work would be ideal for this type of project. Although there were to be artists doing work throughout the shopping precinct, I was given the task of decorating Santa's Grotto. I put my cloths round the walls and black polythene on the floor, hung netting from the ceiling and tied fluorescent stars from it with children's names on each star. We brought in Christmas trees and positioned them so that there was a path to Santa, and another to the exit. I covered the floor with bark and sprinkled luminous pigment on the trees and bark.I researched the shape of reindeer footprints, cut the shapes from luminous sticky backed paper and stuck them down on the black polythene leading to Santa. I set up the music system and used Bill's music from **The Lion, The Witch, and The Wardrobe** to produce the desired ambience. I didn't use luminescence at all; the UV lights were on all the time so it was very colourful. Just before the grotto was due to open, Lorraine took up a new post at Aberdeen.

1999 was to be the tenth anniversary year of North Ayrshire Arts Council and we organised a three-day event in the Magnum Theatre to promote dance, drama, choral and music groups in North Ayrshire. This event titled **Showcase1999** was held on 11-13 March. Our third annual poetry competition attracted over 160 entries from all across the country. The winners were presented with their prizes at a special Poetry Evening held in the Harbour Arts Centre on

Saturday 30 January. Acclaimed Scottish actor Iain Cuthbertson once again recited the winning entries and presented the prizes. As part of out tenth anniversary we published all the entries in a booklet. On Thursday 11 March, before the first showcase, we had a reception to celebrate our birthday and promote our achievements. Gillian and Michael didn't get on. At the North Ayrshire Arts Council AGM on 29 April I was retained as Chair for a second year with Jim McPhie taking over from Michael as Vice Chair. In my report I quoted, "Being a product of arts development myself I understand the importance the arts have in one's personal development and why they must be encouraged. Through determination and hard work, my two hobbies, music and painting, have earned me ten years living as an artist and musician. Self taught in both disciplines and after thirty-seven years of playing music, I am now having music lessons. As well as my creativity bringing me personal happiness, many people have enjoyed it over the years. To me, this tale expresses the importance the arts have in a community." I also stated in my report, "The Arts Services Development Officer, Gillian Wall and I have visited Arts Forums in East Renfrewshire and Inverclyde. We have also had enquiries from artists in East Ayrshire and West Dunbartonshire Council regarding the establishment of local arts councils. I made the point on each occasion that they must operate in partnership with their local council."

George Clark, Country Park Manager at Eglinton had been impressed with the effects of my darkroom during my retrospective at the Racquet Hall in 1997. He commissioned me to produce an installation in the play barn at Eglinton Park, which would run during environment week, 29 May-6 June 1999. The barn was a Nissan hut; eighty-five feet long by thirty five wide and had sliding doors at one end. There was also a small door at the same end as the sliding doors that led into a small foyer before entering the barn. Although there were only the gaps at the doors and a row of windows on one side at the top of the barn, when I blacked them out there was still light coming in from small holes all over the place. The first job I did in my type of installation was to make the venue dark as if any light does get in, it spoils the overall effect. It took me ages to fill in all the holes before beginning the real work. Since this was for environment week I thought that I should use as much material as possible from the park. I said to George that if any trees had fallen throughout the winter storms then he should keep the branches for me. The park also had a bark stripping machine so there was loads that I could use, and it was stored only about a hundred yards from the play barn. A couple of weeks before it was due to open I decided to call it **The Land O' the Leal**. I placed the music system and light switches on the roof of the foyer so that whoever worked them would be able to see where everyone was and this position would not interfere with the effect of the installation. I wrote a short story and recorded it at Jesse's studio. I got a BBC CD of sound effects from the library, but there was a certain part where I wanted to have the effect of panic from passengers on a ship that had hit rocks and was sinking. Jim brought a plank of wood into the studio and laid it on the floor. He set a microphone above it, and Jim, his wife Freda and I ran on the spot shouting, "Help!" and "Over here!" It came out just as I wished. This recording took some time to put together but I was delighted with the finished product. I used my sixteen by ten foot painting and positioned it facing you, about twenty feet from the doors. I kept it to one side, five feet from the left wall of the barn with a black out cloth covering the five feet. This would be the exit from the installation. On the other side I blacked out the remaining fourteen feet with cloth so that all you could see when entering through the foyer was the painting. I placed four UV lights at different locations throughout the area behind the painting and one on the floor that would represent the sun coming up when it was switched on. I wired the four speakers differently than on previous installations, as I wanted a voice coming from one end of the barn. Behind the fourteen-foot blackout cloth I created a twenty-foot path through a forest by tying large branches on each side of the path and also hanging them from the beams overhead. I wheel barrowed tonnes of bark into the barn and scattered it throughout, except for the pathways. At the end of the path was a large clearing with an island of shrubbery and branches in the middle of it. Around the clearing I placed large logs for visitors to sit on while they were waiting for instructions to move out. On leaving that area you had to cross a stream which I created just as I had done before by sandwiching two layers of polythene with fluorescent water in between them. The next area that represented summer had live trees in it and daughter Pauline made me flowers from fluorescent paper. There were paintings of animals on panels on the walls so I overpainted them with luminous and fluorescent paint so that they would be seen in darkness and under UV light. Pauline had bought me one of those wooden birds which when you pull on a string, the wings would flap. I painted it luminous, hung it up high and attached a fishing line to it. The line went down through a picture eye screwed into the top of my large painting and up to the roof of the foyer so that the operator could make the bird fly whenever he felt like it. I used two pieces of music in the recording. The first piece, **The Journey**, was played while the audience entered the forest path. Bill Kerr composed the second piece of music which I titled it for him as **The Land O' the Leal**. It was played as the audience left the clearing. As they looked at the painting, all the lights were on in the barn, including the UV's as they were charging up the luminous paint on the branches and pigment on the ground. The painting i used suited as it was about oil spillage from a tanker into the sea. As I told the story, I put brackets around what happened at certain parts.

The Land O' the Leal

"It was a lovely afternoon as we stood on the deck of dad's ship. My dad was the Captain! Mum, my sister Louise and I were on the trip. I was only six years old at the time but this was an adventure I'll never forget. Suddenly, it got very windy and we could hear thunder in the distance. Before we knew it, we were in a fierce storm. We returned to our cabin as we were very scared. The next thing, there was this terrible crunching sound. We had struck rocks! It was quite exciting as we were lowered down to the sea in a lifeboat. As we drifted away from the ship we could see this huge oil slick following us. Luckily, there was an island near, and as we landed on the beach, darkness fell. (All the lights go out) Dad told us all to keep together as we entered the woods. (First piece of music) After a while we came upon a clearing and dad said that we should stay there for the night. (Insect noises) There were strange noises all around us as Louise and I huddled together and fell asleep. When I awoke, Louise had gone! Then, just as the sun rose, (UV light on the floor at the far end) we could hear her calling, 'Over here everyone.' The only way out of the clearing was to cross a stream. Although it had been cold the night before, all of a sudden it was daylight, and a bright summer's day. (All UV lights on) We could see deer, and two large rodents were playing nearby. We packed up our belongings and headed off across the stream to find Louise. (Second piece of music) Louise was excited when we found her as she had met a little girl who belonged to the island. Mum and dad said we were there for three months before we were rescued, but we never met anyone, including Louise's friend. When we returned home, dad tried to find the island on the map but couldn't. Louise said her friend told her it was, **'The Land O' the Leal"**

As usual, the event went down very well, especially with children. Some of the children came to see it with their schools. It was a difficult job dismantling the installation as all the bark had to be barrowed back to where I had got it, and this time it was an uphill push. The play barn is perpendicular to the Racquet hall in the park and there is a bench in the square outside them. One day while I was stripping out the barn I stopped for a cigarette and while sitting on the bench a man came up to me and said, "You're Jim Collins aren't you? You had an exhibition in there a couple of years ago". We had a good chat and he returned later in the afternoon with two prints that he had bought in America. He said that he liked to travel on ferries between the Western Isles and went on about how planes can fly and ships can float when they weigh so much. He said that if I could come up with an idea for a painting from the information he had given me, then he would buy it.

North Ayrshire Arts Council's third Open Art Exhibition in 1999 was once again sponsored by BNFL with the three prizes of £1,000, £500, and £250, we also managed to secure a prize from Miller's Art Shop of £250 worth of gift vouchers. That year we put up a prize of £250 which would be chosen by the visitors to the exhibition. This was put forward as a suggestion from Jim McPhie and proved to be an excellent addition to the existing prizes. It made people take more interest in the work on show, especially children, who would normally take a quick look round before scurrying off. The judging took place on Thursday 22 July and the winner was Miriam Dokotliver from Aberdeen. Second prize went to Eleanor McGowan from Largs and the third was awarded to James Duffy from Ayr. It gave me great pleasure to phone the winners that evening to inform them of their good fortune. When I phoned Miriam, she couldn't believe it. I tried to talk her into coming down to Irvine the following night to receive her cheque but she thought it was too far. She called me later that evening to say that someone she knew from Aberdeen was coming to Irvine for a wedding and that she would get a lift from him. Wendy Law, the Visual Arts Officer for the Scottish Arts Council came to open the exhibition and I arranged to meet her at the Ship Inn at Irvine's harbourside for dinner. I told Miriam to meet us there so that after dinner we could all go along to the exhibition at Eglinton Park together. It turned out that Miriam went to Glasgow School of Art at the same time as my daughter Pauline. I set up a lectern and a radio mike on a stand for the speakers. Miriam's winning artwork had people talking, as it was a box with a rectangle cut out of the front with a photo of her as a child stuck on in the inside of the back. Fixed to the inside were a toy soldier and a pony. It was titled **Little Pony**. The pony represented the hopes, dreams and aspirations of a child, while the soldier was the dark shape of authority hindering hopes and dreams. The judges said they were intrigued by the piece, and returned to it time and time again, but it was the spark they felt from it which acted as the final decider. Miriam stayed with us overnight and as she was Jewish, Bert had a great time talking to her about the time he was in Israel during the Second World War. The following day I took her down to see the studios and my work. Wendy Law who lived in Edinburgh, was impressed by Irvine and said that she would like to return with her partner and son and I said that she should call me when she was coming and I would let her see the studios. The winner of the visitor's prize that year was Jim Wylie from Stewarton.

Michael went to Norway for the Month of June, then he went to Italy in July, so while he was away for the two months I got down to producing the painting for the man I met in Eglinton Country Park while dismantling **The Land O' the Leal**. He had said that if I could come up with any ideas then he would buy the painting. I said that I would probably just do a drawing, but I just went for it and did a painting. When I phoned him to let him know that I had finished the painting, I told him that if he didn't like it, I would quite happily live with it. The two ghostly arms whose hands hold the ship and plane are their spirits, allowing them to float and fly. Since he enjoyed travelling on ferries to the Western Isles, I painted a Caledonian MacBrayne ship. He came to the studio to see the painting on Friday 30 July 1999. The previous night Bert and I were sitting in company at the Towerlands Sports club and the subject of our conversation got on to Ireland. Bert said that he would love to go and I said, "If that

221

guy buys my painting tomorrow, then we're off." The next day, he loved the painting and wrote me a cheque right away so I phoned Bert to tell him that we were on our way to Ireland. When I got home from the studio I got Tracey's partner Graeme to go on to the Internet and get information on accommodation in Letterkenny, County Donegal. He found a place that suited us so I phoned the landlady and booked it for Sunday and Monday night. My aunt Mary lived in Letterkenny so I phoned my sister Gladys to get her address. Sadly,

she had died the week before and the funeral was only two days before I phoned her. I booked the SeaCat from Troon leaving on the Sunday morning. As we sat at Troon harbour waiting to board, I saw my relations driving off on their return from my aunt's funeral. Helen, Bert, Louise and I, travelled in Bert's car, arriving in Belfast around 1.30pm.

We drove up through Antrim and Londonderry, bypassing Derry and into County Donegal. My father's birthplace, Newton Cunningham was on the way to Letterkenny from Londonderry. Before we left Irvine, Bert filled up his tank with diesel as he was told that it was more expensive in the south of Ireland. It was the complete opposite and he was furious. We settled in to the Bed and Breakfast and went out for our dinner. Bert was surprised that there was a Masonic Lodge practically next door to where we were staying. I got ripped off with the bill by paying with our money as I had no Punts so I changed all my money the next morning. After dinner we went back to the B & B and sat outside with a bottle of whiskey as you couldn't smoke inside. My dad's brother John was in a motorbike accident when he was sixteen and had spent his life in mental institutions. I had never met him and he was now in a nursing home at Stranorlar, fifteen Kilometres from Letterkenny. I only stayed for about fifteen minutes and I'm glad that I went to see him as I had always wondered about my uncle John. From there we went to Newton Cunningham so that I could see my aunt Mary's grave. We went on to Buncranna where Louise and Helen went into the swimming pool. Louise went in at the shallow end and immediately started swimming on her back towards the deep end. Bert and I were up on a balcony watching when we saw her go under and we shouted to the lifeguard, but Louise was fine. We stopped for something to eat after leaving Buncranna. The waitress asked us what we would like to drink and I said "Pochine."

 She went off, and returned saying that it was illegal. I said that I knew that but it was worth a try. After eating we went into Londonderry. This was the only place that we saw guns! It looked like the police were guarding a bank as they were all standing outside it with their rifles. After spending a couple of hours in that fine City we returned to Letterkenny. We went out for a meal and I was hoping to spend some time sampling an Irish pub but it was not to be. Bert didn't want to go as we were leaving the next morning and he had to drive. Helen was too tired and told me to go but it would probably have got me into trouble with her, so I decided just to go back to the B & B and watch television in the huff. We managed to spend some time in Belfast before catching the SeaCat for our return trip to Troon. It was a beautiful crossing, really calm, the sea was like glass, and the sunset was amazing. Ailsa Craig looked stunning basking in the sunset as we passed by quite close to it. We had a really great time in Ireland!

Frank and I played once again at the opening of Marymass on Thursday 12 August 1999. This time we were on the West Sound Radio stage, using their PA. I had written a song called Murmass and we played it that night.

Murmass

Welcome Irvinites tae Murmass, you have gathered here tae see
The Queen elect and her four Mary's, at her crowning ceremony
The Captain of the carters will do his duty soon
He wishes you all a good one, here in Irvine Toon

Watch the parade on Murmass Saturday, full of ancient pageantry
As you listen to the bands play, and catch a piece of history
Join the horse drawn procession; follow to the moor as they pass
The greasy pole and the races, have a great Murmass

See the red coat and the halberd, carried by the halberdier
He's the one who killed the Town Clerk, 1607 was the year
The Carters battled Bruce and Wallace, at Knadgerhill they fought
And at the battle of Langside for Mary, Mary Queen of Scots.

On the following week, artist Anna Kristin Ferking arrived to work in our studio within Michael's space. Michael informed me that she was coming the day before she arrived with her husband Kai and two daughters. I arrived at the studios the following day just as Michael was locking up. He introduced me to Anna Kristin and her family and I asked her where she was from. When she told me they lived in Skudeneshavn, I said that I had been there and it was a beautiful place. They had a floating gallery there to show Anna Kristin's work. It was a glass bottom boat and most of her paintings were of sea life. I would see quite a bit of Anna Kristin and her family over the next month. Helen and I were invited once again to be guests of North Ayrshire Council at Marymass as North Ayrshire Arts

Council got a grant from Awards for All to sponsor young bands at an event in the Harbour Arts Centre as part of Marymass. Anna Kristin had an exhibition at Greenwood Teacher's Centre, which was moved to Nardini's in Largs for the Viking Festival. I attended both of her openings and at the Nardini's one. I was delighted to see Peter Mann and Iain Kirk from BNFL. While speaking to them I said that we were finding it hard to find another major sponsor for our exhibition, as the next year would be the end of their three-year agreement. They both said that there was no reason why they couldn't carry on their sponsorship for a further two years. Peter Mann sent me a letter confirming this. I was invited to the Civic Reception for the Viking Festival at Largs as chair of North Ayrshire Arts Council, and also to a meeting with North Ayrshire Council and members of the Karmoy Kommune to discuss our proposal for the following year's artist exchange.

I had been back into Jesse Garron's studio over the summer months to lay down some more songs. The following song was written as a tribute to all those that have lost their way in the music world. The hazzards of being in the life of rock and roll.

Another Victim of Success

I'm meeting up with an old friend
We used to gig every weekend
Together we'd stand
In the same band
With our guitars in our hand

We grew apart when the band split
He carried on, had a chart hit
Played in the game
Dealing with fame
He was the one with a name

I joined a band doing covers
He played with Lulu and the Luvvers
He was in a mess
A man in distress
Just another victim of success

Gigging again with my old mate
Now that he's back in a fit state
We'll write some songs
We'll right the wrongs
Music is where he belongs.

On 23 October Frank and I played a gig in the Colquhoun Arms Hotel, Luss. It was the hotel used in the Scottish soap, High Road. The Month of October was spent doing a twelve-foot by eight back drop for Jesse Garron. As a solo performer, he would pin this up behind him to represent his backing band. As we approached the third Millennium I wrote a song to commemorate the occasion.

Hear my Call

As we enter the third millennium
Hope it's better than the second one
Peace and love, to us all hear my call

No more fighting, forgive your fellow man
Use your anger, to change things if you can
Peace and love, to us all hear my call

It's getting nearer another century
Hope there's better times for you and me
Peace and love, to us all hear my call.

I resigned from North Ayrshire Arts Council and sent the following letter to the Arts Council's Focus magazine, issue No. 27.

"Regrettably I resigned as chair of North Ayrshire Arts Council at the Executive Meeting on 1 February 2000. I have been an active executive committee member of our local arts council since 1990 and thankfully watched it develop and grow. The success of the many projects I have been involved in is due to teamwork with local council officers, the local arts council executive committee and volunteers who have always came forward when required. I have made many important contacts, and, our success is known throughout Scotland due to Focus magazine being distributed to Arts Officers in all the local councils. Fortunately as a self-employed artist/musician I have been able to give my time freely as chairperson for certain meetings and events within and outwith North Ayrshire. I apologise for leaving before the AGM but I need time to concentrate on my own work. I must stress that if you wish this arts council to continue then the executive committee needs committed representation from all areas of North Ayrshire, representing all art forms. I would like to thank everyone who has helped make the North Ayrshire Arts Council so successful in the last decade and wish my successor and his/her committee to build on that success and take the Arts Council forward into this new Millennium. I would especially like to thank Gillian Wall ex Arts in the Community Officer for North Ayrshire Council for her help and hard work for the Arts Council and wish her every success in her new post at Durham."

I gave up the studio on 31 March 2000. I had to clean out my attic before bringing my work back from the studio. There was so much that I had to dump, as I had no room to store it, or it was too large to fit through the loft hatch. I took my sixteen feet by ten polyptic to Glasgow and put it in Pauline's basement. I had about two hundred and fifty cardboard tubes for my Govan prints so they took up a lot of room in the attic along with my paintings. Some of them were too large to go through the hatch and I had to store them in the cupboard below. I had to dismantle **Bow Assembly** from its stretcher frame and roll up the canvas.

It was a great feeling to have my life to myself after ten years of going to meetings in all kinds of weather. I had been looking forward to the John Byrne @ 60 exhibition at Paisley Museum and was not disappointed when I went to see it on 5 July. I had arranged to meet my daughter Pauline there, as she had not seen it yet. I would like to have attended the opening as it would have been nice to meet with this great man once again but unfortunately I was playing with the band. Although familiar with Byrne's work, I never realised just how versatile he was until seeing this show. His work reminded me of a schizophrenic with his chunky figures as 'Patrick,' and, elongated El Greco type faces as Byrne. I enjoyed seeing the original artwork for the Gerry Rafferty albums and John's artwork on Gerry's guitar and banjo. I had visited John's handkerchief exhibition at the William Hardie Gallery in 1992. He had made up collages from his huge collection and titled them with the usual Byrne humour. Also on display at the exhibition was a recent portrait that John had done of gallery owner William Hardie.

The fourth annual Open Art Exhibition was coming up and I did a special painting for it. Gillian Wall had left the Council for a new post at Durham and Ian Brotherhood had taken over as Chair of North Ayrshire Arts Council. I tried a different technique with acrylics on MDF where I laid on glazes and sandpapered them when dry, so that previous laid colours would show through when the top ones were partly removed. This treatment allowed for different textures in the areas I had sandpapered. My painting was a statement to let everyone know what I was doing now and that I was fine. I couldn't make the opening as Helen, Louise and I went down to Chris and Paul's in Wales. We spent four days there and the weather was great. Their next-door neighbour had an outdoor swimming pool and allowed nephew Jonathan, and neice Bryony along with Louise to use it. We took the kids to the Welsh Agricultural Museum as Helen and I had enjoyed it on a previous visit. I was shocked when on our return train journey, Helen told me that Chris and Paul were not getting on and it looked like they were going to split up. I hadn't noticed anything wrong while we were there and Chris had said to Helen not to say anything to me until we arrived back in Irvine.

When we returned home and the Open Art Exhibition closed, I had volunteered to help them dismantle it. I fell off a ladder onto a sculpture that had won a prize and broke it. The sculptor was fine about it as he said he could repair the piece, and he would also get an insurance claim as North Ayrshire Arts Council insured the exhibition. I was lucky that I didn't break any bones as I also flattened the Plinth that the sculpture sat on.

I had known for a couple of years that I would be involved in an exhibition at the City Gallery, Leicester. The show, **Labour Intensive,** would open on Thursday 24 August and I decided to go down to Leicester for the opening as Mick and Bev Gallagher had offered to put me up for the night. I travelled down by National Express via Birmingham; arriving about an hour before the opening, just in time to freshen up. The artists exhibiting were, David Brouet, David Carpanini, Eva Frankfurther, Valerie Ganz, David Garner, Lulu Hancock, Josef Herman, Peter Howson, Christine Kinsey, Martell Linsdell, Raksha Patel, Andrew Tift, and myself. I was impressed with Andrew Tift's paintings which were executed to perfection on parts of cars such as doors and wings. The evening went well and afterwards, Mick and Bev took me for dinner before we returned to their home for a few nightcaps. As Mick was working the next day I spent the afternoon discovering the lovely City of Leicester. It's not a very large city but there was plenty to keep me from wearying that afternoon before meeting Mick at five o'clock for a drink and chat as I had to catch the coach at seven for my return to Birmingham. My connection to Glasgow was due to leave there at eleven so I had time to catch another few drinks at Birmingham before the overnight journey. I thought the drink would make me sleep, but unfortunately the coach was full and I couldn't get comfortable.

Realising that my polyptic **"Destruction"** in Pauline's damp basement would eventually be ruined, I wrote to Ron Culley at Govan Initiative and asked him if he could find a home for it with all his contacts. I said that an Internet ready computer would be suffice payment for this magnificent work. He wrote back saying that Govan Initiative would have it and that he would let me know where they would like it to go when they had found somewhere large enough to accommodate it. Eventually I was contacted and told to put it in one of the stairwells at the Festival Business Centre at Ibrox. Bert and I spent hours putting it together as we had to cut a piece off one of the panels and also cut a hole through another to allow a light fitting to

be in use. Many people there should see it, as the place is full of offices occupied by small businesses whose customers have to negotiate the stairwell to get to them.

Ron Culley left Govan Initiative on the 15 September to take up the new post as Chief Executive of Scottish Enterprise Glasgow. I was invited to his leaving presentation and gave him my painting **www.paintingmusic@home.ok.** I also received a computer and printer that evening as payment for my polyptic. One of the gifts he received from Govan Initiative was my pastel of the **Hambone** that was one of the images in their 1991 calendar. Granddaughter Louise began Keyboard lessons with Bill Kerr after the summer holidays. I wrote another song that year to commemorate what I was doing with my life now.

What a Life

What a life, doing what you wanna do
Never knowing, what the future holds for you
Painting music every day, Images and words that say
If you want me you will pay, Or here I'll stay

What a life, so different than before
Working in a shipyard, but I don't work there anymore
Painting music every day, Images and words that say
If you want me you will pay, Or here I'll stay

What a life, to have your health and happiness
What more do you need, a little wealth and some success
Painting music every day, Images and words that say
If you want me you will pay, or here I'll stay.

I was unlucky to have missed registration for computer courses that were to begin at Towerlands Community Centre. They were organised and paid for by Community Education with Kilmarnock College supplying the tutors. Tracey, Graeme and Louise had moved next door to us and Graeme grew up with computers so he helped me in the beginning. I had asked him to build me a web site and after he had got fed up with me harping on at him, he gave me a book on Dreamweaver and Fireworks with the demo software. I built a site, all on one page, and then I thought that anyone accessing it would get fed up waiting for my images to download so I started again and put it on four pages. I had uploaded it but it wouldn't all tie together. Graeme came in and linked it all up in half an hour so I was up and running at last. My site was at www.jimcollins-art.com and had some images on it. I managed to register for an IT1 computer course at Towerlands beginning in January 2001.

Pauline and Martin had arranged their wedding for 7 April 2001 but Tracey and Graeme beat them to it when a week before Christmas they sprung on us their decision to get hitched on 3 January. There wasn't much time to prepare for this one and they had decided to get married at Irvine's Registry Office and then to the Gulab Indian Restaurant which had moved from the town to what was the Stanecastle Hotel where we had our silver wedding. When we went to speak to the owner Jack about booking, he  told us that he had just done up a room which was capable of holding thirty-two people. It was ideal for us so we just had our immediate family. I had arranged with Jack to put on a buffet and the price we agreed per head included anyone requiring a western dish from the menu. Tracey booked my mate Doug to do the photos and we had a great night. Jack really did us proud!

From the time my computer arrived and was put into the attic beside my musical keyboard and sound system, there was no room to paint, and when I received recording software, all my time was spent doing the backing for songs and the many other projects offered by this great invention. The computer course helped me to navigate all the office programmes which have allowed me to produce this. I didn't own a CD writer but by the summer I had one and recorded on the computer, burned CD's, and then designed the covers. I downloaded musical notation software from the Internet and wrote music which is why I had been doing the theory of music with Bill. I had written twenty nine thousand words of my memoirs manually in pen and ink and now I was able to transfer all of it to the computer to save it. Family members had bought me a scanner for Christmas 2000 so then I was able to scan in photos relating to my memoirs and position them appropriately.

Pauline arrived to stay with us on the eve of her wedding. My sister Chris also came to stay along with Jonathan and Bryony. Pauline's wedding cake was made to represent the Chrysler building in New York. She came with a polystyrene top for the cake that had to have a number of windows painted on it and I was designated to do the job. I had hoped to relax with a few whiskys but it was not to be. The following morning Tracey, Pauline, her friend Jackie, Louise and Chris all went to the hairdressers to have their hair done and when they returned they were like the hairbear bunch. They returned with croissants, which they had for breakfast with champagne. They got married in the Registry Office at Park Circus Glasgow, and their reception was held at Pollokshields Burgh Hall. The photographs were taken at the entrance of this stunning the building. It was a beautiful red sandstone building and unbeknown to most, was tucked away at the edge of Maxwell Park. After the photos were

taken, Pauline, Martin, and their pals went into the park to have a carry on before the caterers were ready. Martin was giving Pauline a coal carry when he fell, ripping his suit trousers and cutting his leg. He had to send home for another pair and the blood from the cut had seeped through the plaster on his leg on to the emergency pair of trousers. They had friends came over from Germany for the wedding and on a previous visit to see them by Pauline and Martin, they had brought home boxes of schnapps which they laid on the tables. Their German friends also brought bottles of wine with them that were laid on the tables. We decided to do the speeches before we ate as that would get them out of the way which allowed us who had to speak enjoy our meal without any nerves. The best man was Martin's pal Kenny. Bert had done so much work in Pauline and Martin's flat that Kenny presented him with a Superbertie, DIY Wizard medal that he had made from cardboard with red white and blue ribbons attached. Bert was embarrassed but it was a nice touch! The meal was excellent with extras for anyone who wished to gorge themselves like me. I got a pleasant surprise when Pauline stood up after the meal and told everyone to rattle the small schnapps bottles off the table and then open them and down them in one gulp. I thought to myself, "Good on you Pauline." The band was brilliant and made the night. They were called Clachnacudden and played all sorts of music electro acoustically all night. We had been in the hall from 3pm until 1am the next morning and all the whisky I consumed over the hours took its toll near the end of the night when Pauline's boss spun me round

 while I was jumping about like a mad Scotsman. I hit the deck! When I got up there was blood coming from my right eye, I just carried on jumping about, so they tell me. I didn't feel a thing until the next morning. Raymond carried me out of the hall over his shoulder

just as he used to do when he was roadying for the band many years before. Helen was in her element the next day watching me suffer and taking photos of my eye every now and then as the colours changed.

Chapter 13

Although I was still a member of North Ayrshire Arts Council, I hadn't heard anything from them since October – November 1999. A letter arrived at the beginning of June advertising the post of Exhibition Co-ordinator for the forthcoming fifth Open Art Exhibition. I read the letter, made myself a coffee and after reading it again decided to go for it. I could not have applied if I hadn't been doing the IT1 computer course I had been on since January, as I knew that you would need to look into databases and also create them. There would also be press releases to write weekly and many letters to compose. It was rather embarrassing writing a CV for this position as my educational background reflected the fact that I left school at 15. I knew I was capable of doing the job as I had been involved in three of the four previous exhibitions and knew exactly what had to be done. The exhibition had been too successful to let it disappear and there was no one available within the local Arts Council who could afford the time to put into it and that is why they advertised the post. I went to an interview on 14 June 2001 and the panel was Martin Bellamy, Curator of North Ayrshire Museums, Suzanne Le Blanc, Vice Chair of North Ayrshire Arts Council, and Ian Brotherhood, Chair. It was strange as I knew all of them and they all knew me, and we all knew that I was capable of doing the job. Suzanne was firing all these questions at me and then I produced three copies of my strategy for the job which I gave to each of the panel. Evidently I had covered everything that the other two were intending to ask me so my interview went well and I was offered the job. There were things which needed to be attended to that should have been resolved months before. North Ayrshire Arts Council had called a Special General Meeting on Thursday 21 June and it was decided to wind it up. They employed me as Exhibition Co-ordinator and after only a week on the job they were dissolved, but I was assured that I would be paid. I had six weeks to pull the show together. I had to find three selection judges, two prize judges, and a guest to open the exhibition. When I sent a letter to Peter Mann at BNFL to arrange a photo shoot of the presentation of the large cheque I was to find that he had left and was replaced by Dr Paul Harding. Ian Kirk had also left and I had to fax a letter I received from Peter Mann acknowledging the further two years of sponsorship from BNFL, as no one knew exactly what their commitment was to us. I got the use of office equipment within the Arts Services department of North Ayrshire Council and went in most days to send out exhibition packs to artists and enter his or her information in an enquiry database. North Ayrshire Council's Convener Sam Taylor agreed to speak at the opening and to supply the wine as the Council had done for previous exhibitions. David Miller of Miller's Art in Glasgow agreed to sponsor a voucher prize of £150 and Iain Crosbie Printers of Beith sponsored all our printing as they had done in all previous exhibitions. I had been speaking to Norma McCrone about a guest to open the exhibition and she advised me to contact Adrian Wiszniewski who had been involved in a previous project for North Ayrshire Council and she said that he was a nice guy. Adrian lived in Lochwinnoch so after he agreed to open our exhibition, I arranged for Suzanne to meet him and his wife at Kilwinning railway station and take them to the Claremont Hotel for dinner before coming along to the preview on Friday 27 July. I booked fourteen-year-old European champion piper Tommy Turner from Kilwinning to play outside the Racquet Hall before the official opening. When the time came for speakers, Tommy marched into the hall still playing and when he stopped, I welcomed our guests and introduced the speakers. It was a fine summer's evening and there were around a hundred and fifty to two hundred guests. The prize winners that year were Roy Fitszimmons once again taking first prize for his unusual sculpture, "Going Over the Wall". They said that for the opportunity to win £1000, artists had not bothered to put much effort into their work and that Roy's sculpture was by far the best work on show. Gayle Calderwood from New Cumnock took the second prize with her Portrait, "Primary 4", and the third prize was awarded to Eoghann MacColl for his work, "Maybe Hecla." On Monday evening 30 July I got a call from Bryan Garvie at the Irvine Times asking me about the North Ayrshire Arts Council folding. We didn't want this information to go public until the end of our exhibition. After speaking to Brian I phoned Ian Brotherhood to let him know that the paper would probably contact him as I had given them his phone number. On the following Thursday I went up to my local newsagent to get the paper and noticed we had made the headlines with A BULLET THROUGH THE ART. As I walked home reading the article I could have crawled into a corner when I read what I had said to the journalist on the Monday. "Providing we get support from North Ayrshire Council it is feasible the exhibition could go ahead without the Arts Council. There's a lack of interest from the members, which is a shame. Since I bailed out it's gone to the dogs. I'm not being big headed, it's just I was fortunate enough to be working as a freelance artist, so I had the time available to put into it. When I left there was no one there to do it. BNFL at Hunterston have provided cash prizes of £1000, £500 and £250 for the past four years. But if the Arts Council goes under BNFL will be free of their commitment and could drop out if funding is not found – meaning artists who currently entered from all over the UK would also lose interest." I went home and sat all day with my stomach churning, expecting the phone to be red hot with comments such as, "Who do you think you are," but I received no calls. That weekend I had to be at the exhibition with other committee members and their attitude to my comments was, "Well it's true isn't it?" I was so relieved at everyone's comments! The exhibition was the most successful to date with sixteen paintings sold totalling £5045. We had artists exhibiting from Birmingham, Ilkley, and Errol Kukor from Worksop won the visitor's prize of £250 sponsored by North Ayrshire Arts Council. Errol's metal sculpture "She Dragon" was way ahead in the voting and was worthy of taking a prize. The turnover for the exhibition was £9000 and I didn't think I would have to deal with that sort of money but it was all accountable, and hopefully, the exhibition would continue in future years.

Our exhibition committee agreed to form a new group for the sole intention of promoting and running this annual event. I contacted all the sponsors after the exhibition and received expressions of interest from BNFL and Miller's asking me to provide our proposals for the next year when we had our new committee set up. Claire Komiski, a crafter from Largs whose small business Skoskie had offered to sponsor a visitor's prize of £200 for the following year.

I began another computer course at Towerlands farm in September. This was the ECDL (European computer driving licence) and had nothing to do with driving. The course consisted of seven modules, basic IT, managing files, word processing, spreadsheets, databases, presentations, and information & communication. There would be a test at the end of each module and the results put into a little book that would be your driving licence. The tutor Richard Robbins was supplied by Kilmarnock College. The course was set up by Community Education and paid for by a European fund. This qualification is recognised throughout Europe, hence the reason for its title.

Martin Bellamy had been writing a book about shipbuilding, he told me that the book would be about the people who worked in the industry. As I had told him that I was writing my memoirs, he asked me if he could have a look at it so I gave him pages from my time in the shipyard, and also some shipyard newspapers which may have been of use to him. He returned them and I asked no questions until the book, "The Shipbuilders" was delivered to my home one Monday at the beginning of November. The first thing I did was look at the acknowledgments at the back of the book and when I saw my name, I then discovered that Martin had used six short extracts from my unpublished memoirs. I had said to him when I gave him my script that he could use anything he wanted so I was quite happy to see my words in a book.

The Vennel Gallery in Irvine had asked me if I would be interested in contributing to an exhibition of ex shipbuilders who had gone on to do various disciplines in the Arts. This exhibition, **Over the Wall** was due to open on Friday 7 September and run until 27 October 2001 and before it had began, interest had been shown from various places throughout the UK to house it. Contributors to the exhibition included, Tom McKendrick, Roy Fitszimmons, Peter McDougal, Kevin McDermott, Ken Ryan, Kenny Little, Stuart Orr, Jim Sweeney, Willie Moran, Tom Mills and me. Tom Mills was an employee of the sponsor Fairway Forklifts Limited, and was commissioned to produce a sculpture for the show. As he was an engineer, his piece was made from machinery parts and was a memorial to his father and uncles who had suffered early deaths due to asbestos. Because there were so many artists involved in this exhibition, the Vennel was buzzing on the opening night and Kevin played an acoustic set which we all enjoyed. John Gray from the gallery had organised a party at his house in Dreghorn which took place directly after the preview. He had a blues band playing in his lounge and he and his partner Joyce laid on loads of food and drink. We had a great night and left by taxi at 3.15am. I went in to see John at the Vennel on the Monday and asked him what time had the party finished at. He said, "After we got rid of you." Everyone who was there when we left just crashed out where they lay.

Helen and I had put aside most of the money accrued from my fee as Exhibition Co-ordinator and booked a week in Ibiza for the school October break. We also booked for Louise but as she was an impatient eight year old, we decided not to tell her until we were at the airport. Everyone knows that when it comes to school holidays the Tour Companies put up their prices, so we got a deal leaving from Stanstead as it would not be a school break in England that week. We

are only fifteen minutes from Prestwick airport so we got Ryanair flights to Stanstead from there. Tracey picked Louise up from School at 3pm on Friday 12 October 2001 and brought her to our house to get her clothes changed for seeing Helen and I off at Prestwick. I said to Louise in the car on our way to the airport that we had to use her small case, as we didn't have enough room in ours for what we were taking with us and she was quite happy with that. As we checked in

our luggage and show our passports I had to whisper to the woman on the desk that the wee yin didn't know yet that she was coming with us. Tracey, Graeme and Bert were with us as

244

we sat down in the waiting area. Louise had not been happy since we booked the holiday that she wasn't going with us, but we kept reminding her that she had been to Majorca during the summer and now it was our turn. After sitting for about ten minutes I called Louise over and said to her, "Do you remember when you went to Majorca you took a photo of me and your Gran to remind you of us. Well we're taking one of you to remind us of you," as I pulled her passport from my pocket and handed it to her. As soon as she saw it was hers she knew she was going with us and her face lit up. She was even more excited when we handed her spending money which all her uncles and aunts had given us to pass on to her. Louise was full of questions after that which was one of the reasons we didn't tell her sooner or we would never have heard the end of it. So off we went to Stanstead having plenty of time for dinner at the airport before our flight to Ibiza. We arrived at Can Sanso Apartments at Santa Eulalia around 4am on the Saturday morning and I let Louise sleep in the twin bedroom with Helen as I thought it would be safer for her. The apartments looked lovely in the Thomson brochure but they were next to a main road and ours was right next to it. Half an hour after going to bed whoever it was that had the apartment above us began moving furniture about. That, and with the traffic on the road outside, I got no sleep on our first night. Where our balcony was situated we got the sun as it came up in the morning so I was out there at sunrise, bleary eyed. After a hearty breakfast at the complex Helen and I just lazed about in the sun while Louise was happy playing in the pool. There was plenty for the kids to do within the complex as they had crazy golf, a play area with swings chutes etc. and a tennis court. They were all lit up at night and as the complex was fenced in, it felt safe for the children to run around in groups while their parents sat at the bar next to the pool. Can Sanso Apartments had won all sorts of awards which were displayed round the walls. I would say that one of the main reasons for this was their head waiter, Emilio. He was there in the morning to serve you breakfast and apart from a short break in the late afternoon, he was back until the bar closed at 1am. He didn't mess about after closing time. If you hadn't finished your drink, he told you to take it to your room and bring the glass back to him in the morning. There was entertainment every night in the bar area except for two and one of them was happy night. The first night we were there it was a magician and all the children were lined up in front of him sitting in a row on sun beds. On the Sunday night it was bingo and Emilio was the caller. The guy was a star with his broken English as he had everyone in stitches. He was better entertainment than the bingo itself! We won three litre bottles of white rum and a litre of vodka. It looked as if it was going to rain on the Monday and as this was our first time in Ibiza, we were told not to miss Ibiza Town. As we were trying to find the way to the Old Town I heard someone call out my name. It was Raymond, a guy I knew from Irvine who was on holiday with his wife and another couple. They pointed us in the right direction and we met them another two times that day before we left to return to Santa Eulalia. Louise was bored as it had turned out a fine day and we had dragged her away from her friends and the swimming pool. Like most kids, she didn't like walking and it was quite a climb up to the Old Town. We took her to MacDonald's in Santa Eulalia before we went back to the apartments so that cheered her up. While Bert and I were in the club at Irvine on the evening before our departure, we found that one of our neighbours was going to Playa D'en Bossa, which was near the Aquamar water park. We arranged to meet in Aquamar on the Tuesday morning at 11am. By sheer coincidence, the trip organised by Thomson's to the water park was on the Tuesday and just as we stepped off the coach outside the park, our neighbours tapped us on the shoulder and said, "That was great timing." We were there with them until five o'clock when we had to leave to get our coach. They stayed not far from the water park. Everyone was on the slides and in the water except me. I went in up to my knees and decided that it was too cold so I just sunbathed all day. The next day was the Hippy Market at Es Canar, which wasn't too far from us so we got a taxi there. Louise was fine with that as it gave her the opportunity to get gifts to bring back. Evidently the hippies went there in the sixties and used to make craftwork to sell at this market, but there wasn't much of that on display then. I suppose it was typical of any market selling the usual nonsense but the thing that most impressed me was the live art. You saw what looked like a sculpture, and then it would move, scaring all the children. We took a boat trip back to Santa Eulalia from Es Canar and the skipper was deliberately making it rock at times making Helen uncomfortable as she doesn't like boats. We spent our last couple of days just lazing about at the apartments, which kept Louise happy. One day Helen took her top off as we lay at an area away from the pool but within sight of it. When Louise realised that her Gran was topless she pulled over an umbrella and tilted it so that no one from the pool area could see her. She said, "What do you want to get your boobs tanned for Gran?" I felt sorry for Louise on our return as we were picked up from the apartments at 1am and taken to the airport for our 3am flight to Stanstead. We got through customs at 5am and our flight back to Prestwick wasn't until 8.35am. She kept falling asleep and we would have to waken her but when we got to Prestwick she was full of life. Tracey and Graeme picked us up and as we turned the corner into our street Louise said to me, "Granda, if you're going to take me away again, could you give me a couple of days notice so that I can pack my own case." I went straight to bed as I had a gig to do that night at the Transport Club, East Kilbride.

I attended the launch for Martin Bellamy's book on Wednesday 12 December 2001 which was held on the Tall Ship at Yorkhill Quay, Glasgow.

My Mum was eighty on the 12 March and I had volunteered for Frank and I to play at her party in the nursing home but my sister Gladys had already booked someone before I mentioned it. However, she booked us for an afternoon in June. We seemed to go down well so she booked us for the two Christmas parties on the evenings of 17 and 19 December 2001. George Nimmo, our bass player from Frekels, and his wife Anne Marie, were at the gig on the seventeenth as George's dad was then in the nursing home. It had four houses, Beaton, Seaton, Carmichael, and Fleming, and each party was for two of the houses with most of the residents and their families attending. My Mum was in Fleming but attended both parties because I was playing.

Bill Kerr and his wife Jill organised an afternoon's entertainment for the patients and their relatives at the Douglas Grant Rehabilitation Centre in Ayrshire Central Hospital every Christmas for the last twelve years. Bill asked me to go along to that year's party on 20 December 2000 and do some songs. It would be different to anything he had in the past, in other words they'd never had an old rocker. Bill's daughter Mairi also sung and Lynsey McConnell played the horn, so along with his virtuoso keyboard playing, the afternoon's entertainment was very varied. I was pleased to see my old mate Tam Gardiner who I used to go to Arran with. He was now 91 and unfortunately was resident in the hospital. Bill also knew Tam as he used to go along to see Bill playing in the Cross-Keys at Irvine's Harbourside some thirty years before.

While writing this I had enjoyed contacting people from my past. Just before Christmas that year I thought I would try to contact Bob McGoran. Someone had told me that his parents had moved to Paisley Road West. I looked up the phone book and found his father Joe's number which I wasn't sure of until I spoke to him. We had a good old blether about the old times when Bob and I ran about together. He sounded great for being eighty-five and I was pleased that he was still living. I remember that he used to have one of those tiny blue three wheeled invalid carriages as he had lost an arm and a leg in the Second World War. He informed me about Bob's brothers and sisters, where they were, and what they were doing now before giving me Bob's address and phone number. I didn't call him immediately, but when I did, Bob was expecting my call as his Father had already phoned him to tell him about our conversation. Thankfully he was pleased to hear from me and we spoke for nearly an hour about the old times in Pollok and what we had been up to since then. Bob and his English wife Sheila lived in Brussels for a time in the seventies before he trained as a teacher. He taught English in a secondary school on Islay before moving to Dumfries in 1985 where he taught at St. Joseph's secondary school until his retirement. They moved from Dumfries to Moffat in January 2001 and have a daughter named Hannah who was twenty-one and a thirteen year old son James.

The exhibition,"**Over the Wall**", had now moved to the Pumphouse Gallery of the Clyde Maritime Centre at Yorkhill Quay Glasgow. The sponsors of the show Fairway Forklifts Limited gave us another preview there on 22 January 2001. Their Director Frank Brown had his staff going round with trays of sushi and topping up our glasses all evening as well as laying on a scrumptious buffet. I only had three paintings on show at the Vennel but I had seven at this exhibition.

George Nimmo's dad passed away at the end of January. George told Frank and I at the funeral that his dad was excited the day after we played at his Christmas party which was only weeks before. He said it was a great night, and hopefully, that night will stay as a good memory for George and Anne Marie when they think of him in future years. He had his first stroke thirteen years earlier and most

250

recently had another, but he battlied on. It was a chest infection which took him in the end.

Dougie Henderson and his partner Gillian came to see Frank and I playing at the Kilbryde Arms on Saturday 9 March. I had taken along the draft of my memoirs to have him check out what I had written about him. He has his own memories of the times he came to gigs and played with the Five Interns. He said that he would write them in his own autobiography, but I was happy to include them in my memoirs if he so wished. Dougie has a good sense of humour. At the end of our gig, he came up to me and said, "Jimmy I was just reading about me staring at Allan all night when I was fourteen, well tonight I've been staring at a drum machine!"

We changed our phone line from BT to Omne Communications on 18 March so I sent an email to all my contacts to inform them of my new email address. Bernhard Oestebo replied on 10 March and let me know that he had a solo show opening in Norway on 6 April. At the end of his message he wrote, "PS Your 'Welder's Graveyard' painting looks great in our house. It is placed by the stairs between the ground and the first floor. A lot of people make comments on it, and especially young people tend to like it. A 19-year-old girl (a very creative and artistic one) made very positive comments on it as late as yesterday." The painting that Bernhard was speaking about was actually **"The Dimming Light of Life"** which represents the welder's graveyard. When he was here in 1996, I exchanged the painting for one of his monoprints.

The exhibition, "Over the Wall" moved to Summerlea Heritage Park at Coatbridge. It opened on 23 March and ran until 12 May 2002.

I had a pleasant surprise on Friday 29 March when I received a call from Ian Cooper letting me know that he was at Polly's mum's

in Dailly and if I had nothing important to do, then he would pick me up and take me for lunch. It was great to hear from him as I knew that they had moved to the Rhondda Valley from Bournemouth at the turn of the year. Polly had secured the post of Arts and Culture Manager for Rhonnda Cynon Taf County Borough Council, and they lived in rented accommodation at Pontypridd until they found somewhere to buy after they had sold their property in Bournemouth. He arrived at 11 am and I let him send an email to Bernhard to inform him of his new address before we left to go for lunch at the Ship Inn. Jamie O' Dea came into the pub with some people while we were eating and was surprised to see Ian and I. I had been in to see him the day before and we were both wondering why we hadn't heard from Ian. After lunch Ian and I spent the rest of the afternoon in Jamie's studio reminiscing.

At the time I hadn't done any artwork for nearly two years and Ian hadn't done anything since he gave up his studio at Stalbridge in 1998. Their son Flint was born on 1 December 1998 after which Ian spent the next three years as a househusband. When Flint went to pre-school, Ian told me that he now had more time to himself and had just finished designing icons for his Brother Steve's computer Company. It didn't seem that long ago we were both toiling away happily at the studios in Irvine!

Every Thursday evening at 10.30pm Bert and I went to Towerlands Sports club for a drink from the time we lived in Irvine. We were always in the company of Jeff Love who originally came from Glasgow and went to school with George Nimmo from Frekels. Jeff had lost his wife in 1998 and was getting married again on 31 May 2002 at Gretna Green. That was the same day as Bert's seventy seventh birthday so Bert Helen and I intended to go to the wedding and stay the night at Gretna. On Thursday 4 April Jeff said that he and his future wife Ann were going to Gretna the following day to put their bans in. I realised that they would be going past Moffat and asked Jeff if he wouldn't mind dropping me off there so that I could at last meet up with Bob McGoran and his family. I phoned Bob the following day to make sure that they would be at home, and then cancelled my music lesson with Bill. We set off at 10.30am and they dropped me off at the Moffat exit from the A74 at ten to twelve. I took Helen's mobile phone with me and called Bob as soon as I got out of the car so that he could pick me up. Moffat is only a mile and a half from the motorway so I didn't have to wait long before seeing my old mate again after 30 years. Bob said that as I came into view that he knew it was me because of my walk. On arriving at his home, he introduced me to his wife Sheila and son James and we had a good old blether before Sheila made lunch. We then went up to James' room to have a jam on his Les Paul and electro acoustic guitars. I was impressed with his playing for a thirteen year old. After a stroll round the town with Bob and Sheila, I got a call on my mobile phone from Jeff saying that they were about twenty minutes from Moffat so unfortunately I had to leave. I left Bob my memoirs to correct grammar etc.

As the North Ayrshire Arts Council had folded the previous year, we held a meeting in the Vennel Gallery on Tuesday 23 April to reconstitute as the North Ayrshire Open Art Exhibition Committee and began to plan the 2002 exhibition. Norma McCrone and I met with Dr Paul Harding at Hunterston A power station regarding continued prize sponsorship. He agreed to give us £1500 which was £250 less than we had got for the last four years and we decided that the prizes would be £1000, £300, and £200. We opened a treasurer's bank account with the Bank of Scotland with no funds and required money to pay for insurance before the work arrived. As secretary of the exhibition committee and exhibition co-ordinator, I managed to get £200 from Fairways Forklifts and another £200 from Goldrealm Properties. This was enough to pay for the insurance! Clair Komiski of Scoskie in Largs gave us £200 as the visitor's prize, and Miller's Art Shop in Glasgow once again gave £150 of gift vouchers. Iain Crosbie Printers of Beith also sponsored all our full colour printing as he had done in every previous open exhibition. We were all set with our sponsors in place!

On May 24 2002, a week before Jeff and Ann's wedding, Helen and I were at Brian Craig and Alison Scott's wedding at the Seamill Hydro Hotel in West Kilbride while Bert was at a family function in Glasgow. He had not been feeling well earlier that day but decided to go. He ended up in the Southern General Hospital with a urine infection and that had caused other health problems. He was supposed to take Jeff, his best man Ronnie, along with Helen and I down to Gretna the following Friday and was kept in the hospital until Thursday 30. He didn't feel like going, even as a passenger.

Bride Ann's cousin Ronnie drove Helen and I along with Jeff on Friday 31 while Ann's daughter Jennifer took her and Ronnie's wife Fiona. Another couple who we sat in the club with on Thursdays were Drew and Angela. They also went and as we were approaching Gretna, Ronnie got a call from the office of the taxi firm he worked for saying that Drew couldn't find the Crossways pub where we would all be staying that night. It was right next to a roundabout and as we approached it, we saw Drew pulling into the pub's car park. As we pulled in beside them and we all began taking our baggage out, they then realised that they had left their change of clothes behind. Drew was dressed in a Celtic football top and trainers! We couldn't believe it when they told us that he had lifted their clothes up from their bed to get a camera that was under them. There was a shopping Mall nearby so Drew and Angela went there to purchase clothing while the rest of us settled in to prepare for the wedding at 4.30pm. Drew had a people carrier, which came in handy, as there were nine of us altogether and the Smiddy was five minutes drive from the Crossways. The sun had shone since we left Irvine, and fortunately remained for the rest of the day. Ann's brother Jimmy, her aunt Margaret, twin cousins Cathy and Trisha, with Cathy's twins Amy and Darren all came down for the wedding and were driving back to Irvine later. Jeff and Ronnie looked smart in their highland regalia, and Ann was radiant, as were her bridesmaids, daughter Jenny and Ronnie's wife Fiona. The reverend Isabella Pennington conducted the service by the anvil. She was brilliant! She was small, with thick glasses and hair that was grey and bushy. Originally from Inverness, her highland accented humour had us in stitches. On the serious side, it was interesting listening to the history of the Smiddy and the difference in Scot's and English law regarding a marriage ceremony. You can only marry in a church in England, but in Scotland, the church comes to you, wherever you wish to get married. After the ceremony and photographs outside the Smiddy, we all went back to the Crossways for dinner and drinks. The 'return to Irvine brigade' all left after dinner and the nine of us who were staying the night carried on drinking in the lounge. There was a small lounge upstairs next to the rooms and Ronnie suggested that we get a carryout and carry on partying upstairs as he and I had brought our acoustic guitars with us. Ronnie went for the carryout and I think we went up around 11.o'clock and had a good old drunken singsong until about 2am. I couldn't believe that I was the one who said that we should go to bed as we had a long day ahead. There was a reception that night in the Dunlop Hall, Dreghorn and Frank and I were to play at it. As you can imagine, we were all rough in the morning and Jeff could only manage a coffee. The rest of us had a large fry up! We left around noon for the drive back to Irvine and I went for an afternoon nap so that I would be fresh for the gig. Bert came along to the reception for a short time, just to show his face. We had another great night, all in all a weekend to remember.

Frank and I played at Kirkintilloch Miner's Club on June 22 and Allan Craig came along with his wife Cathy. It was good to see them again. It is always strange to play in front of someone that you used to play in a band with; fortunately my experience has never let me down!

The Sixth North Ayrshire Open Art Exhibition was opened once again by Wendy Law, Visual Arts Officer for the Scottish Arts Council. It opened on Friday 12 July 2002 at the Racquet Hall in Eglinton Country Park and was open daily until Saturday 27 July. The winner of the £1000 prize was Edinburgh artist Gerald McGowan. At the opening a guy came up to me and said, "You don't know me, do you? I'm Gerry's brother Neil." I vaguely remember a Neil McGowan from my young years in Pollok. It was the very man! We had a painting stolen from the wall on the day following the opening. This was the first time in six years that we had came across this problem and would be looking for a more secure hanging system for the future. We sold eight paintings totalling £2480, which gave us £620 commission. The exhibition had always made a loss, but for the first time we made a profit of £622.89.

I had completed my European Computer Driving Licence (ECDL) and felt that I should learn more about computing, so I enrolled at Kilmarnock College's Irvine Campus to do a full time NC course which started on Monday 26 August 2002.

Andy and Marion Neil came along to a gig we were playing in the Rob Roy Club, Kirkintilloch on 31 August. We were supporting cabaret act Gerry Anderson and didn't do much playing as Gerry wanted to hog the limelight. "Fair enough mate, we still got the same fee as we would have got for playing much longer"! We had worked with him twice before so after his first set when the bingo came on, Andy and I went to the games room as he had spotted retired boxer

Jim Watt. He was still there so when he was free from talking to anyone I approached and introduced myself. I said that he used to see Frekels playing in the Star and Garter pub at Maryhill in the seventies. Andy and I must have spent about an hour and a half talking to Jim and his wife Maggs. Jim gave me his phone number and asked me if I would come to his home some time in the future for a jam. He asked me if I could play Sultans of Swing by Dire Straits. I said "yes" and he replied, "Even when you're pissed!" When we went back onstage I played it after a couple of numbers and as I was pissed, I managed to adlib my way through it. A committee woman came on to the stage and handed Frank twenty pounds. Frank passed it to me and said that Jim Watt had sent it. I phoned Jim the following night and said that we should leave my visit to his house for the time being as I had just started college. I also thanked him for the twenty pounds and he began to laugh. He said that he told the committee woman that she should pay us extra and that was how the twenty pounds came to us.

The fee I received for co-ordinating the exhibition in the summer meant that I could once again look for a holiday during the October school break. I booked an apartment at Calas de Majorca for Helen, Louise and I. Two weeks before we were due to go I got a call from Sky Holidays saying that the apartments were closing down early as it was the end of season. They said that I should look in their holiday brochure and pick wherever I liked in Majorca, and if it was available, then we could transfer. As Louise was quite happy playing by the pool, Helen and I thought that the Martinique Apartments in Magaluf had the best pool. Magaluf is also nearer Palma airport than Calas de Majorca and we had never been there before so we chose that and departed from Glasgow on October 12. We didn't arrive at the apartments until the evening and were put on the fifth floor overlooking the hills. When we got up the next morning, Louise had noticed that we were not far from the two water parks which we could see from our balcony. She had been at Cala 'Dor once again in June and had been to the Western Waterpark and wanted to return there as it wasn't far from us. We had a great day out there! Louise spent most of the day in the water which was absolutely freezing, but it didn't bother her. Helen and I went to most of the shows that were on throughout the day and sunbathed in between shows. We all went to Oliver's Water show, which was funny but also quite scary as Oliver dove into a small pool of water from fifty metres above. We had another good day out at Golf Fantasia in Palma Nova. We met a Scottish guy on our first night and he told us that there was bingo in Gow's bar just below where we had dined so that was Helen and Louise happy every night for the week. There was entertainment at the Martinique most nights from 10pm, so we would go to Gow's after we had dinner so that Helen and Louise could have a few games of bingo before returning for the show. Our return flight on 19 October was at 7.30am so we were to be picked up by coach at 5.30. As we were waiting alone for the coach, another couple came out of the apartments and we got talking. They were Scottish and when I asked them where they were from, they replied, "Whitburn." I said, "I play in a band and I'm playing at Blackburn tonight." I knew that it was right next to Whitburn. Another of those strange co-incidences which kept cropping up in life!

I had been asked by Norma McCrone a couple of months earlier if I would be interested in creating an installation in Kilwinning for National Tell a Story Day which would be Friday 25 October. It was being organised by North Ayrshire Council's Libraries Department who had booked storyteller Malcolm Green for the event. I acknowledged my interest and contacted Malcolm to give me an idea on what his stories would be about so that I could create an appropriate setting for him. He reckoned that the baobob tree was important so I painted it in inks on a calico backdrop. He said that there should be a fish appearing out of a dry riverbed, so I also painted a catfish on a small piece of calico knowing that it would be placed on the ground. I purchased some canes and tried to construct a hut for Malcolm to sit in and after some frustration decided to finish it on site. The venue for the installation was the music room in the

Abbey Primary School at Kilwinning. Primary seven pupils from all seven primary schools in Kilwinning would attend the storytelling either on Thursday 24 or Friday 25 October. I ordered loads of grasses and bamboo along with a cube and a half of bark so that I could turn the classroom into a jungle. I only had one day to set it up so I got my mate from college Stewart Howat to assist me. It was a hard day's work, as the bark seemed to be never ending, but in the end, it did look like a jungle and we managed to build the hut. We had blacked the room out and hung two UV lights from the room's fluorescent fittings. I returned the following morning to make sure Malcolm was happy with the setting and after a few minor alterations, he was ready to go and I left him to it. The Council had also booked storyteller Kenneth Steven to recite at other venues in North Ayrshire. I was invited to dinner on Thursday evening along with Malcolm and Steven prior to their sharing an event in the Abbey primary which was open to the community. Helen, Tracey and Louise came along to the school to hear their stories. Steven told stories about the environment and Malcolm, about Africa. We were all impressed with Malcolm's performance, especially his facial expressions. I arrived at the school the following day at ten to three to strip down my backdrops, lighting etc. I went into the room as Malcolm was ending his last story. As soon as he finished, he told the children that I was the creator of the setting and had them all bowing to me. The grasses had to be left in the room until Monday morning as they were all hired from McLaren's nursery near Lugton. The nursery closed at 4pm so I returned on the Monday to remove them. The event was well received by everyone who attended it and I hoped that I would get more installations to create in the future.

My mum was to hear me playing another couple of times as Frank and I did another two Christmas parties at the nursing home. Helen's Uncle John Hester was now in the same house as my mum and didn't know me as he had dementia. His wife Betty who was my mother in law's sister had passed away only a couple of weeks earlier and he was unaware of it.

The lyrics of the song were inspired by having to go outside for a cigarette while at college. I tell people that it was inspired by the smoking ban in 2006. Friday 24 January 2003 was the end of the first semester. The subjects had been Microsoft Office Word and Access, Communication, Computer Hardware, Computer Networks, BSAD (Business Systems Analysis and Design), Computer Programming (Q-Basic), The Internet, and Numeracy.

Slaves to the Nicotine

It's no joke if you feel like a smoke
And you have to stand out in the rain
There was a time when there was no crime
To have a cigarette on a plane

We are the scourge of society, slaves to the nicotine
Only those addicted like me will know just what I mean

I would be healthier and a lot wealthier
If I had the will to kick
I've tried it before, but then I adore
That little bit tobacco stick

It's kinda rough if you feel like a puff
Sitting in a restaurant
Watch the heads turning when they smell that burning
Feeling guilty as you know what they want.

Over the Wall exhibition opened at the Lillie Gallery, Milngavie, on Friday 10 January 2003 and ran until 12 February before moving to the Museum of Levenmouth, Lower Methil, Fife, from 27 February until 19 April. This would be the last venue for the exhibition that had been touring since September 2001.

I completed my computing course in June with one HN unit, two highers, eleven Intermediate 2's and three Intermediate 1's. At long last I had some academic qualifications.

Frank and I played at the Harbour House Hotel at Portpatrick on Saturday 5 July. Pauline and Martin had booked a caravan there for a week beginning on Saturday the fifth. Bert, his brother George, Helen, Tracey, Louise, Pauline and Martin all travelled down in the afternoon. Frank and I went there in the evening to do the gig. They all turned up in the evening along with Bert's mate Willie Laing, his wife Margaret and another couple. Frank went home after the gig and I stayed on until the Tuesday evening as I had to be back to set up the Seventh North Ayrshire Open Art Exhibition on the Thursday. The exhibition was successful once again with The Moffat Charitable Trust sponsoring the £1,000 prize, Kingscroft Logistics Ltd of Irvine sponsoring the £250 prize and Miller's Art of Glasgow giving a prize of £150 gift vouchers to spend in their shop. The show was opened on Friday 18 July by film journalist John Millar and ran until Saturday 2 August.

I had decided that I might as well carry on learning and signed up with Kilmarnock College to do the HNC in computing. The course started on 1st September 2003. This time I would have to travel to Kilmarnock for four days every week. I was too old for a student loan and received no travelling expenses. After a few weeks April Macphail who stayed near me joined the course and she had a car. April had done some of the subjects online and was able to drive me to college most days. Suzanne Hanvey, Ally McCabe and Jason Lyndsey from the NC course all returned to do the HNC. I would discover that this was to be much harder than the NC and that much of my time outside college would be spent writing essays and

261

researching.

Helen Louise and I went off to Cala Dor from 11 – 18 October 2003 staying at the Barcelo Ponent Hotel. Louise was excited as she had been to Cala Dor twice before and would be able to show us where to go. We felt sorry for her as it was a SAGA hotel. There were only another two couples with their grandchildren; everyone else in the hotel was over sixty five. She did keep us right with directions and where to go for entertainment as our hotel had organised entertainment to suit SAGA.

On the morning of Saturday 13 December 2003 I got a phone call from my sister Gladys to tell me that our mother had just passed away at Darnley Court Nursing Home. We were told that she had a stroke and suffered no pain. The funeral was on the following Wednesday 17 December and Frank and I had to play at a Christmas party in the nursing home that evening. It was in a different house from the one my mother was in but we had to play at another party in her house two nights later. She had said to me two weeks earlier that she was done. I said, "Maw you've been saying that for years. Are you telling me that I've not to bring a mike for you? It was a difficult time!"

Pauline gave birth to her daughter Rosslyn on 30 January 2004. It was a good start to what would be a great year for me.

Norma McCrone arranged a meeting in March to ask me if I would be interested in taking the best of North Ayrshire artist's work from the forthcoming eighth Open Art Exhibition to Mallorca along with my own work. As if I was going to say "No"! Norma went to Mallorca the week after our meeting and when she returned, she told me that the gallery required images and artist biographies as soon as possible. As the North Ayrshire exhibition was not happening until July, this meant that we could not go along with our original plan. It was decided that we would take my work along with four other North Ayrshire artists. Each artist would supply four paintings. The other artists were to be Michael Durning, Chick McGeehan, Jamie O'Dea and David Reid. I had to gather digital images and descriptions of work from the artists along with biographies. This information would be translated into Catalan and Spanish for the catalogue.

All of my time in the first half of the year was spent studying and by the end of the course on 18 June, I managed to get my HNC in computing. Project Management was the only subject that I did not complete as I had not spent enough practise time using Microsoft Project software. It was not a core subject so I wasn't too bothered.

The Eighth North Ayrshire Open Art Exhibition 2004 was opened by Dr Anne Lorne Gillies on Friday 16 July. Although there was no £1,000 prize that year, the exhibition still managed to attract 184 entries of which 104 were hung. Eighteen paintings were sold totalling £3,760. Anne kindly wrote the following poem for me and recited it at the exhibition preview

North Ayrshire Exhibitionism

This year I planned to start in May, paint something just for me – and not for Mr Collins's selection committee.

This time I would be organised: this was the year that I'd not pace the floor the night before praying the paint would dry.

I'm amateur: that means I've painted all my working life. (To be professional I'd need a full-time working wife.)

I don't want prizes: fame is such a burden – as Matisse once sighed "Mon Dieu, each work I do must be a masterpiece."

Art for art's sake's the thing: I learned this lesson in my teens,
though the teacher never told the class exactly what it means.
When business men go out, they sip rare wine and talk of art.
When artists get together they sit in grotty pubs and – f – f – fret
about money (or the lack of it!)

But I digress: May was so stressful – tons of extra work
thanks to my boss – the philistine cappuccino-swilling berk.

Doesn't he know the North Ayr Show needs peace, light, inspiration,
and you don't get that on the commuter track between Largs and
Central Station.

So in June I went to GOMA just to concentrate my mind,
then Miller's down in Stockwell Street to see what I could find.

I spent three hundred pounds – you ought to see the stuff I got!
I couldn't wait to go home and paint, then it hit me: who? Or what?

A still life or a portrait, or an Ayrshire view instead?
Tracy Emin could make art out of the mess inside my head!

Relax, I said: remember, kids paint pictures without thinking,
and everyone's an artist after several hours hard drinking.

Just locate your inner feelings through subconscious analytics,
then prepare a level surface and expose them to the critics.

I know all Van Gogh needed was a humble painted chair,
but would it have been art if he had bought it in Ikea?

I'll try to be like Martin Creed, I told myself at first,
but after fusing all the lights I turned to Damien Hurst.

I planned an installation with my goldfish: how I tried –
But I couldn't bring myself to feed wee Gus formaldehyde.

On the eve of the selection I took several caffeine pills,
then worked all night, and phoned to tell the office I was ill.

I laid down my brush at lunch-time, packed my painting without swervin',
then drove in seven minutes all the way from Largs to Irvine.

My masterpiece is over there: a conclusive demonstration
that for artists, deadlines are the only sure-fire inspiration.

It's still sticky round the edges; I'd have framed it if I could,
but then again if it was finished it might not have been so good.

© **Anne Lorne Gillies 2004.**

    With all my studying and coordinating the exhibition, I couldn't wait until October for a holiday and managed to get 11 nights all inclusive for Calella in the Costa Brava from 2-13 August 2004 for Helen, Louise and I. On the morning of August the second I was stripping down the display boards at the Racquet hall and putting them up on the balcony for the following year. When I got home, there was only time for a shower and quick lunch before heading to Glasgow airport. We flew to Gerona, arriving at dusk. I was impressed by the scenery at Gerona airport. We stayed at the Hotel Osiris in Calella and could use the all inclusive facilities at the nearby hotels Olympic and Amaika as they were in the same group. Our room was just above the restaurant and looked onto the pool. Louise made friends with a girl from Manchester and her parents looked after Louise more than we did on this occasion. Our hotel had three open air Jacuzzis on the roof, a bar, music and sun beds and was only available to adults, making it the ideal escape from the noise around the swimming pool. Helen and I spent quite a bit of time relaxing up there. We both took a trip by train to Barcelona and found that there were many resorts that we had never heard of between Calella and Barcelona. As we were heading for the Picasso Museum, we were told to get off the train at the Arc De Triumph. The queue for the Picasso Museum was very long and I had been told by my friend Eoghann MacColl that there was a bar that sold cheap champagne nearby. He had written the name of it down on paper so I asked a Spanish gentleman where it was showing him the piece of paper. It was across the road from where we were standing but was closed until September. I told the man the reason we were looking for it and he took us to another area nearby and pointed out that across the road was the main centre in Barcelona for electrical goods. He said that in the centre was a small shop with hams hanging outside. It had no name but sold cheap champagne. When we eventually found it, we went in to find that it was crowded with local people obviously having lunch. You had to buy something to eat before you could order wine or champagne. We got two rolls with cheese and a bottle of Cava for just over six euros. I had bought a map of Barcelona and wanted to see Gaudi's Temple Sagrada Familia. It didn't look too far on the map so we just followed it until we got lost. It was really humid in the city making it tiring to walk any distance but we got there eventually. The Temple is a formidable sight, towering above all the buildings around it. Although it was a long way from completion, I hope I live long enough to see it completed. We spent quite a bit of time inside the Temple looking at the Gaudi's drawings, plans, and of course the architecture itself. We decided to head back to the Arc De Triumph train station as we were shattered with the heat. One afternoon while Helen and I were at the hotel bar area I heard two young guys speaking with Irish accents. I believe that I can tell the Donegal accent so when I was passing; I stopped and asked them if they were from Donegal. When they replied "yes", I said that my father was from Newtoncunningham. One of them actually lived there, and the other one lived in St Johnston which is not far from

266

Newton. I asked them their names and they replied, "Do you want our names or nicknames"? I said "Give me your nicknames". One of them replied, "I'm Annie and he's Bender". Annie was actually Gerry and Bender's name was Mark. Both their partners were called Caroline. Marks Caroline was Gerry's sister. We enjoyed their company and would spend some time with them until they left a week before us. Bender was quite a character. He owned a horse, did pony trapping and various other activities in order to survive. Helen, Louise and I had a great night out at a Medieval Show in Tordera which was about a half an hour trip by bus. You went over a drawbridge into a fort, and then introduced to the Queen before being led to your seat to watch a jousting tournament. In front of you were bottles of wine, juice and water and you were brought a full chicken and roast potato which you ate by hand. After the show you went to another area where a band played before another show was put on with flamenco dancers. Since Helen likes her bingo, there were a couple of bars nearby that had it in the evenings so I used to walk her to the bar and return to the hotel for drinks then return to collect her. On the Tuesday of our second week when I met her at a corner just along

from the bar she had been in she said, "I met someone, come on back to the bar". It was her cousin Andy McGhee, his wife Pamela and two of their children. They had been staying at the hotel Olympic since the Sunday before we met them. We enjoyed socialising with them until the end of our holiday on Friday 13 August.

Chapter 14

Four weeks later on Monday 13 September 2004 I was off again to Palma Mallorca to organise the exhibition which was to be held at Claustre St Domingo in Inca. I was met at Palma airport by Norma and Margalida Vidal who informed me that the apartment that I was supposed to get in Inca had no electricity or water. We were to meet someone at a bar on the outskirts of Inca and I was to get his mother's house for the five nights I would be staying. After we met the guy, he took us to his mother's house and showed us round. Norma and Margalida returned to Palma city and the guy took me to the Claustre so that I would know where to go the following morning for 9.00am. I told him to drop me at the Claustre and looked for a phone box to phone Helen. By this time it was around 10.00pm and I realised that I did not have the address of the house I was to stay in. I had an idea where it was so I phoned Helen from the railway station and went in search of the house. After I located it I went to a local bar for a couple of drinks before retiring for the night. The house was on the ground floor with the door opening onto the street. It had two bedrooms and the one I stayed in had a window that also looked onto the street. The window had louvre shutters built into the wall from the outside, double glazed windows and another set of louvre shutters that could open. I didn't want to mess with the windows so I went to bed with the window closed. It was so hot that I couldn't sleep. I got up at 4.00am to go to the toilet, put on the hall light and noticed a large cockroach running along the floor of the hall. After going to the toilet I closed the bedroom door to keep the cockroach out which made the room even hotter. Needless to say I didn't sleep at all that night. I got up and left the house at 7.00am to explore Inca. I had been there at the weekly market on a previous visit to Mallorca but which only occured on one street. I wandered around getting my bearings, went for a coffee and arrived at the Claustre before 9.00am. I had been told to ask for Joan but he was already waiting for me and introduced himself. He then showed me the crate which held the paintings that were sent to Mallorca by freight a month before. I had taken a power screwdriver with me so we had it open in five minutes. We had to take the paintings up two floors and Joan had positioned the crate near to a small lift so it was done with no effort at all. After unpacking the paintings, I then positioned them around the walls asking his approval. Joan spoke no English at all but we still managed to communicate. The gallery was a u shaped corridor with the paintings being displayed on the outer walls. We then began to hang the work and I would find that arriba poco meant up a little, and abajo poco, down a little. We managed to get all the paintings hung by the end of the day and I had been asked by Norma and Margalida to take the train to Palma and meet them at 8.30 that night in a bar at Plaza de Espana which was across the road from Palma railway station. After meeting them we then drove to a restaurant at Algaida, which is about 20 kilometres from Palma just off the Palma to Manacor road. When we arrived, we met two people from Scottish Opera and Sebastia Vidal. Sebastia had translated all the English text for the exhibition catalogue into Catalan. The people from Scottish Opera had been in Mallorca to discuss the possibility of an education project. As we were about to discover the delights of Mallorquin cuisine, we left ordering food and wine to Sebastia and Margalida. They ordered various starters and we all sampled a little from each dish. Each one was delicious. I had meat balls in gravy for my main meal, and it was so different from any I had tasted before. The wine they ordered was also excellent. Sebastia ran me back to Inca after the meal. When I entered the house, there were cockroaches running around everywhere, it was quite creepy! I found a large can of insect repellent which I sprayed on them causing them to flip on their back. Again I found it hard to sleep and by the morning I counted eight dead cockroaches.

The exhibition preview was changed from Friday evening to Thursday and explanation cards for the paintings and the exhibition catalogues were delivered on the Wednesday, so I let Joan know that I would see him on Thursday morning. I took the train from Inca to Palma on the Wednesday morning as I intended to head for Cala D'or. By the time I reached the bus station in Palma, I had just missed a bus for Cala D'or and the next one wasn't until 2.00pm. While pondering what to do with myself, a young English couple arrived at the bus stop. When they realised that they were in the same predicament as me they were discussing whether to get a taxi to Cala D'or. I said that I would give them twenty euros if they wished to share a taxi so they agreed and off we went. They had been staying at Santa Ponsa and the girl's parents were staying in Cala D'or so they were going to visit them. We arrived there around 11.30am and the first thing I did was to go and have a full English breakfast as you couldn't get one in Inca. I then went to the Tartan Arms bar hoping to see Bill and Annette but it didn't open until the evening. Unfortunately I couldn't wait until then as the last bus to Palma was around 6.00pm. I just strolled around reminiscing and having a wee bacardi and coke here and there before catching a bus to Palma. While I was on the bus there was a torrential rain storm that ended before I arrived in Palma. I wandered the streets there and was amazed by the beauty of the city. In my previous visits to Mallorca I had never thought of visiting Palma city. I eventually found myself at the enormous Palau de L Almudaina and the Cathedral. I walked down the steps from the Cathedral, crossed the road and onto the promenade where I walked until I came to the beach. There was a little beach bar there where I had lunch and a couple of drinks. There had been no rain since I arrived in Palma and the sand had dried in the heat of the sun so I managed to get an hour or so sunbathing before it got dark. I then headed up Villalonga as there were signposts for Plaza de Espana. I continued to discover Palma, went for dinner near the train station and headed back to Inca. When I got back to the house, all the cockroaches had gone. Someone had been in and cleaned up the place. I went round to the bar which I had visited on my first night and had a few drinks before retiring. It was really strange sitting around people who could not understand me, or I them. We did our best to communicate but it was difficult. I returned to Claustre St Domingo at 9.00am on Thursday morning to mount the explanation cards. The cards were in English, Spanish and Catalan. Each set was wrapped separately, so I opened the English set and began placing them on the floor below their respective paintings. Joan did the same with the Catalan cards. When it came to the Spanish ones, we were both baffled with four of them and had to get another employee at the Claustre to decipher them. We then mounted each set of cards on the walls alongside their respective paintings and laid out some catalogues on a shelf just inside the door of the gallery. When the cleaner arrived to polish the floor I went for lunch before going back to the house for a lie down on the couch which was outside in the patio. I had a shower, got dressed up and headed back to the Claustre for 6.00pm. When I arrived, I remembered that I had forgotten to bring the camera with me which belonged to North Ayrshire Council as I was supposed to take pictures at the preview, so I had to return to the house for the camera. It was only a ten minute walk from the Claustre. Norma and Margalida were setting out the food and refreshments for guests at the preview when North Ayrshire Provost Drew Duncan arrived with his wife Rosemary and Director of Education, John Travers. I made my way up to the gallery to greet them and show them around the exhibition before any of the invited guests arrived. There was a PA system set up in a corner of the gallery and the officials consisted of Balearic Government Ministers and the Mayor of Inca, along with our Provost. They all gathered in a semi circle and the Mayor insisted that I joined them. There I was, in the official party when I was supposed to be taking photographs of them. There was a video camera on us that I believe was from a television company and an official photographer. All the speeches were in Spanish or Catalan and I was pleasantly surprised at how well our provost delivered his speech in Spanish. After the official opening most people went immediately downstairs to the cloisters for food and refreshments. There were two tables laid out, one with

Mallorcan cuisine and one with Scottish that had oatcakes with Scottish salmon, shortbread, and of course good single malt whisky. I would sample all there was on the Mallorcan table including the locally made gin and herbas. Herbas is a local liqueur that is based on aniseed and herbs. While we were enjoying the hospitality, there was a drama group rehearsing at the other side of the courtyard from us and their performance was quite visual. Norma had told me that Sebastia would be taking me for dinner along with a Mallorcan pornographic artist. I believed that we were going to the artist's house and got changed into my jeans which I had brought along with me. Sebastia introduced me to the artist whose name was Tomeo. I put my jacket and bag into Sebastia's car. I had purchased a special bottle of Glenmorangie whisky which was just on the market at Glasgow airport, and brought it with me expecting us to savour it at Tomeo's house. I was walking along the road cradling my bottle of whisky. We eventually came to a restaurant which was an old wine cellar. Tomeo could not speak any English so Sebastia translated for us. He said that I had been carrying my whisky around like a baby, as if it was so precious. I explained that I thought we were going to Tomeo's house and that is why I brought the whisky. We all had a good laugh! Once again I left the ordering of food to Sebastia and enjoyed his recommendations. We finished off with coffee and Sebastia opened the bottle of whisky and poured some into each of our coffees. I called to the waiter and offered him and his colleague a shot each. He took the bottle away and poured two glasses, returning with the bottle and a cigar for me. When we left the restaurant we went to a bar where there was a rock band playing. A perfect end to a perfect night! We left Tomeo in the bar and Sebastia ran me back to the house as he had brought me local figs, cheese, bread and tomatoes to take home to Scotland. The figs and tomatoes were from Sebastia's own garden.

I asked Norma if I could have the Friday to myself as we were supposed to go to Inca town hall for dinner. She said that I could so I got the bus to Alcudia in the morning. . Again, the first thing I did in Alcudia was to find somewhere that did a good English breakfast. I noticed a couple having breakfast at one of the bars and asked them if it was good. They recommended it so I sat down at the table next to them and asked them where they were from as they were Scottish. The woman replied "Irvine". I told them that I was from Bourtreehill and they said they were from Broomlands, which is in the same area. It was good to be able to have a conversation with people from back home as I had not been doing much talking during that week. Although I got Spanish at school, I really struggled along at Inca as they speak Mallorquin. I enrolled at Kilmarnock College's Irvine campus to do a Spanish course which started on the evening I arrived in Mallorca. I had my huge breakfast, bought a bottle of suntan oil and headed for the beach to toast. Apart from visiting a beach bar for a couple of drinks and another for lunch, I spent the whole day soaking up the sun's rays. When I returned to Inca I had a shower, packed my case and went to find the restaurant I had been in the night before with Sebastia and Tomeo. It didn't take me long although it was twenty minutes or so from where I was staying. When I got the menu I remembered Sebastia had told me what dishes were meat. I don't know what I ordered but enjoyed it. I think it was lamb which was on the bone with various vegetables on top and chips. Sebastia let me taste ice cream the night before that was made with almonds and I managed to order that. It was absolutely delicious. As I was finishing my ice cream, the waiter brought me a bottle of herbas and a small glass. He told me that he made it himself and it took eight years. I poured myself a small glass and took a sip. This was the daddy of the one I sampled at the exhibition preview. I had another glass before the waiter came to take it to another table pouring me a third glass. My tongue was burning for the next three days. I left there and went to my local bar where it was the same crowd that had been there on my two previous visits. I sat beside two couples, one of which had a baby in a pram sleeping. One of them could speak English, not very well but at least we could all

274

communicate through him. He asked me if I would join him at another bar so we went in his car. The other couple walked there with the pram and we had some more drinks before I left. I hadn't a clue where I was and got lost. This wasn't due to the drink; I had been walking in the wrong direction before asking someone where the town hall was. When I reached it, I knew which way to go to get home. Norma phoned me the following morning and asked me if I would take the train to Palma and get a taxi to her hotel arriving there at 11.30 as we would be leaving from there for the airport. I phoned the person who showed me the house, to ask him what I should do with the keys and he told me to leave them at Claustre St Domingo. I locked up, went to a café round the corner for a coffee and asked the waitress to phone a taxi. When the taxi came, I dropped the house keys off at the Claustre while the taxi driver waited for me, and then on to Inca railway station for the train to Palma. When I arrived at Norma's hotel, all our party were waiting in the foyer. Drew, Rosemary, Norma and I went for refreshments at a bar which looked over the marina that was close to the hotel. John Travers had to stay at the hotel as he was meeting the Director of Education for Mallorca there. Margalida accompanied us to the airport, dishing out gifts of food on the way. The food that Sebastia had given me was to be shared with Norma but Margalida told me to keep it as she had got her some more. She also gave me a Mallorcan sausage to add to what I already had. John Travers dropped me off at Pauline's house where I just had time for dinner before she ran me with my case to Pollokshields Burgh Hall where Frank was waiting for me and we played at a wedding there. Helen, Bert and I would enjoy our Mallorcan bread with cheese and figs for our Sunday morning breakfast. The sausage and tomatoes were consumed in the following weeks.

I started my Spanish course on Monday 27 September. Helen and I went back to Mallorca on Sunday 17 October. I booked it all on the Internet. We flew out with Flyglobespan and returned via

Stanstead with Easyjet on Friday 22 October. Since I was impressed with Palma a month earlier, I booked a hotel in Can Pastilla which is near the airport and Palma city. We got a taxi at Palma airport to take us to the Orleans Garden hotel. When we arrived, the hotel was closed but there was an arrow pointing up the road. I noticed when I was on the Internet that there were two buildings, one on either side of the pool, so I didn't panic yet. The taxi dropped us off at the other building which was opened. This was the Orleans hotel. When we arrived at the reception the receptionist said, "Mr and Mrs Collins? Come with me". He took us round the corner to the Alexandra hotel and left us after speaking to their receptionist. Our room overlooked the Orleans complex and we both agreed that we were in the best hotel of the three. We were half board and the food was excellent. We noticed immediately that we were in another saga type hotel that was full of Germans, Spanish and Italian pensioners. It didn't bother us but we were glad that Louise wasn't with us as she would have had no friends. We arrived late on the Sunday night and missed dinner, so we went across the road for a pizza. The hotel was just across the road from a small beach and it was in a very quiet area. Maybe it was just because it was the end of the season! We just lazed about near the pool on the Monday and spent the evening in the bar. We had a bottle of champagne with our dinner and another at the bar. There was entertainment every night in the hotel. We were in bed by eleven that night as I felt sozzled with the champagne. The following day while we were at the pool, a crowd of people passed us by and we noticed that they were Scottish. Some of them were from Kilwinning and they recommended two bars for us to go to. The first one was just across the road from the hotel, near the beach. We went there after dinner on the Tuesday and a Manchester United game was about to start so we stayed there and watched the game. The second one was called The Secret Garden and was owned by a Scottish guy. We went there after the game and met the owner. His name was Liam and he was originally from Prestwick which is not far from where we live now. While we were talking he asked me if I knew an Alex Frew.

Earlier in the year I received a call from my cousin Ronnie's wife Gwen. She said that she was in the Horseshoe Bar in Glasgow and she was talking to a guy who knew me. It was Alex! She put him on the phone and he told me that he was living in Palma. I had said that I would be exhibiting in Mallorca in September and would be coming over so he said that he would contact me nearer the time. He never did! I told Liam that story and he said that Alex had lost his mobile phone, losing all his contacts. He took me through to the secret garden which was an area through from the bar which was exposed to the elements. He pointed up to a large painting of a dragon on one of the walls and told me that Alex had painted it. Lower down around one of the walls were prints of rock stars which Alex had also produced. He phoned Alex and we arranged to meet up at the Telegraph bar the following night. Liam had spent ten years in the Far East helping unfortunate people before taking over the bar in Can Pastilla. We met Alex at the Telegraph and had a good old chat and I performed some of my own songs with an acoustic guitar which belonged to one of the owners who was also Scottish. Helen and I went into Palma one day and we went down to the beach for lunch at the place I had visited the month before. We left Mallorca in the afternoon of Friday 22 and had dinner at Stanstead as we had five hours to spend there before our flight to Glasgow.

My installation for the storytelling project that year was at St Bridget's primary school in Kilbirnie. I set it up on Tuesday and Wednesday 26 and 27 October. The theme was "Stepping Stones to Sea Stories". I don't know who thought of that but it was a brilliant title for the project. I didn't hire any plants this time as it would have been inappropriate. I dismantled the installation after the last session on the Friday and picked it up on the following Monday.

I attended Kilmarnock College's graduation ceremony on Thursday 4 November to collect my HNC certificate. My friends Jeff and Ann Love came along with Helen and then came back to our house for a drink to celebrate. Bert, Jeff Ann and I then went up to Towerlands Social Club as we did every Thursday.

Portrait of me by David Reid

I was offered another project by Jo Leviton, Arts Development Officer for North Ayrshire Council. The Harbour Arts Centre had received lottery funding to refurbish and extend. The first exhibition when it reopened in the autumn of 2005 was a portrait exhibition of

North Ayrshire people painted by David Reid. My project was to purchase and distribute disposable cameras throughout North Ayrshire, have the photographs developed and pass them on to David. He then selected people he wished to portray and arranged a time with them so that he could take better quality photographs. I distributed cameras in all seventeen libraries within North Ayrshire during November. I had also been given a list of potential candidates that I should contact by Jo; some of them were cryptic clues. One of the people on the list was Julie Fleeting who was born on 18 December 1980 and is the daughter of Jim Fleeting from Kilwinning. Julie had played football for Scotland's woman's team since she was 15. She joined Arsenal from Ross County in January 2004 and played for San Diego Spirit in the 2002, 2003 and 2004 seasons, when the league was disbanded. Julie played for Ayr United in the women's league for nine years before signing with San Diego Spirit. She was also a PE teacher at Charleston Academy, Inverness. Julie's father Jim also played for Ayr United and Norwich City. This information was obtained by typing Julie's name into Google search engine on the Internet. At that time I read in an article that Julie was a PE teacher in St Michael's Academy in Kilwinning so I phoned them, only to be told that she had moved to Inverness or Aberdeen. Knowing that Julie played for Scotland's women's team, I went back to Google and typed in SFA. I got their telephone number from the SFA's web site, telephoned the number and explained to the woman who answered about the project and my reasons for trying to contact Julie. She told me that the women's section were not based there but asked me to hold. When she returned, she told me that Julie's father worked there and he wanted to have a word with me. I was surprised and introduced myself to him telling Jim about the project. He then gave me Julie's mobile number reminding me not to try and contact her through the day as she would be teaching. I phoned her that evening and she agreed to having her portrait painted, and told me to pass her number on to David Reid so that he could arrange a meeting which would be suitable to them both. David did many small portraits and several large ones. My portrait on the previous page was one of the bigger ones.

The Interns had a reunion of sorts a few years ago but no one knew where singer Johnny Campbell lived. I received an email from a John Keith at the end of January 2004 informing me that Johnny was the kit man at Manchester United. A friend of his, Veronica Kelly from Pollok who now lived in Vancouver directed John to my website as she had noticed the photos of the Interns. They used to come to see us when we played in Pollok all those years ago and he contacted me as an interested reader after visiting my site. I emailed Manchester United around May and asked them to confirm if their kit man, Johnny Campbell, came from Pollok. I explained that I had played in a band with him in the sixties and would like to get in touch again. I received an email a week later from Johnny's son Stephen giving me Johnny's address and mobile telephone number. This was just pure coincidence as Stephen had akso been contacted by John Keith. I phoned him from my mobile and said, "Is that you Johnny"? "Aye". "Are you still in Barnbeth Road"? "No I'm in Denton". "Where's that"? "Manchester, who's that"? "Jim Collins". We then had a good old blether and Johnny said that he had been given my message at Manchester United. He told me that he had been coming up to Glasgow every New Year for the past 27 years. We kept in touch throughout the year and arranged to meet in the Mire bar in Glasgow on Thursday 23 December 2005. Helen and Bert came along and as the three of us walked into the bar, Johnny shouted from a corner. I didn't know what to expect, probably a fat baldy guy, but he was just an older version of the guy I knew forty years ago. Johnny was with his mate Tam. He has phoned Tam every Friday night for the last 27 Years and met him every year when he came up. It was good reminiscing about the old times. I went through again to meet him on 2 January 2005. We met again in the Mire bar and then went to his sister's where Bert brought his brother George along when he came to pick me up. George used to come along to some of our gigs in the sixties.

My sister Gladys phoned me on Wednesday 5 January 2004 to tell me that our Aunt Iza had passed away the day before. Her husband was my father's brother Willie and they lived in Cowdenbeath, Fife. The funeral was to be on Monday 10 January and if I wanted to go, then I could travel there on the Sunday and stay with Willie. I contacted him and arranged for him to pick me up at Dunfermline bus station at 4.30pm. We picked up suppers on the way to his house and spent the night chatting. I had always liked Uncle Willie who was 85, and am glad that I was able to spend more time with him than I had on previous occasions which were mostly at funerals. He told me many stories and I found out that his brother, my Uncle Harry, was best man at he and Iza's wedding in 1956. I am ashamed to say that I never knew my Aunt. I had also never met their daughter Jean who lived nearby with her husband Dave and son Lorne, but I would meet them the following day. Willie told me that when he was a boy, he left school at Newtoncunningham, Donegal at 14 to work in a farm for two years and was only paid just over two pounds for the entire period. He worked in Jersey in the Channel Islands selling ice cream. He said that the license for this was fifteen pounds for non residents and two pounds if you were resident. The person who gave him the job got him a two pound license and he soon ended up at the police station along with the person who got him it and a third person. That was the end of this job! He told me that when he was coming over here to Scotland in 1947 to work in the coal mines, the ship that he was on ended up on the rocks somewhere in County Antrim due to a storm. They eventually got free and were towed to the Clyde. Willie was sent to work in a pit at Dunfermline. He got out of the pit and then worked on the roads. While working at that side of the country with his brother Harry, he drove him home to Glasgow to visit their sister Grace who lived at Barlanark. Willie took a severe pain in the stomach before they left

Fife and suffered it all the way to Glasgow. He dropped Harry off at the Edinburgh Road in Glasgow and carried on to Grace's. He said that he lay on the settee and fell asleep. The next thing, when he opened his eyes he could see a blurred Grace and her husband Quentin standing over him before he was put on to a stretcher and taken to the hospital. The doctor told him that he would have been dead if it had been another twenty minutes before receiving attention as he had a burst appendix. Uncle Willie told me other stories about his life such as having a small holding which he looked after while working at a normal job. I would also find out that my Uncle John had passed away in September 2003. At aunt Iza's funeral the following day I met many cousins that I had never met before. Pat, Mick and Celine were sons and daughter of my Uncle Michael and aunt. Ilene, Caroline and Theresa were daughters of my Uncle Pat and Aunt Ilene. Both families had another three brothers and sisters who had not attended the funeral. I stayed with Uncle Willie that night and travelled back to Irvine on the Tuesday, arriving at 4.00pm as I had an exhibition meeting at 7.30. The weather at Irvine was horrendous as a storm was expected that night with winds gusting up to 120mph. I cancelled the meeting until the following Tuesday.

Pauline and Martin had a party for Rosslyn's first birthday on the afternoon of Saturday 29 January 2005. It was actually a day before her birthday as Martin had to work on the Sunday. I bought Louise an electric guitar and amplifier before we went to Rosslyn's party as she had shown me that she was keen to learn and was playing well in the three weeks that I had been teaching her. At that time there were only three of my father's family left, Pat, Willie and Kathleen whom I had never met as she lived in Corby, and as far as I knew had never came up to Scotland.

I was working on my pc on the Tuesday evening, 15 February 2005, when Helen shouted to me that Tracey wanted to see us. Louise was at the pictures when we went next door. This was one of the reasons why Tracey wanted to speak to us as she had just done a pregnancy test and it was positive. Helen and I were delighted and I suppose Tracey and Graeme were still coming to terms with it as Louise was now 12 and they didn't know how she would react. Louise came in to see me the following day and told me that she burst out crying when she was told but she was fine about it later.

Helen and I went back to the Osiris Hotel, Calella from 21 June – 1 July 2005. Louise was off to Switzerland with her school at that time. While we were there we did the official day tour of Barcelona visiting Gaudi's temple once again, Camp Nou, La Rambla and the fountains at Montjuic in the evening. We didn't go into the Sagrada Familia Temple this time and only had twenty minutes to wander round outside it to take photographs. As our courier took us to a souvenir shop this voice said, "How's it going Jim"? It was John Boyle, an old friend from school who was on the same bus as us but staying at a different resort. He was now living at Stewarton and had actually spoken to me at the time of the Open Art Exhibition at Eglinton Country Park the previous year.

The 2005 exhibition was the best since it began in 1997 as we sold 32 paintings totalling over twelve thousand pounds. We had three and a half thousand pounds sitting in our bank account at the end of the show.

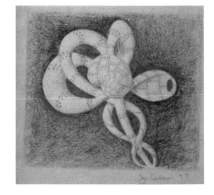

Photo by Steve Hunter

Tracey's son Zander was born on 20 October 2005.

My Aunt, Sister Theresa who was a nun had spent most of her life in England teaching nuns and priests and was now in St Francis nursing home in Govan with a suspected brain tumour. I phoned my Uncle Pat to see if he had heard anything about Sister Theresa as she had been waiting for results of a brain scan. He said that my cousin Patricia had been to the hospital and was told Aunt Theresa had a tumour that was malignant and that she had only six months to live. A couple of weeks later I did a gig and when I arrived home, Bert told me that Aunt Theresa had passed away. So much for being told that she had six months to live. It had only been two and a half weeks since being told that and I never managed to go to see her.

We had never been to Benidorm because we had been told that it was Spain's Blackpool which I do not like. Helen's dad Bert and I went with Jeff and Ann Love on 28th November until 1st December 2005 staying at the Hotel Dynastic in the Rincon area. I absolutely loved it, first class entertainment everywhere and places where you could eat all night. There was a Spanish guitarist playing at our hotel and he let me go up and play a few of my own songs. I remember being on the beach on 1st December with my top off. This would be the first of many trips to Benidorm in the future

Tracey ran Helen and me to my Uncle Pat and Aunt Ilene's golden wedding at North Queensferry on Saturday 7 May 2006. It was good to meet my Fife cousins once again along with others I hadn't met before. We had a great night although I had overdone it with the whisky. Helen and I went to Benidorm on 31 July 2006 for 11 nights staying at Evamar Apartments. Frank and me played at the Ballachulish Hotel on Christmas Eve and Friday 30 December 2005. We were fortunate to get there and get home on both dates, each journey stopping for a break and a dram for me at The Drover's Inn. We got the same dates in 2006 and also made it there and home.

The 10thNorth Ayrshire Exhibition ran from 15 July until 29 July 2006. Twelve paintings were sold totalling £3,420

I sold my Eko Ranger 12 string guitar on EBay and it was purchased by a guy from Manchester. I phoned my friend Johnny Campbell and asked if he could put me up for the night. He said yes so I took the guitar down on the bus on Tuesday 27 March and Johnny met me at Manchester bus station. We went to his club in the evening for a drink and catch up and he ran me to the bus station the following day where I met my customer and gave him the guitar.

Helen and I went to Calella on 29 April 2007staying at the H Top Calella Palace Hotel which used to be the Osiris. Helen would be 60 the next day so I had written to the manager, in Spanish of course, informing him of her birthday and asking if he could have flowers and champagne sent to our room on the morning of the 30th. Sure enough, the manager and his assistant knocked on our door at 9am with a lovely bunch of flowers and a bottle of cava. Helen's dad Bert, his brother George, her brother George and partner Ellen had booked a hotel at the next town Pineda De Mar and came through to us later that day to celebrate Helen's birthday by our pool. They were only in Pineda for a few days and we were in Calella for a week. The day they were leaving, we went through to their hotel, the Pineda Palace. While they were waiting to be picked up for the airport a message came over the intercom for Mr Robert Morrison to come to the reception. When the maid was cleaning his room she found his false teeth under the pillow. We all had a good laugh about that!

The 11th North Ayrshire Exhibition ran from 7 July until 21July 2007. Twenty two paintings were sold totalling £6,875.

Helen and I returned to Benidorm, once again at the Evamar Apartments from 23 July until 2 August 2007. We were married 40 Years on 28 October, so on Sunday 11 November we went back to Benidorm with Helen's dad Bert, his brother George, our daughter Tracey, her 15 Year old daughter Louise and son Zander, and Pauline's daughter Rosslyn. On this occasion we stayed at the beachfront Torre Principado Apartments for a week. It was Fiesta time and we saw the firework displays at the old town from our balcony. There was kid's playground equipment on the beach facing the apartment, so that kept Rosslyn and Zander happy while we adults took in the sun. I remember Tracey and me taking Louise out one night and she drank us under the table. 13 years later and she still can. We all had a lovely day at Aqualandia in Benidorm. There were dolphin and seal shows on at certain times of the day and most of us got soaked by the dolphins.

TUSK

Chapter 15

Jeff, Bert and I went to Gerona on 14 January 2008 and stayed at the Hotel Ultonia. We went on a Monday arriving in the evening and spent most of the night in an Irish bar. I had became friendly with Juan the waiter from the rooftop bar in the Calella Palace Hotel, Calella as Helen and I had stayed there twice. He had a bar called D'artagnion not far from the hotel. We found that it was possible to get a train from Gerona to Calella that involved one change of trains. On the Tuesday we took a train to Calella arriving at Juan's bar around mid-day. He served us large bacardi and cola all day and we left the bar at seven pm. The train station was only around one kilometre from the bar and the last train to Gerona was at seven thirty nine. We never made it! The station master told us that the only thing we could do was to take a train to Barcelona where we could get an express train to Gerona. I don't remember getting on the train or getting off at Barcelona but I remember not having any cigarettes. A security man at Barcelona station sent me to a bar across the road where I was able to get a pack from a machine. I had a cigarette outside the station before the security man showed the three of us to the correct platform for the Gerona train. We were sitting together when sometime later a train pulled in. I turned to a woman sitting next to us and asked her, "Por favor señora, esta tren por Gerona"? "No no", so I continued speaking to her in Spanish. I turned round to notice Bert and Jeff had vanished. I then saw Bert standing up inside the train and shouted at him to get off as it was the wrong train they were on. He moved towards the doors with Jeff directly behind him as the doors closed but the train pulled out! Still feeling the effects from my afternoon's drinking I caught the correct train to Gerona. When I arrived I went to the police station to report them missing but the police sent me back to the train station to tell security. When I arrived the station was closed. I then went to our hotel, told reception and then went to the pub. When I returned Bert and Jeff were in bed. Jeff was sleeping but Bert stayed awake in case I had arrived by taxi from Barcelona and didn't have enough money for the fare. In the morning they told me that the train they were on stopped at the next station and everyone got off. They got off and began looking for a bus that would take them to Gerona. Not having a clue where they were or how far it was to Gerona, they decided to take a taxi. They hailed one, got in and told the driver, "Gerona". He told them "No" and pointed to the door. Jeff had a map of Gerona and had circled where our hotel was. He showed the map to the next taxi driver and he decided to take them at a cost of 135 euros. I hadn't phoned Helen the first night and I couldn't on the second as I didn't know where her dad was. I phoned her at work on the third day and she thought our story was funny. I wrote the poem on the following page for Jeff's sixtieth birthday a couple of months later. By then everyone knew the story and could understand it all.

Los Tres Amigos En Espana

Los Tres Amigos went tae Gerona a couple of months ago
Jim knew a guy wi' a bar in Calella and they decide tae go
They spent a' day drinkin' large bacardis till they couldny staun
By the time they got tae Calella station the last train hame had gone

The stationmaster said to them there's one thing you can do
Just take the train tae Barcelona and another will take you
To the city of Gerona where you want tae be
So on they got and off they went Los Tres Amigos three

Barcelona tae Gerona is a hunner mile
Noo here's the bit a know will gonnae make ye smile
They were waiting there in Barcelona when in came a train
Making sure they wurny gonny miss a train again
Jeff n' Bert jumped aboard as Jim was talking Spanish
Tae a wummin next tae him then noticed they had vanished

He saw them standin' oan the train and waved them tae get aff
As they moved towards the doors they closed, it didny make him laugh

He put his hands upon his heid and said aloud "Oh Fuck"
Imagining them hitchhiking oan some Spaniards truck
For they were oan the wrang train, God knows where it wiz gaun
The right wan trundled in and one amigo just went on

They said that efter wan stop they got aff without a fuss
An' walked aboot four bus stops lookin' fur the Gerona bus
Whereaboots in Spain they were, they didney huv a clue
So efter some discussion thought a taxi hame wid do
They hailed wan, jumped in, sat and told the driver where tae go
"Gerona"! said the señor before he told them "No"
They didney realise how far away from there they were
Until the next wan took them. A hunner an' thirty five euros wiz the fare

Meanwhile in Gerona Jim had went tae tell the cops
Hoping they could find oot where the amigos' train stops
Still reekin fae Bacardi, his questions wurney filed
They chased him oot, but later, amigos reconciled

Noo if los tres amigos go tae Spain again
There's wan thing they'll make sure of that they willney take a train
But when ye get tae sixty, the brain cells start tae go
Happy Birthday Jeffrey, that's it mate, cheerio.

The North Ayrshire Open Art Exhibition ran from 11 July until 25 July 2008. Twenty eight paintings were sold totalling £8,009. Our fourth grandchild Helenna was born on 20 July 2008 to the delight of Pauline and Martin, and of course Helen and I.

A bit of useless information that I wrote in my gig diary was that when I played at the Regent Club Greenock on 8 November 2008 it was the first time since January 1973 that I hadn't taken my 1972 Fender Stratocaster.

Helen's dad Bert, Jeff and I went to Lloret De Mar on 9 November to bring back cigarettes and tobacco. We stayed at the H Top Casino Royal and had no intention on taking any train journeys, but we did. The hotel was all inclusive and there were people staying paid by others to bring back their cases filled with tobacco and cigarettes. They took advantage of the all inclusive for the couple of days they were there. I remember Jeff liked dancing and bought a pair of patent Cuban heels. I bought a black leather jacket with fringes and beads in the style of an American native. We went to Calella on 11 November to see Juan at his bar to tell him about our adventure earlier that year getting back to Gerona. This time we did not have much to drink!

Frank and I played Hogmanay 2008 at Beith Masonic finishing at 1am. When we got to my house we unloaded the gear and both went to Jean Reader's house as she had invited me. Her daughter Eddi Reader was there, and her son Frank and his wife Tanya over from Los Angeles. Frank is the singer in the band Trashcan Sinatras. John Douglas also from the Trashcans was there. I can't remember if John and Eddi were together then but would later be husband and wife. My friend Frank didn't stay long and I left not too long after him as we were playing New Year's Night at Garlieston in the south west of Scotland, about a two hour drive.

On Thursday June 11 2009 Frank and I played at Lanark Thistle Bowling Club for Lanark Lanimer's Day. Every June, the town holds its Lanimer Day celebrations. Festivities reach their high point on the Thursday of Lanimer week when the children parade in fancy dress with floats, pipe bands, the Lanimer Queen and her Court. Two nights later we played at Beith Gala dance in Beith Community Centre. On 20 June we returned to Garlieston to play at a sixtieth birthday party.

The Open Art Exhibition opened on 11 July and ran until 25 July 2009. Thirty five paintings were sold totalling £10,975. One day while I was looking after the exhibition with another committee member, Country Park Visitor Centre receptionist Rae Millar came into the hall to inform me that there was a woman on the phone from Australia saying she wanted to purchase a particular painting. I went back to the reception armed with an exhibition catalogue. Evidently, the woman's mother was an exhibiting artist and she had been raving about artist Rosalind Summers' painting "Islay Pony (Ready For Action). The price of the painting was £1200 so I gave the lady our bank details and the money was in our account the following morning. At the end of the show, I had to wrap it up and give it to her mother who was really surprised but delighted.

Helen and I went to Rothesay with Bill and Jill for the night on the sixteenth of July. We visited Mount Stuart by day and went for an Indian meal at night, returning to Irvine the following evening

Helen and I also went to Strathpeffer on 27 July 2009 with David Urquhart Coaches and were based at the Strathpeffer Hotel. The following day we went to the Gairloch, Poolewe and Ullapool. We went to Skye on the twenty ninth spending time and a few drams in Portree. The next day we went to Inverness and Nairn. On our return to Strathpeffer from there we stopped at champion haggis makers Geo Cockburn & Sons to buy some to take home. Our driver said that our hotel would keep it in their fridge until we left the next morning after breakfast. We got a haggis, venison burgers and some venison. We all agreed that it was the best haggis we have ever eaten and was really moist.

On 8 March 2010, Bert and I went to Benidorm staying at the Dynastic Hotel. We knew that Jeff and Ann, Ann's daughter Jennifer and her husband John, his brother Graham and their mother Betty were all going to another hotel further up the hill from us arriving the following day. Bert and I had been keeping it a secret to try and surprise them all. My old school friend Frank Cusack knew we were coming over and said that he would meet us at our hotel on the morning of the ninth. Bert and I were waiting for Frank to arrive and as the Irvine crowd were due to arrive at 1pm, Bert went on up to their hotel while I waited for Frank. At 12.45 Frank still hadn't showed so I left a message at our reception to let him know where we would be and I hastily made my way to their hotel. Bert and I were watching out for them when Jeff came up behind us and said hello. He said that he saw a guy walking up the hill that looked like me and had sent me a text saying so. So much for all the secrecy! Frank arrived but said he couldn't stay too long so eventually I walked him back to where he had parked his car near the Hotel Venus and Bert went back to the Dynastic. When I got back to our hotel, I was met by our friend Steve Cosgrove as he and his wife Senga had come to visit from Algorfa where they were living at the time. We had entertainment in the evening and were all inclusive so Bert gave the waiter a good tip which let Steve and Senga also enjoy the free drink. Jeff and Ann visited us the next afternoon and we spent it by our pool. That night we went to their hotel and enjoyed a free night and entertainment as they were also all inclusive.

On 7 May 2010, Helen and I flew down to Cardiff as there was going to be a party on the 8th to celebrate Mark, my sister Chris' partner's 50th birthday. They had a lovely house at Glynogwr near Bridgend with a lot of ground, chickens, ducks, two cats, two guinea pigs, and Harry the wee Jack Russell. They had a marquee erected at the side of the house with a singer guitarist on at night and a hog roast which had been cooking slowly for hours. What a great night and I got up and did Kingston Town using the guy's gear. We flew back the following day.

The tenth North Ayrshire Open Art exhibition ran from 10 July until 24 July 2010 and 16 paintings were sold totaling £3,885.

We went to Lloret De Mar for a week on 2 August 2010 staying at the H Top Hotel Alexis. This was a small hotel on the hill facing the beach that didn't have a swimming pool but had three Jacuzzis on the roof. There was a group of ex British Army guys that were on a stag. One of them did not drink as he was looking after the one that was being married, that is loyalty and I was impressed with it. We took a bus up to Tossa De Mar since it was not too far away and the old guy I worked with in the parks in my late teens used to go there on holiday often. Jeff, Ann, Bert and I went off to Torremolinos from the first of December to the third staying once again at the Buensol Apartments, using the usual cheap Ryanair flights to stock up with tobacco and cigarettes.

Frank and I played the 2010 Hogmanay gig at Gairlochead Bowling Club and the Alternative Hogmanay Party on the second of January 2011 at the Lighthouse, Kilcreggan. This was for all those that had to work on Hogmanay so the night was treated just like the real one with "Happy New Year" at midnight. There was a great atmosphere in the pub that night!

On Thursday 24 February 2011, while Bert and I were at our club, one of Bert's friends said that his son was driving down to Cardiff to check out a flat he had there as he had been working in Scotland recently and staying with his mum and dad. I asked his dad Neilly Campbell if he thought his son Jim would give me a run down so that I could visit my sister Chris . He took my phone number so that Jim could contact me. Jim phoned me the next night and said that he would pick me up from my house at 3am on Sunday 27 February. I remember Neilly telling me that Jim didn't smoke so I knew that I would not be smoking throughout that long journey to Wales. I phoned my sister and she arranged to have me picked up from a service station on the outskirts of Cardiff and Jim was fine with that. On the Saturday I went down to Boots Chemist in Irvine and bought large nicotine patches. I played at the Ashton Helensburgh on the Saturday night and finished at 1am. I had rolled cigarettes before going and smoked them all night. When I got home, I had time to have a cup of tea and my last cigarette before Jim picked me up. So off we went on my cigarette free trip as no one where I was going to smoked. We came home on the Monday and I went into my local chemist on the Tuesday and signed up for the smoking cessation plan and was given free nicotine patches by Annie Marshall. I can't remember exactly how often I was checked to see if I had strayed but I didn't and as I write this will be smoke free for 10 years on 27 February 2021..

The 15th Open Art Exhibition ran from 16 July until the 30 July 2011. Twenty one paintings were sold totalling £4,893.

Bert, Jeff, Helen and I went to

Helen's dad Bert and his brothers. Alex, Bert, Jim and Donnie at the back. Thomas and George at the front.

Benidorm 21 September 2011 for a week staying at the Hotel Rosamar. Our friend

Jeff had been diagnosed with pancreatic cancer some months before. Bert and Jeff had the room next to us that had an adjoining door which could be locked from both sides so it was handy. Jeff's wife Ann was coming over a couple of days later with some of her friends.

On the day they were arriving, the four of us went to their hotel to surprise them. When they got settled in we had a good session and ended up staying in for the night. One day while we were sunbathing at the pool, Jeff got up and said he was going for a newspaper. He came back with a walking stick! Jeff was obviously unwell throughout the holiday but didn't complain at all. He didn't drink much when we were out in the evenings, sometimes just water. All the women came to see us off when we were leaving for the airport in the early hours.

I got a shock on Saturday 19 November 2011 when I got a call from Cathie Craig telling me that her husband Allan had passed. Allan was the drummer in our sixties band, The Five Interns. Allan, Johnny, Andy and me had been meeting up on the

third of January for the last couple of years. Days later, on the Tuesday 22 November, a large soft lump appeared on the back of my head. It wasn't until some years later, it came to me that my uncle George had the very same so it seems that I have inherited it. On Friday 25 November my good friend Jeff passed. Bert and I had been going round weekly to see him as he deteriorated, but he always made us tea and a chocolate biscuit. Jeff was a gentleman and I really miss him!

A good night out in Irvine with Davy and Maree Hughes.

TUSK played St Peter's Men's Club Paisley at Hogmanay and at the Alternative Hogmanay Party once again at the Lighthouse, Kilcreggan on 2 January.

On 27 January Bert and I met up at the Crystal Palace, Jamaica Street, Glasgow, with some of the sheet iron workers that I used to work with. They included Willie Ferrie, Gordon Wilson, Waddy, John Gray and his son Jason, along with others that worked with them then at Yarrows. It was good to see them all as we had worked together for many years. Bert didn't really know them as they all began their apprenticeships after he left the yard.

Frank and I did a strange gig at Port William on Saturday 18 February 2012 in the Monreith Arms Hotel. This was a strange one for us as we were playing for the community council who were going to announce the new Queen for their Civic Week which would be on the first week of August. The Queen would be a 3rd or 4th year pupil at the secondary school and should live within the parish of Mochrum. Candidates would previously have done a presentation to the council in the community centre at Port William. Civic Week would begin on the first Sunday and a marquee would be erected on the green next to the statue and there would be various events all week until the following Sunday. There would be nothing on the Wednesday of Civic Week as everyone would be at the Wigton Cattle Show. Anyway, after the history lesson, we had a great night, were fed, watered and complimented on our performance.

Bert and me, his brother Donnie and partner Ellen, and Helen's cousin Joan and her husband Jim all went to Torremolinos on 23 April 2012 staying once again at the Hotel Cabello. We spent quite a bit of time walking along to Benalmadena Marina and one day further on to the bird park up the hill from the whirlies. We decided that we would all like to take a day trip to Gibraltar. We met a lady who ran trips and was looking for customers. Unfortunately, the next trip was on Thursday 26 April. We said that we were flying home that evening. She asked us the time of our flight and organised that we take our cases on the bus and the driver would drop us at the airport in time for our flight as she lived near to it. We had a good day in Gibraltar, had our brunch, a few drinks and duty free. Sure enough, after dropping everyone off in Benalmadena and Torremolinos, we got dropped at the airport and gave the driver a good tip as we would have had to get two taxis from our hotel if we had left from Torremolinos.

On 10 May 2012, Bert, Helen and me, her brother George and his partner Ellen all went back to Torremolinos staying all inclusive at the Hotel Puente Real to celebrate Helen's and my 65th birthday. While we were there, Bert's brother Thomas, his wife Irene, their daughter Liz and her husband with their kids were staying at the Hotel Bali in Benalmadena. On the day of my birthday, we took a bus through to Benalmadena and went to their hotel in the hope that they would be there. Luckily, they were all by the pool so we had a good day with them. During the day at our hotel they had various activities for adults and children. Bert, George and I went to the bow and arrow day. There was netting behind the target and one of my arrows went straight through it and into a field that had horses grazing. Now I tell people that I nearly shot a horse.

As I liked The Shadows since the early sixties and been on Charlie Hall & Friends forum for like minded fans, I found out that there was a gathering at Scarborough Rugby Club on the weekend beginning Friday 25 May 2012. Helen and I went along and I remember it was a long journey on the trains. Irvine to Glasgow Central, then Glasgow Queen Street to Edinburgh Waverley, then Waverley to York, and finally York to Scarborough. We stayed at The Tudor House near Peasholm Park. We went out on a pub crawl on the Friday night; saw a singer guitarist at one and a great young band at another. On the Saturday, we took a taxi to the Rugby Club as the day was to begin at 11am or mid day, I can't remember. There were many Shadow fans there and dozens of red Stratocaster guitars. It began with individuals going up to play using backing tracks. Every one was worse than the one before and a band would get up in between. A lot of mistakes were made, even with the bands. In the evening many of us went for a fish supper at a restaurant out of town and the food really was first class. On the Sunday Helen and I spent the morning at the seafront rather than go to the Rugby Club too early. The afternoon was much better than the previous day and someone loaned me a guitar to play Apache and Midnight. That evening we met up in a hotel near us and had a jam session. We left for the long journey home on the Monday morning.

The 12th North Ayrshire Open Art Exhibition ran from 7 July until 21 July 2012. Twenty one paintings were sold totalling £5,256. I had been co-ordinating this exhibition since 2001 and decided to resign after this show as it had grown so big over the years and I had started to make mistakes. It was time for someone new to inject some life into it. I still intended to help out with the setting up and hanging. After the following year's show which I had nothing to do with, someone complained about me. Unbelievable!

On Monday 30 July 2012 we took our family to Torremolinos for 8 nights staying at the Hotel Sol Timor. Bert, Helen and me, Tracey, Graeme and Zander, Pauline, Martin, Rosslyn and Helenna all went on the 30th. We flew from Prestwick to Malaga and had a minibus ordered to pick us up. Louise and partner Nic came on the 31st July. While I was booking all the flights with Ryanair on the Internet, when it came to paying with my credit card, it was blocked and my phone rang at the same time. It was my bank asking me what my last three transactions were. After getting everything cleared up

and going through the booking procedure again, it cost me another £200. The bank was looking after me but it came at a cost. One day while we were all by the pool Zander went missing. We all split up and searched all over the hotel grounds and throughout the hotel. There was a gate from the hotel to the promenade, so we became worried that he had went out of it. Eventually I spotted him lying on a sun bed, he had been watching us all the time. One day we all went out on a fishing trip from Benalmadena but Zander was the only one fishing. There was an Ice Bar at the marina and we all went there one evening. They supplied everyone with a warm cloak and cocktails were given to us in ice glasses. Another day was spent at the crocodile park, definitely a good experience. The park owner fed the crocodiles chickens by throwing them, and they fought to get them. He also walked over their backs. Bert, Zander and me all held a small crocodile that had its mouth taped. We also took the tourist train which travelled on the roads up to the bird park at Benalmadena. All of us except Louise and Nic spent a day at the Bioparc in Fuengirola. We returned home on Tuesday 7 August feeling good as it was great to have a holiday with all the family.

Frank and me did Hogmanay 2012 once again at Gairlochead Bowling Club and the second of January 2013 at the Lighthouse Alternative Hogmanay Party, Kilcreggan. This would be the third time we have done this gig at the Lighthouse. We returned to play The Anchor Gairlochead on Saturday 5 January.

It's holiday time once again! This time Bert, Helen and I went off to Salou for a week staying at the H Top Molinos Park Hotel at Cap Salou from 23 April 2013. The area was nearer to La Pineda than the centre of Salou. We flew from Prestwick to Reus and got a transfer bus. The hotel entrance was halfway up a hill and I pulled our cases to the reception. This was the first time I felt exhausted while doing that, and it was obviously due to my COPD. While we were there we went to the Gaudi Experience in Reus. I remember Bert being happy that Gaudi's father was a boilermaker. I really liked the hanging strings and weights upside down that represented the Sagrada Familia in Barcelona. There was a mirror on the floor that showed the reflection of the hangings as The Sagrada. It was a pleasant walk from our hotel to the centre of Salou and we did it many times. We went to the market in La Pineda one day and spent our evenings at the hotel entertainment.

Bert, Helen and I went to Benidorm on 7 August 2013 for a week staying at the Flash Hotel. Helen's brother Robert dropped us at

Prestwick Airport at 9am, we walked to the check in desk and I gave the girl my passport after putting my case up. She said, "Sorry sir your flight has just gone" and I laughed. . Sure enough, it had gone. Days before, I had booked flights to Malaga for Bert, Helen and I, Bert's brother Donnie and his partner Ellen, and Helen's cousin Joan and her husband Jim. Those flights were to be checked in at 9am. I never thought I could make a mistake like that. We were given the option to fly to Alicante the next day, or to take one to Murcia at 4pm. I decided on the second option, booked and paid for the flights, then phoned Helen's brother Robert to come back and pick us up and take us home for a few hours. When we arrived at Murcia Airport we got a taxi to Alicante intending to take the tram to Benidorm. When we arrived at Alicante tram station the last train for Benidorm was about to leave and we had to get tickets from a machine. With the help of staff, we managed to board just as it was leaving or it would have been another expensive taxi journey. Arriving at Benidorm station, we took a taxi to our hotel arriving around 9pm. The whole exercise cost £500 and we got to the hotel around eight hours later than we would if we had got our original flight. I thought Helen would be annoyed but she was impressed that we actually got there on the same day, only later. Helen's cousin Rosina and her husband Louie along with friends came to see us one day as they had been staying in a resort near Benidorm. Rosina noticed Uncle Bert lying at the pool with his socks and sandals on. My old school friend Frank Cusack and his wife Helen had moved from Algorfa to Ciudad Quesada, south of Alicante. He drove up to us one day and took us to his new house. He had friends over and we had acoustic guitars out for a session, stayed the night and he drove us back to Benidorm the next day.

Helen's brother George and his partner Ellen got married on Sunday 8 September 2013 and Frank and I played at the wedding reception at the Neptune Masonic lodge in Clifford Street. This was a second wedding for both of them.

We flew out to Torremolinos on 17 October 2013 and stayed at the Buensol Apartments. This was the group booking that caused me to miss my flight earlier in August. We picked a nice spot where we could all lie together and sunbathe. Helen and her cousin Joan were the only ones that dared to go in the pool. Jim and Joan's granddaughter and her boyfriend came to our apartments for a few days. We all booked a day trip to Gibraltar. We got breakfast across from our apartments at Mirage ran by Mick and Debbie before catching the bus. Jim and Joan did the taxi trip up the rock and Bert, Helen, Donnie, Ellen and me just did the walk from Grand Casemates Square up the Main Street looking in all the duty free shops until we got to the Angry Friar for something to eat and a couple of drinks before heading back to where the bus had dropped us off. The two young ones did their own thing and got charged far too much for everything as they were using Euros which shops would gladly take instead of British Pounds.

Sam Stellard and Bill Kerr invented a country called Swahovia and in 2013 I put it on a map in the Baltic between Poland and Denmark. They gave me information and I built a web site that was constantly updated. Bill was Sidimir Kovlovski, Minister for Tourism. Sam was Keur Stashaan Yabeesh, Mayor of Mauvia and I was Broshnak Malokov, the mad monk. We kept the website going for two years and a facebook page still exists.

Bert, Helen and I went to Benidorm on Friday 06 December 2013 staying at the Evamar Apartments. It was pretty chilly at that time of the year and we had an electric fire on most of the time. The kitchen of the apartment looked across the road to the outdoor market which was on every Sunday and Wednesday. On the Monday morning while making coffee, I looked across to the market and there were three wild boars obviously feeding on what was left behind, mammy, daddy and baby. Behind the market is waste ground so they were probably living there. It really was a surprise to see something like that in what is normally a busy Benidorm.

The three of us were off again to Torremolinos on 15 January 2014, again at the Buensol for four nights. It was cold this time but not as cold as Bonnie Scotland. It wasn't too bad through the day and the bars and restaurants had heaters. Fortunately they were only across the road from our apartments. The three of us went back to Benidorm's Acquarium II Apartments for a week on 23 April, returning home on Helen's birthday 30 April. I enjoyed spending time listening to live rock music at Heartbreak and Daytona Rock, both on the Promenade of Levante Beach near the old town. Bert liked going to watch a Rangers football game and Helen liked her bingo. In

Benidorm it is sometimes possible for us all to do the things we love at the same time. Our apartment was at a corner and we could look into the Sol Pelicanos pool where they filmed the television series "Benidorm". Unfortunately, they were not filming while we were there. Helen went back to Benidorm a couple of weeks later with her brother Robert's wife Rita, her cousins Marion and Betty Garty and some other girls, they stayed at the Hotel Pueblo. This would be the first time Helen went with them all but they had been doing that for years, and while they were away, Robert went fishing to Loch Awe with some friends.

I had made the mistake of booking Bert and I to go to Salou on 20 May 2014 for a week thinking that this was when Helen would be in Spain but I was wrong. Helen was home before we went. We stayed at the Hotel Santa Monica Playa, on a hill close to the town centre. We went to Tarragona one day and took the street train tour. It wasn't very good as it rained all day. We really spent most of the time at the hotel and watched the Champions League final between Real Madrid and Atletico Madrid on 24 May. You will have gathered that I have never had time for football, but there was a great atmosphere in the town that day especially after the game that Real beat Atletico 4 – 1. One of my friends from my time in the shipyard Andy Crowther and his wife Bev were in Salou at the same time so we met up one day for drinks.

I had booked for the three of us to go to Carcassonne on 5 June 2014 for three nights. Tracey said that she had planned us to look after Zander then as Graeme and her would both be working. She asked us if we would mind taking him, and of course we said yes, but booking was rather strange. I booked his flights, but as he was only nine at the time, I had to go to the Ryanair desk at Prestwick to link his booking to ours. We stayed at the Hotel Au Royal. It was the worst place we have ever stayed in, luckily it was only for three nights. There were two rooms and each had an en suite if you could call it that. Bert and Zander were in one room with Helen and me in the other. One time Bert was having a shower when he slipped and fell, what a noise! Helen rushed into their room to see her eighty nine year old dad naked, upside down with the water running into the room. He was fine but the three of us couldn't stop laughing. Carcassonne is a beautiful town with an impressive fortress. We walked there one day and spent hours behind its walls. We found out that there was a manmade beach near to the town of La Cavayere and could be accessed by a bus so we decided to go there. We bought a punnet of strawberries at the market in Carcassonne before boarding the bus. When we got round to eating them, I believed they were the best Strawberries I have ever tasted. The lake was lovely and the sun shone all day and Zander spent most of the time in the water, while we watched him play with other children. Carcassonne is a destination I would like to visit again.

On 24 July 2014 the three of us went to Malta with Tracey, Graeme and Zander and stayed for a week at the Hotel Diplomat in Sliema. . Our board was bed and breakfast and had a fridge in the rooms Tracey and Graeme's room was two floors above ours. One evening Helen was standing leaning over our Juliet Balcony when something whizzed past her head landing on a car below in the street. She could see that it was a bottle of water and was shouting that it had come from above. Later when we met with Tracey, Graeme and Zander, Helen was telling them about the hooligans above us. The hotel had a pool on the roof and Zander spent a lot of time jumping in and soaking all of us. Bert, Helen and me took a day trip to Gozo while Tracey Graeme and Zander went to a water park. A bus picked us up from outside the hotel and took us to the ferry terminal at Cirkewwa for the short crossing to Mgarr on Gozo. It was

a pleasant sail, passing Comino and the Blue Lagoon. At Mgarr we booked the open bus jump on jump off tour around the island. I had been advised by one of my friends Andy Irvine the best places to get off at and have a look round. The first was Marsalforn, passing the impressive Ramla beach on the way. Next was the Azure Window that would collapse in a storm in 2017. Most impressive was Xlendi where we had lunch by the bay watching divers from St Andrew's Diving Club swimming amongst all the mullet. I could understand why my friend had stayed there many times. Gozo is green and beautiful, while Malta is also beautiful but rusty in colour. One day Graeme and I went on our way to visit Valetta. Still in Sliema, we came across a small bar called Changes. A quaint little place with football scarves from all over the world and a really hospitable owner called Joe. We spent too much time drinking bacardi there before getting the ferry across to Valetta. It was a very steep hill from the ferry terminal to the Cathedral which was closed by the time we got there. We had a bite to eat, more bacardi and eventually got the ferry back to Sliema. So much for our cultural day out! On another day, we all caught the bus up to Bugibba and did the street train tour of Qawra, Bugibba and St Paul's Bay. We were impressed with this part of Malta and would hopefully return another time. Life is too

short and you should always make the effort to visit somewhere you that have never been before, or return to discover new places of interest! On the flight home, Tracey revealed that it was her that dropped the bottle from above us. She said that she was putting bottles in the fridge and some had rolled along the floor with one going straight out and down to the street just missing her mum. We all had a good laugh about it.

All three of us went to our favourite little beach in Can Pastilla Mallorca on 26 October 2014 staying at the Hotel BQ Anfora. The hotel faced onto the beach and the weather was fantastic for late October. We walked all the way along the promenade to Playa De Palma and Arenal, stopping now and again for refreshments. We returned to Can Pastilla by the street tourist train dropping us off

next to our hotel. The Secret Garden pub that Helen and I visited in 2004 had gone. It is always sad when you return to a place that you visited and it is no longer there. Such is life!

Once again Frank and me played Gairlochead Bowling Club on Hogmanay and the Alternative Hogmanay Party at the Lighthouse, Kilcreggan on 2 January 2015.

On Tuesday 10 February 2015, Helen found a lump on her right breast and made an appointment to see the doctor. The doctor referred her to Crosshouse hospital and she had a mammogram and biopsy in the morning of 6 March at Crosshouse Hospital. In the afternoon we were told that it was cancer. She had an appointment with consultant Mr. Osman and surgery was set for 31 March. Helen went for her pre op on Monday 16 March, saw the anesthetist on 23 March, and went for an MRI scan on 24 March. She saw Mr. Osman again on 27 to discuss the operation. Helen had already decided to have her right breast removed. She went in to hospital on the 31 March, had a mastectomy, and was collected by Tracey and me at 2'30pm on April 1st. Helen phoned me at 9am to say, "This isn't an April Fool, I am getting out today. What a woman! She came home with a drip in which was taken out on Wednesday 8 April. We had a meeting with another consultant Ms Elgammar on Friday 17 April and were told that the lump was 14mm, grade 2 and there was nothing in the lymph glands. Helen had more fluid drained on the 21 April.

Helen had intended to go to Benidorm again with eight other women including her sister in law Rita, but cancelled after what she had been through. She felt good at the beginning of May, and asked the doctor if it would be safe to go ahead and she confirmed that it would be okay to travel. Yours truly got on the net, booked her an outbound flight with Easyjet from Glasgow on 17 May and a transfer to the Hotel Pueblo. I managed to get her on the same return flight as the women with Ryanairto Prestwick. She would arrive hours before the women, so I suggested she should stay around the pool area until they arrived, then surprise them. Everyone was delighted to see her and they had a great time.

Helen's dad Bert was 90 on 21 May 2015, so we had a surprise party for him on Friday 29 at Lodge Neptune in Ibrox. He wanted a party and we were all saying that there was something on in the lodge on the 31st and instead we would all be go for a meal that day. We managed to surprise him on the night with all branches of the family in attendance, and a good time was had by all. Bert was in his element, and quite rightly so!

Thankfully, Helen got the all clear on Thursday 4 June.

316

Chapter 16

Our present to Bert was to take him to Malta for a week in June. We left from Prestwick Airport on 11 June, this time going to the Hotel Coral in Bugibba as we had liked the area on our previous visit. We noticed that Bert was really off his food, once only ordering rice and curry sauce when we were out for dinner. He really wasn't himself so after three days when we were ready to go out for dinner, I looked at him and said, "Bert, you need to see a doctor". He agreed with me, so I went to the reception and asked advice from the hotel manager. He phoned for a taxi to take us to a clinic in Mosta next to the Rotunda where a bomb had fallen into during the Second World War but didn't explode. When we went in, Bert was given a ticket, just like in Argos. We waited quite a while and having missed dinner, I went across the road and got two large slices of Pizza for me and Helen as Bert didn't want anything. I finished my slice then let Helen out to eat hers as I waited with Bert. Eventually all three of us went in to see the doctor who asked Bert what was wrong. His answer was, "Doctor I'm jiggered". The doctor looked at us with smiles on our faces and we explained to him that Bert was feeling exhausted and had been off his food. The doctor examined him and then sent him to another room for an x ray. After the x ray we went back into the doctor and there it was on the doctor's computer screen. He didn't like what he saw in Bert's chest and advised him to go to the hospital. The taxi driver who took us to Mosta gave us his number and told us to call him when we were out of the clinic. He came and picked us up, taking us to the hospital near Sliema. Once again we waited quite a while to be called. After Helen complained to reception, Bert's name was called and off we went again. He was treated very well, bloods taken, oxygen given, his heart checked, a really good once over. Following all that he was released and given his results to pass on to his own doctor back home and once again we phoned the same taxi driver. As soon as we got to our hotel, we poured three bacardi's.

This was in the early hours of the morning, but after all we had been through, especially Bert, well deserved! One evening while we were having a drink in the front of the hotel, we could hear what sounded like the noise from a football match. It turned out that not far away was Malta's home ground and they were playing that night. We didn't go very far from the hotel for the rest of the week.

Helen and I flew down to Bristol from Glasgow with Easyjet on Thursday 9 July 2015. We then got a bus from the airport to Bristol bus station and another bus to Cardiff. We were picked up by our niece Bryony, so as it was a lovely day sat outside a pub with our favourite pina coladas as we waited for her. It must have been graduation day in Cardiff as the city was full of graduates with their gowns on. When Bryony arrived we had another drink and then headed off for my sister's house in Glynogwr. We had a pleasant four days there with Chris, Mark and Bryony, and not forgetting little Harry the Jack Russell.

On Monday 20 July 2015 at 9am, my 64 year old sister Gladys phoned me to say that she was in the new Queen Elizabeth University Hospital (Southern General) in Govan and was having major surgery.

318

This was also Helenna's 7th Birthday and we went through to see her. I went to the hospital and I was told to return the following day as she had not returned from theatre. I got the 34 bus from outside the hospital to Battlefield and Helenna's house where Helen and Tracey were. Before going home to Irvine we returned to the hospital and were turned away again as they said she was in intensive care. The following day my brother in law Robert took Helen and I to the hospital. My cousins Irene Tees and Patricia Dixon met us there. This time we got in to see her and she was all wired up. The two surgeons that operated on her came to speak to us along with others. They said that she may not recover from the operation. I felt her stone cold legs and I was sure she was already gone. We went home and I got a call after midnight telling me to come as Gladys was not going to last the night. Robert ran us there. I had phoned Irene who phoned Patricia and her husband Eddie and they all came with Irene's husband Billy. They switched the equipment off bit by bit until Gladys passed at 4am on Wednesday 22 July 2015. We went home and returned later with Tracey to collect the death certificate. The person we met with asked if we were having a cremation so wouldn't require a post mortem done. We got the certificate and Gladys was cremated on Friday 31 July 2015, thereafter to the Crookston Hotel. We all thought that something not right went on with Gladys' death. She did not want to tell us she had been so unwell because of what Helen had been going through since early March.

EULAGY written by Pauline Collins and Martin Tierney 2015.

Gladys Ann was born in 64 Braidcraft Road in Pollok on 28 January 1951, the first daughter of James Collins and Gladys Bremner. Gladys attended Damshot Crescent and Braidcraft Primary followed by Lourdes Secondary. She was Jim's baby sister and three years later would have a younger brother Fred followed by baby Christine. The family lived in her mother's parents' house in Pollok with her Aunt Peggy too. Peggy was a kind, warm hearted woman who was great with children, always taking them on days out and giving them treats when their mother was busy running the household. Peggy remained with the family till the end of her days. Gladys' cousin Irene, born only 11 days after Gladys, would become a lifelong friend, even to the last where Gladys, embracing new fangled technology, would text Irene regularly to keep her up to date with any news – and indeed gossip. Gladys' dad James had settled in Glasgow from Ireland. They would occasionally return to Ireland with the family in the summer to Newton Cunningham and have immense fun there. The house in Braidcraft Road was always full of life and bustle; Gladys enjoyed helping her father in the garden where he grew vegetables, keeping the garden pristine. Gladys laboured passionately in the garden and proudly displayed her immaculate beds and borders. Always shy, on leaving Lourdes secondary, Gladys was advised to work in jobs where she would meet a lot of people. This took her into the thriving textile industry at that time and she was soon found work and an outlet for what would prove to be a considerable talent, at Cohen's textile factory in Pollokshaws where she learned to make garments. Her skills were soon recognised as her precision and her attention to detail in sewing soon gave her the opportunity to find more challenging, specialised work. She began working for a well known fashion designer at that time, Marion Donaldson, where she became really good at creating exquisite dresses. She often wore these Liberty inspired patterns herself. For many years she had an amazing array of dresses in a variety of styles and patterns. She was probably the only woman in Pollok parading around in limited edition 'Designer' dresses, long before the concept became an obsession that it is today. Naturally this would raise a few eyebrows and it wasn't long before her friends began to ask Gladys to make them clothing and allow them to join this very exclusive club. Indeed she was so skilled that many of her very young nieces were soon sporting miniature versions of these rare colourful dresses as they caroused around the earthy streets and lanes of Pinmore Street in Nitshill. It didn't stop there. The nieces' dolls were similarly elegantly outfitted. Those dolls tea parties must have been a sight to behold. This provided a nice little income stream for Gladys and no small amount of pride and would eventually lead to many commissions to make wedding dresses. You can be pretty sure her attention to detail combined with her nimble skills must have made many brides and bridesmaids happy. Before Gladys' father died he asked her to look after her mother. She continued to work in the textile industry in addition to the selfless task of caring for her mother whose eyesight and mobility were becoming increasingly diminished. In 1988 she met Roy Patterson who she fell in love with and married soon afterwards. Gladys and Roy travelled to America where Gladys had a wonderful time. Roy introduced Gladys to the Spiritualist church which they regularly attended and they also participated in the social life that the church provided. Gladys always spoke fondly of the time she spent with Roy who sadly passed away in 1990. Gladys' mum moved to Darnley court Nursing Home. When a job came up Gladys applied and became the activities coordinator in the home. Using her driving skills she took people on days out and organised events. This was a welcome change for Gladys who enjoyed working many years at the home. In her youth Gladys often visited the Inner Hebrides and it was a passion she would sustain in her regular journeys that would see her travel the length and breadth of Scotland. Mull in particular was a great favourite where she would have holidays on the Isle of Iona. Here she began her love of photography. She would always have a camera and would often get the family huddled together to snap the moment. Her photograph albums chronicled her life. Gladys like a good blether and... Indeed... a wee whisky. She enjoyed travelling to visit friends who had moved away as well as her family who had moved from Glasgow. More recently Gladys spent her free time in Luce Bay with friends enjoying the wood burner collecting wood on the beach and relaxing. She was part of the Pollok History group, went to her exercise class and knitted blankets for the dog and cat home. She was content with her own company in her retirement and became something of 'a lady who lunched' although she was never one for Spartan portions and liked nothing better than getting tucked in to a hearty lunch, even though it didn't show as she remained lean most of her days. Following a recent illness, she died peacefully in the Southern General hospital after a difficult final few days.

On 3 August 2015 Helen and I went to Fort William with our friends Bill and Jill Kerr. By now, they both had their bus passes so we got there and back for nothing except for the seat reservations that were only £1 a journey each. I had asked Bill if they had ever been to the Drovers Inn at Inverarnan, just north of Loch Lomond. They hadn't, so I booked us to be dropped there on our return where we could have lunch and get the next bus two hours later. We stayed at Fasnahuille BB in Fort William. After settling in, we sat outside with a couple of drams before going out for dinner in town. We had

booked the steam train journey to Mallaig for the next day so did not stay up late. Bill and I had a couple of hip flasks each for the journey and Jill was ready with her camera. Helen had her cargo of bacardi and coke. What a brilliant journey passing Ben Nevis as you leave Fort William, Loch Eil, stopping at Glenfinnan Station, then over the Glenfinnan Viaduct, Arisaig, and finally Mallaig. A highly

recommended journey! We had a bite to eat in Mallaig and got back on the train for the return trip to Fort William. Helen and I went into Morrison's Supermarket for another bottle of Jura for me and Bill, and flowers and chocolates for our hosts at the B&B while Bill and Jill waited at the taxi rank. We joined them leaving our messages on the ground while we waited for a taxi. When we got to the B&B, as we were getting out of the taxi, I asked Helen if she had the Jura. She thought I had picked it up and I thought she had, so some lucky person enjoyed our whisky. . We got the bus for Inverarnan and the Drovers the next day. The Drovers Inn is a unique Inn that was used

by the Highland drovers while taking their cattle to the lowland markets. It is mainly used now by walkers doing the West Highland Way. On entering, you are met with a stuffed grizzly bear and an assortment of other animals. It is also supposed to be haunted. Anyway, I had my long awaited venison for lunch and a couple of drams. Then we were back on the bus to Glasgow, and then Glasgow to Irvine. Another fine trip with our friends! Helen went to Benidorm in September with the girls.

Bert, Helen and I went back to Can Pastilla, Mallorca on 28 October that was our 48th Anniversary. We stayed in Embat Apartments at our favourite beach Cala Estancia. One day we took the bus into Palma getting off at the Placa De Espana. From there we took the Ferrocarril train to Soller in the mountains, then the tram down to the Port De Soller. What a beautiful place it is. We spent a bit of time at the port and then went back to the town. By this time it was late afternoon and Bert just wanted to sit inside a café as he was cold. We got the train back to Palma and the bus from Placa De Espana to Can Pastilla. We went into a restaurant to have dinner and my wallet was gone. I think it was taken from my pocket as we were getting on the bus in Palma, our food kitty, two hundred Euros was gone. I remember when we were leaving the airport we were the last Ryanair flight to leave the island until 2016.

The three of us were supposed to go to Torremolinos on Monday December 14th 2015. Helen and I came back from our old neighbour Cathie McAree's funeral on Thursday 10 December and Bert was sitting with a housecoat on, something he never did. Our sister in law Catherine said, "look how fat his legs are". His legs were like tree trunks so Robert and Helen took him round to the doctor's surgery immediately. He saw Doctor Campbell who gave him water tablets, telling him it was fine to fly on Sunday. On the Friday his legs were no better and after calling the surgery got a call back from doctor Black who said to give him 2 tablets on Saturday, Sunday and Monday and it should be okay to fly, "But I have not seen him"! On the

Saturday, our granddaughter who is a nurse advised us, "Don't go". On the Sunday we asked one of our neighbours in to see him and she said that he shouldn't fly. She is an occupational therapist, so we didn't go! On the Monday doctor Alexander came to see Bert and said that he needed to go to hospital. We took him at 3.50pm and he was admitted to assessment ward 3E at Crosshouse Hospital. The following day he was in ward 2D. We visited every day or night and as the days went on, his hands and legs were weeping. He got a biopsy on his liver on Wednesday 23 December and we got him home from 10am until 6.30pm on Christmas Day. Helen had got him his favourite whiting fish fried in breadcrumbs but he hardly touched it. We brought him home for the Rangers Hibs game on Monday 28 December as he had been looking forward to this match. Rangers won 4 – 2 and he was delighted. we took him back to the hospital that day. Next day he wasn't good, and on the following day, we were told to come to the hospital and speak to the palliative care nurse. Helen and I, her brothers Jim, Robert and Raymond all went to be told that the biopsy results showed liver cancer that had possibly came from the mole he had on his forehead a couple of years before. Robert and Helen went in with the nurse to assess Bert. She asked him if he would rather be in hospital or home. His reply was, "Hame"!

Frank and I played at Garfields, Ardrossan on Hogmanay. Not a pleasant time for me to be celebrating, but I was happy that it wasn't too far away. We were sent for on Sunday 3 January 2016 at 11.30am. We all went to the hospital and Helen said to me that I should go to Glasgow and meet my Five Interns friends Andy and Johnny as we were to meet in the Crystal Palace Glasgow at 2pm. I got the bus into Kilmarnock and then the Glasgow bus, had just a couple of drinks with them and returned to the hospital. Helen and I went for dinner at the hospital canteen knowing it would be our last opportunity for food. Helen and I, Robert, George and Jim were at Bert's bedside until he passed at 4.50am on Monday the fourth of January 2016. The man was a legend! Bert's funeral was on Thursday

14 January at Holmsford Bridge Crematorium, thereafter to Towerlands Sports Club, Irvine. The following Eulogy was written by our son in law Martin Tierney

BERTIE

Some knew Robert Morrison as Bert or Bertie. Some knew him as Burlington Bertie. Others called him Bertie Bassett or Bertie Rajah. His family called him Uncle Bertie, Granda Bertie, Dad or simply - Da'. Few can boast so many names but few squeezed so much from life. Fewer still, have been as respected or indeed loved, by so many. The turnout here is clear testimony to that.

CAMPS AND CARAVANS

As we all know Bert was a great believer in the active life and as a young man with a young family they were always on the go getting into the countryside travelling Scotland as often as possible. Bert and his brothers built a hut in Carbeth and the family, along with their cousins, spent all their free time playing in the open air. Camper vans followed. Bert being Bert built an interior of a van to allow him to drive people to work but at weekends it would convert to a camper. Over the years there were caravans from east to west and the clan would fish, dive, pick mussels and sail in boats. Soup and all sorts of fish would be cooked and consumed with Bert showing off his culinary skills. If you ever took a trip with Bert and Nellie to whichever caravan Bert would inform you "I just need to go in and see......" It could be a long drive. He had always wished to visit his long time family friend Andy who had emigrated to Australia decades before - he finally managed it - THREE TIMES. Robert accompanied him on the first trip where Robert even won a motorbike that was typically donated back to charity. Bertie could have built his own anyway. Wee Porgie - Wee brother George - went on the second and for the third trip, George had won their fare in a competition. You can picture this pair of mischievous tikes, battering about Oz, talking Glaswegian, asking the locals if they had any 'hingwys'...

JIM AND HELEN MOVE IN

After Nellie's sad passing in the Spring of 1989 Jim and Helen moved into Fintry Terrace with Helen running the home, Jim painting, playing in the band, adding to his guitar collection. Meanwhile Bert would be building – sometimes in the living room.

SPAIN

For years the three of them would go on regular trips to Spain. The heat did Bert the world of good invigorating him and he would get to meet new people. One time they all went to Barcelona, Bert, Big Jim and their great friend Jeff. As anyone who has travelled outside the sea resorts will know, where English is widely spoken, it's not the same in the cities. With a day's solid drinking achieved the chaps realised it was time to catch the last train. Train stations are confusion at the best of times, so you can envisage a slightly panicked group of inebriated Scottish guys. It's not the best way to read a Spanish Timetable. Fortunately Big Jim had just sat a module in Spanish at Kilmarnock College and he made a valiant attempt to find the correct platform. His happiness at communicating with the locals was short lived as he turned to see the doors of the wrong train closing, wee Bertie and Jeff planked firmly on a seat inside, the train slowly moving off, Jim narrowly pulling his ponytail from the closing doors. They got a costly Taxi back but not before being thrown out of the first Taxi where Bertie, who hadn't done a module at Kilmarnock College, found that flapping his arms like a fevered chicken, shouting 'no aeroporto, no aeroporto, no aeroporto' was not the best way to convey unwillingness to be driven to the airport by a driver whose Glaswegian was worse than Bert's Spanish.

FAMILY CLOSENESS

Bert's family lived close by, indeed Fintry Terrace is known as Morrison Avenue, making it easy for the family to keep Bert active and, in turn, for him to motivate them. George would pop in to tell his Da the latest intrigues. Jim would come along with his many ideas, usually involving a boat. Robert visited every day with one of his many wonderful jokes. And Raymond would make daily trips with wood supplying Bertie with enough wood to build the new 'Bertie Sark'....That's one of Roberts by the way. It was a very busy house.

DIFFERENCES OF OPINION

Helen and Bert frequently had differing views, such as falling rust from boat propellers not being the best match for a cream coloured, newly laid carpet. They would regularly disagree and try and explain their differing world views. Not being one to give in Bert had to make his point. He would do so; using very colourful, rhythmic language that was so descriptive he seldom failed to communicate his views. Helen was also an expert in colourful, rhythmic language. Nobody knew where she got that talent from. But surely that honesty is the sinew of an open, healthy family, one like Bert Morrison's – one that sees things differently but never uses petty spitefulness to score points or gain advantage. He had a special relationship with all his family each person knowing him well; he gave his time generously to all, always asking "What's new"?

BERT AND ATTITUDE TO WORK

Bert believed in a barter system, you find the screws, wood, metal, even better if it was from someone who knew someone. There was no clearer example of this than when Bert would do little jobs for his pal Peter, who owned an Indian takeaway on the Paisley road. 10 Biryanis was better than a tenner.

LIVING TO 90

Bert never complained about his aches or his pains. He just shrugged his shoulders, smiled, stuck his thumbs in the air and said "sticking out" - usually followed by 'have ye seen ma' hingwy?' at which point you would be flinging mental cartwheels in your head trying to figure out if he was asking for a crank; a spanner, a piece of piping -30mm diameter, - or a bit of 2" by 2". Or was it 4" by 2"? Each day he would perform his stretching exercises – Patented and rubber stamped in Govan, like so much of what he brought to the world. After this he would focus on what he would make that day, every day. He liked pipes and metal but was able to turn his hand to just about anything, woodwork, plumbing, laying floors or hanging doors. Indeed if it had been Bertie stranded on that island instead of Robinson Crusoe, and the boat came by 5 years later, they would have found Bertie on a beach with a wee home distilled whisky and coke brewed from palm trees and crushed pineapples. He would have been lying there resplendent in his cut off chinos, black socks curling round his ankles, a knotted hankie on his head - and an entire city built out of seashells. The generosity of the time he gave to help his family and larger family of close-knit friends is astonishing. No one ever really thought the day Bert slowed down and hung up his overalls would come.

Legacy

Bert and Nellie's legacy is immense. They have left behind a clan who help, care and depend on one another. Their lust for life and laughter is continued in how they live their lives through their own families. On the days after Bert's death, amongst tears, the sound of laugher could be heard as the family reminisced about childhood, their youth into adulthood. Their parents always central to the stories. Bert never wanted to be remembered as an old man, he rejected his hearing aid, walking stick and wheelchair as something only 'old' people do.

BERT MORRISON – A LEGEND!!

Alas even legends have to say 'Maj Salaami Effendi.'

Eulogy written by Martin Tierney in 2016. Thank you Martin!

Being at the front in the crematorium, I didn't realise the number of people that were there, but back at the club, it was absolutely packed. I had never seen so many people in the club. Bert certainly had a good send off, and will be missed by many!

Berty Morrison 1925-2016

Wreath from Rangers Football Club

Chapter 17

I spent a lot of time dealing with Gladys' estate in 2015. I cleared the house, had it painted and then sold it. Fortunately she had made her will with me as executor and Tracey, Pauline, my sister Chis's son Jonathan and daughter Bryony were beneficiaries. After the house at Braidcraft Road Pollok was sold, the family was paid out early January 2016. Tracey and Pauline gave us money and I had already taken a sum out of our savings for the holiday fund so we had a healthy amount to enjoy, and we certainly did! Helen and I had fourteen holidays in 2016. The first trip was to Maspalomas in Gran Canaria on 27 January for a week where we stayed at the Oasis Playa Apartments near the beach and sand dunes.

We had never been to Dublin so we went for three nights at the end of February staying at the Arlington Hotel by the river Liffey. It was absolutely Baltic while we were there so we dined in the hotel as they had a show on every night consisting of Irish dancers and a singer. We spent time in the bars in Temple Bar, going there over the famous Ha'penny Bridge. There were a couple of old guys in one of the bars who were playing traditional Irish songs. When they had a break, one of them had some grapes and a cup of tea, changed days I bet! We went into the pub called Temple Bar and I spoke to the owner about whiskey. I said that I found Jameson's too sweet, and asked him if there were any peaty Irish malt whiskeys. He recommended Connemara and I managed to get a bottle at the airport to bring home. Nearly all of the holidays I booked were between Sunday and Friday so they did not affect my gigs with Frank.

On Thursday 10 March 2016, I opened Ronald A. Smart's Exhibition at Irvine's Harbour Arts Centre. Ron is a local artist and has been a friend since I moved to Irvine in 1989.

We went to Haggerston Castle with our daughters and grandchildren in April during the school break. We were only a couple of days back when we returned to Bugibba, Malta for a week with Tracey, Graeme and Zander. Our next trip was to Villamoura, Portugal for a week in June. We were going to Albufeira in December so we thought we would check out the hotel we were going to. So we went to the centre of Albufiera where we boarded the tourist train from there to the old town where we would be staying. The Hotel Rocamar looked great, sitting on a cliff overlooking the beach with the old town downhill at beach level. There was plenty going on and some entertainment in the evenings. So then we had something to look forward to in December.

On 4 July we did another David Urquhart bus trip to Torquay with Helen's brother Robert and his wife Rita along with her cousin Joan and her husband Jim Moody. We stayed at the Ashley Court Hotel which was on a hill. Fortunately, there was a car park with a lift next to the hotel which took you down to the main streets where all the shops were. We were also not far from the Marina. It was a long journey from Irvine to Torquay so we had all made our minds up that we were not doing any of the organised tours. There was a swimming pool in the hotel so after breakfast and a walk into town; we sat by the pool and ordered sandwiches and tea from the hotel kitchen. It

335

was always quiet as everyone else was away on their day trip. We had a ride on the big wheel down at the Marina one day and had great views of Torquay and the Marina. We did our own day trip to the quaint harbour town of Brixham. There is a replica of the Golden Hind in the harbour and not far from it, a statue of John Knox. I asked the management to get some single malt whisky for the bar or we would be drinking out at night. He asked me my preferred brands and got two bottles in. Now that was sorted, most nights were spent in the hotel as they had entertainment. We went out one night to a bar at the marina which had a band on. We had a great time but the journey home on Friday 8 July was a nightmare with all the traffic jams. If we went to go down to the south coast again it would never be by a bus or car.

My painting from the window of 153 Crossloan Road, Govan, 1971.

Our friends Bill and Jill Kerr had booked a cottage on the Isle of Mull for a week in July 2016. They invited us to stay for any number of days we wished, so we got the bus to Oban and the ferry

across to Mull on Monday 18 July. Bill and Jill met us at Craignure ferry terminal. . The weather wasn't too good all the way up and a bit drizzly on the sea crossing, but as we neared Craignure the clouds broke and the sun was splitting the sky as we pulled into the pier. Bill and Jill were patiently waiting for us, and laughed when telling us that it had been raining all day until we arrived. Every holiday they have had in the UK, they have had great weather and we call it "Kerr Weather". We got in the car and Bill drove us up to Tobermory where we went to a restaurant next to the distillery for dinner. Bill then drove us up the hill behind all the brightly coloured houses where we had an excellent view of Tobermory Bay. I remember there was a cruise ship moored out in the water. We left there and headed for their cottage at Benmore. Bridge Cottage is situated by a bridge over the River Ba, with the mountains on one side and surrounded by forest. We had a few more drams that night with good company. The next day Bill and Jill had planned a cracking drive round the Island. We left the cottage at Benmore Estate, through Gruline, Kellan, skirting the north shore of Loch Na Keal. At Acharonich we could see Iona in the distance, then onward up the west coast to beautiful Calgary Bay where we stopped for a while and had an ice cream on a wonderful sunny day. We carried on to Dervaig, Achnacraig, Salen, and back to Benmore. That evening while we were having refreshments, Helen was looking through binoculars after I mentioned that there were deer on a ridge at the top. Bill said to me quietly, "Photo". Then he said, quietly again, "Nudists". Immediately, I

created a post on Facebook with the photo of Helen looking through the binoculars with the comment, "Helen is looking out for nudists". We were leaving early afternoon on Wednesday 20 July, so Bill took us on another run. This time we took the south shore road of Loch Na Keal to Dhiseig, round  to Balnahard, turning inland until we got to Loch Scridain, then onward to Loch Beg passing through Craignure. I remember us going through the clouds on that stretch of the road. Bill got us to the ferry just in time for our departure. The sailing to Oban was foggy all the way; it was eerie with the shop's foghorn blowing away every now and then.

On Sunday 21 August 2016 Helen and I went to Riga in Latvia for four nights. When I told her where we were going, she wasn't pleased but it was a beautiful city and we had a good time. We stayed at the Hotel Victorija on Aleksandra Caka Iela. The room was fine, but we had no view from the window as the outside of the building was

being shot blasted at the time and netting obscured any view. It was situated fifteen minutes walk from the city centre and railway station, and there were plenty of places to eat nearby. The old city has beautiful buildings such as The House of the Black Heads, St Peter's Church, Riga Cathedral and Riga Castle. The Freedom Monument is impressive, opened in 1935 to honour soldiers killed in the Latvian War of Independence. We spent an evening in this area, had dinner and then went to a bar with a band on. We went for dinner one night at a shisha bar next to our hotel. On another day, we took the train to the coastal resort of Jurmala and I dipped my feet into the Baltic Sea. Just as well it was August!

We had a great adventure going to Spain on 20 September. I had planned this trip at the beginning of the year. We flew to Malaga and got the train into the city of Malaga. We stayed at the Hotel Don Paco which was near Maria Zambrano train station where we would leave the next morning for Ronda in the mountains. Next Morning we had breakfast and headed for Maria Zambrano Station and were surprised that we had to put our bags through a scanner just like the airport. We got a train to Santa Ana and had to wait an hour or so for a connection to Ronda. Our Hotel Colon in Ronda was about a mile from the station. It was downhill so we just walked. The hotel was recommended to us by our friend Jill Kerr who had stayed there. We arrived early afternoon, checked in and headed out to explore the destination I had wanted to visit for the past few years. Five minutes walk from the hotel there was a sensational view of the surrounding countryside and mountains as we were looking from a cliff top at Alameda Del Tajo. We walked along the cliff until we came to the

viewpoint, Mirador De Ronda and then went on to the historic bridge, Puente Nuevo. We then had a walk round the town and found a guitar museum. The owner was also an accomplished flamenco guitarist and did concerts there some evenings, so we booked for that evening. The guy was a great player and gave us a history of flamenco and we were enjoyed a free glass of wine. The following morning I was up early and took a walk to the bottom of the gorge and found Puente Viejo, the old bridge. There is a superb view of the countryside from there. I came back up the gorge and followed the steps and gardens of Jardines De Cuenca De La Mina. I took loads of photographs to take back to the hotel for Helen, saving her a lot of energy. I was shattered and this was before breakfast. The hotel was run by two sisters. They were both lovely and very helpful. They made our breakfast and we had a blether with them after we finished. There was a mural on the wall of the Santa Maria and the writing, Cristobal Colon. (Christopher Columbus). I tried to book the dinner and flamenco show at El Quinque but it was full that night. We just wandered around the town for a while and took in the atmosphere, went for a nap, and then out again to find a nice restaurant for dinner. The following morning, we left after breakfast. We strolled at leisure up the hill to Ronda train station and caught the Madrid train to Algeciras. It was one of Michael Portillo's train journeys that I had seen on television. The scenery was wonderful as we sped through the Andalucían countryside ending at Algeciras train station. We went to La Linea de la Conception on the bus which left from across the road from the train station. We stayed two nights at the Hotel Asur Campo de Gibraltar which wasn't far from La Linea bus station. The room they gave us had a great view of the Rock of Gibraltar. We got out what we thought we would need for our short stay from our bag, and headed to Gibraltar which was about a twenty minute walk from the hotel. There is something special about Gibraltar, just like being in the UK but with sunshine. We had only seen the Main Street and duty free shops on previous visits, so now we would see more. We had lunch outside an Irish pub on the Main Street, got our Duty Free Bowmore single malt whisky and bacardi, plus cigarettes for Helen. We then went to the Ocean Village Marina for cocktails and headed back to our hotel where we remained that night. Next day we had breakfast in the hotel and headed once again to the Rock. After we went through customs, there was a tour agent, so we booked a minibus tour of the rock. We had to wait until enough people booked to fill the bus. Eventually we left and headed for Europa point where we could see Morocco quite clearly. Then up the rock to Saint Michael's Cave where we saw the wonderfully lit stalactites and stalagmites. We kept climbing up to the monkey feeding station. I don't know who was scared the most when I took a photo of Helen with them. Further up again, we visited the World War II tunnel. From the entrance, you go down a fair distance with only a limited amount of time given so we didn't go too far in.

Through holes in the rock, you could see the airport runway. At

various points there were mannequins dressed in military uniforms. There was what looked like a prison cell. Helen went to investigate and a voice shouted, "Who goes there"? You could hear her scream echoing throughout the tunnel. This was the last part of the tour, so we got on the bus and got dropped off near the Ocean Village. Once again we had cocktails. I had a knickerbocker glory and Helen had chicken drumsticks. We didn't want to eat too much as we had planned for friends Eileen and Russell Dick to visit our hotel and then go out for dinner in La Linea. We took a bottle of Big Peat and

Smokey Joe blended malt whiskies through this time. We had never

met Eileen and Russ before. Eileen was a friend of mine on Facebook through musician's pages. Eileen was from London and Russ from Scotland. At one time they were a duo living in Carluke. Eileen's father was Spanish and they have been living in Spain for many years. Like us, they have two daughters who live near them. They also have a son who lives in Seattle. They came along in the evening and we had a drink at the hotel. They drove us to an Indian restaurant on the Mediterranean side of La Linea. We had a lovely meal and catch up. Russ knew some musicians I knew from the sixties in Glasgow. On Sunday 25 September, we left La Linea by bus and headed for Torremolinos, staying this time at Hotel Los Jazmines at Playa Bajondillo. It was close to the beach and there was an Irish bar next to the hotel. There was also a complex nearby which had some restaurants and a bar with entertainment. We spent five relaxing nights here and headed home on Friday 30 September.

Another short trip was to Rome on Tuesday 25 October for four nights. It was another destination I have always wanted to visit. I had booked to fly from Prestwick to Ciampino Airport, but on the dates booked they intended to work on the runway, so it was changed to Rome Fiumicino which was a lot further from the city

than Ciampino. I managed to get a private taxi booked for a reasonable price considering the distance. We got to the Hotel Pratinn Vatican in the evening and a short walk from there took us to the Vatican. It is very impressive when lit up at night and we discovered that the Pope would be coming out the following day. I booked a two day city tour bus, plus a Vatican tour and picked the tickets up from an office just outside Piazza San Pietro on the Wednesday. We walked to St Peter's Square that Wednesday morning and sure enough, the Pope was in the Popemobile going through the enormous crowds that were gathered. We collected the bus tickets and Vatican City fast track tour tickets and as it was raining, we decided to do the Vatican Museums that day. We met in a small bar at Viale Vaticano, on the hill across from the entrance to the museums. A small group of us were gathered, registered and tickets taken so that we would not have to queue. Once we were through security, we were on our own to discover the huge collections of artwork. We went through some of the museums and took a tour of the gardens. Because it was raining, it was hard to see out of the plastic windows on the normally open minibus. We went back in and

eventually came to the Sistine Chapel and Michelangelo's famous ceiling. This was the only place you were not allowed to take photos. It was very impressive, but so was the work in the other museums. After the Sistine, we came out and went through a separate entrance to St Peter's Basilica. It is an amazing place, and so rich in history. We went for a bite to eat near the River Tiber and afterwards got the Tour Bus all the way round the city taking note of stops we would take on the second day of our tickets. In the evening after dinner in a restaurant on Via Andrea Doria, we found a small bar to have a couple of drinks. The rain was really pouring down when we were leaving and they gave us a large golf umbrella to help keep us dry. On Thursday 27 October we took the tour bus to the Colosseum.

It was a glorious day and even though we had fast track tickets, there were so many people that it seemed to take an eternity before we actually got in. They were a bad lot the Romans! I hadn't realised that as well as having the gladiatoral contests and executions, they could also flood the place and have mock sea battles. I am so glad that I managed to pay the place a visit as it was one of the most impressive buildings I had ever been in. We spent quite a bit of time in the Colosseum so when we crossed over to the Roman Forum, we decided that it was too much to see in one day. We travelled on the tour bus to the bus station to find out where the bus stop was for our return transfer to the airport. We then had lunch in a small Trattoria. We got back on a tour bus and got off at The Altar of the Fatherland (The Vittoriano) which I noticed on the previous day's tour. This monument was built from 1885 and opened in 1911 in honour of Victor Emmanuel II, the first king of a unified Italy. It incorporates the shrine of the Italian Unknown Soldier. It is a really impressive piece of architecture and on the inside it houses various museums, one of which is military. We took the metro from there to the Spanish Steps and then on to the Trevi Fountain but we didn't stay long as there were too many people. We walked from there to the Pantheon, went inside and saw artist Raphael's tomb. We then sat and had a glass of wine while enjoying the buskers in the sun. We returned to the Hotel for a shower and short nap. I was lying on top of the bed and Helen was sitting on a chair putting on her makeup when we felt the building shake, evidently there was an earthquake in Perugia and it was felt in Rome. We went for dinner and returned to the bar where we were on the previous night to return the umbrella. They were very appreciative that we came back with it as they didn't expect us to return it. After a drink it started to get very busy with families and lots of children. It was for a kid's birthday party and we thought we should leave, but we were told to stay and had a lovely night with such nice people. On the Friday we went to the cylindrical Castel Sant'Angelo, on the banks of the Tiber and within walking distance of our hotel. We spent a couple of pleasant hours there and afterwards while walking around, came across Piazza del Popolo which looked as if it was intending to have a concert of some sorts. It was a lovely day so we went for lunch nearby returning to a square which was gradually getting much busier than before. It was some sort of political demonstration. There were speeches and music all afternoon. There was a Leonardo da Vinci exhibition in a museum off the square, so we went in there for a break. So that was Rome, time for home and our own bed on Saturday the twenty ninth of October.

A musician friend of mine, Jimmy Campbell told me of a meeting of musicians from the sixties and seventies organised by musician David McCallum who lived in Troon at that time. I contacted David and as the meeting was in Lime Deli East Kilbride on Friday 11 November 2016, he said that he would pick me up and take me there.

I can't remember exactly who was there. I think it was Tommy Gordon, Charlie Sands, John Williams, David and I. It was great talking about some of our adventures on the road back in the day. David called it CTF, Chewing The Fat. Seemingly, David and Tommy's friend, keyboard player Charlie Taylor had the vision that it would be great to get all the musicians together to talk about their experiences of playing music in the sixties and seventies. For me, that day was to be the beginnings of something huge.

On Wednesday 7 December 2016 we went to the Hotel Rocamar in Albufeira for a week through Mercury Holidays. When I booked this in January, it was for a week in Sri Lanka, but I chickened out when I found out that the area we were going to had an outbreak of dengue fever, a mosquito borne disease. Mosquitoes like me a bit too much so I changed the booking to Portugal. We had a nice room but not a sea view this time. The hotel was situated on a cliff, and there was an elevator down to the beach just two minutes walk from the hotel. My friend Jacqui Cunningham's mum and her partner John were going to Albufeira at the same time as us. They were staying at the Hotel Sol E Mar, five minutes walk from us.

We had never met Jacqui's mum Babs so made arrangements to meet up with them. They had been there many times and knew the best places to go in the evenings. We had a couple of pleasant nights out with them in the old town bars. Helen and I took a bus trip to Silves and Monchique. First stop was the delightful town of Silves which was once the ancient capital of the Algarve. We visited the castle and cathedral, and were able to spend a little time in the local food market. We went on into the mountains at Monchique and onwards to the highest point in the Algarve, Foia. There were some great panoramic views from there and we bought delicious honey from the shop at the top. We stopped off for lunch at a restaurant somewhere in the countryside. If you don't write it down, it's gone! We carried on to Portimao and back to Albufeira. One thing we noticed was stork nests on the roofs in Silves and on the top of lamp posts in other places. One afternoon we had left our hotel and gone down the steps to the old town at the tunnel to the beach. At the bottom of the steps is a shop with souvenirs outside it. I was in front of Helen when I heard her shout, "Isobel". It was Helen's childhood friend and her daughter. Isobel McNaughton and Helen had gone about together at Kintra Street in Govan when they were children. Since we were next to the tunnel we went through to the beach and had a few drinks and a catch up at a hotel bar. They really were delighted to see each other and it is fortunate that we went down the steps, as we normally took the street route down to the old town and they would have completely missed each other. They were staying at the other end of Albufeira and we never saw them again. We had some good nights at Sir Harry's Bar at the square in the old town. I was in the infinity pool at our hotel just over a week before Christmas. The weather had been great all week, wonderful for that time of year.

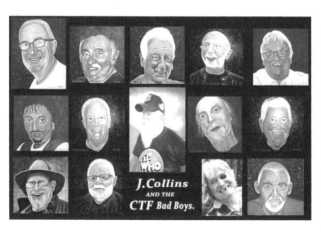

David McCallum picked me up for the next CTF meeting in Lime Deli East Kilbride on Friday 16 December. Frank and I played at Polmont Bowling Club on Hogmanay. We had only done a total of twenty four gigs in 2016.

348

Johnny Campbell, Andy and Marion Neil, Cathie and Graham Craig, Helen and I met up in the Crystal Palace Jamaica Street Glasgow on Tuesday 3 January. Marion sadly passed four months later on 4 May 2016 and Andy on 4 May 2020.

Still in holiday mood, Helen and I went to Caleta de Fuste in Fuerteventura for two weeks on Sunday 15 January 2017. We stayed at Castillo Playa Bungalows not far from the beach and close to the town. We had two sun beds on our patio where we used to lie most days after breakfast. I would put my Bluetooth speaker under the bed and listen to Frankie Miller's Double Take most of the time. Love that album! Sometimes we would have a fried breakfast at the bar in the complex, or somewhere outside, but two weeks of fried breakfasts is not good for the waistline. I began going out for croissants with butter and cheese. I had taken a block of my favourite mature cheddar with me. . One afternoon we heard music coming from a bar. It was a bar you looked down to from street level and there was a duo playing outside. We went down and as we were looking for seats, a Scottish voice told us to sit at their table. It was a high table with two high chairs available so we sat down and ordered drinks from a waiter. The couple was George and Geraldine McGuinness known as the two Gs and they came from Blackpool. We had blether when the band had a break,

so I asked George, "What do you do"? He said, "I'm a skydiver, and Geraldine packs the chutes". I will write more about that subject later in the book. I had taken a ukulele with me as we were away for two weeks and didn't want my fingers to go soft. One day we were out and about and had cocktails, a jug of sangria and wine with our dinner. We were in our bungalow early evening and I felt like playing my uke in an underpass we had found next to the open air market. The acoustics were good as I had given it a wee sound check previously. I picked up my uke and Helen said, "Where are you going". I replied that I was going to the underpass and asked her if she would like to come. "No way" she replied, "You're embarrassing". So off I went with my uke and a small stand for my phone so that I could video my performance. I was singing away when a couple tried to give me money. I said, "I'm a professional, I don't want money". I was blootered! Anyway I recorded three videos and enjoyed the

process. We met up with the two Gs a couple of more times and one night they had a party. The bass guitarist from the duo which was playing when I met them came with his partner, his bass and acoustic guitar and George also had an acoustic guitar. We had a good session.

Helen's cousin Rosina, her husband Louie, and their family had a villa on the hill at Caleta and we also had a party there one night. We did a tour of the Island as this was our first time on it. We were supposed to be picked up outside our bungalows. Half an hour after the pickup time there was no sign of the bus so I phoned the tour company. They sent a taxi for us and we caught up with the bus at Antigua and seemingly we didn't miss much. I can't remember all the places we visited but it is a beautiful Island with impressive mountains and deserts. I remember we stopped at El Cotillo in the north of the Island; we passed through Corralejo and stopped again at the sand dunes south of Corralejo for photos. The social convener from Grangemouth Railway Club Richard, his wife Betty, his brother Gordy and his wife Linda were in the classy Gran Hotel Bahia Real in Corralejo and I had arranged for Helen and me to visit them. It was a fair run on the bus up to their hotel, but we got there one day of our second week and spent a lovely afternoon with them. Richard paid for everything and wouldn't let me put my hand in my pocket.

Another person I got friendly with at our bungalows was Kevin Grenville from Milton Keynes and we still keep in touch through Facebook. That was a most enjoyable couple of weeks and we met some interesting people.

On Tuesday 7 March we were off on another adventure to Castelldefels, Sitges and Barcelona. I booked us into the Hotel HP Castelldefels for ten nights and the Hotel Madison Bahia in Sitges for three nights. We took the train from Castelldefels into Barcelona as I wanted to see Gaudi's work. We made our way by metro to Casa Mila and Casa Battlo. The building next to Casa Battlo was also impressive. I believe it is called Casa Amatller and was designed by Josep Puig i Cadafalch, a contemporary of Gaudi. We went back on another day to explore Park Guell which is situated on Carmel Hill and quite a walk from the nearest metro station. When we eventually got there we had to wait for about another hour to go in with the next group, as they only let certain number of people into the park at any one time. This was an incredible place and we spent hours admiring Gaudi's creations. He was definitely way ahead of his time! There was a great view from the park, and you could see the Sagrada Familia towering over all the other city buildings. There is a small house in the park where Gaudi lived for a time and is now a museum. The park is full of fascinating structures, buildings and colourful tile work. It was a beautiful day

and it was quite exhausting walking all around it, so we just made our way to the train station and went back to Castelldefels. One of the staff at our hotel was Malaysian and invited us to her home one evening for dinner. We Scots can get a piece at any door! She had a young son and her husband worked away. I think she told us that she lived 21 streets away so we started walking; it turned out to be miles. Her son was lovely and so was the soup she made, but the chicken tasted like fire and we had to give up. On Sunday the 12 March we got the short train journey to Sitges, taking only what clothes we would need for three nights away. Our room at the HP Castelldefels was paid for, so we were fine leaving our other clothes etc. The Hotel Madison Bahia was on a small street, fifteen minutes walk from the railway station. The entrance was next to a bar, and I got friendly with manager Johnny and waiter Jordi. We would call in there in the evenings before going back into the hotel. The interior of the hotel was really old and we had sun beds on the terrace which overlooked the town rooftops. Sitges is a lovely, typically Spanish town and there were plenty of sculptures around to keep me amused. The town, viewed from the sea is dominated by the old church, Esglesia de Sant Bartomeu. Behind the church is the Bacardi Museum, but was closed when we were in Sitges. Jordi told me that bacardi was invented in Sitges but I believe it was in Cuba, hence the drink Cuba libre, rum and coke. We came across an Indian restaurant on our first night in Sitges. We ordered two bacardis and coke before our meal, another two during it, and when we asked for the third lot, they left the bottle on the table. Now that clinched it, we would eat there the next two nights we were in Sitges. We returned to Castelldefels on the morning of the fifteenth and just relaxed in the hotel grounds. The following day we walked into town and paid a

visit to the castle. I was a bit disappointed as it was a ruin and not particularly pleasing to the eye. We just spent time in the town and had dinner there before going back to the hotel. We loved the hotel, particularly the staff that comprised of different nationalities.

I don't know what happened to the March CTF meeting on 7 April at the Scotia, it was absolutely crowded, and many had brought acoustic guitars. Bob Bradley brought an acoustic bass and small amp. What a day that was! I met friends I hadn't seen for years such as Brian Denniston, George Leggat and Henry Wright who I used to see in the Flamingo with the Raiders when I was 14. Henry Played with Lulu and the Luvvers. I made many new friends that day. It was obvious that the Scotia was too small to accommodate our growing band of brothers.

Helen was 70 on 30 April 2017 and our daughters Tracey and Pauline gifted us money to pay for our trip to celebrate. I planned another one to Ronda, La Linea and Fuengirola. As we had been to Ronda by train from Malaga some months before, this time we would go by bus as I had been told that it was a journey with spectacular scenery. We flew to Malaga on Monday 24 April, got the train from the airport to Torremolinos, and the bus from there to Ronda. The bus went down the coast to San Pedro then into the mountains and the views were superb. We stayed at the Hotel Colon again, and the sisters were delighted that we had returned. On this occasion we had a penthouse with a large solarium and great views of the town. On the first evening I previously booked and paid online for the flamenco show at El Quinque. We had a three course dinner and the flamenco was performed by a family. The father played guitar, the wife sang and the daughter was the dancer. I don't think Helen was overly impressed but I enjoyed all of it. The next day while walking near the Puente Nuevo, I decided to venture down the gorge while Helen sat and had a pot of tea. I soon discovered that this was something I should have undertaken when I was younger. Luckily, I had my inhaler with me and on my return I had to stop many times out of breath. However, I got some good photos, but I think Helen had the right idea. We had drinks and a snack at a restaurant on the outskirts while watching vultures circling above. In the evening we had tapas in a restaurant which was in a large square full of families enjoying their food and children playing all around the square. It was a really happy place, noisy, but lovely to be there. We left Ronda on Wednesday 26 April and once again took the train to Algeciras and onward by bus to La Linea where we spent another two nights. We checked into the Hotel Asur Campo de Gibraltar as we had enjoyed our stay the last time we were there. Once again we got a room with a good view of the rock, and that's where we headed after settling in. After crossing the border we headed for Grand Casemates Square and Main Street. We walked all the way up Main Street and had lunch at The Angry Friar. If you're lucky, you can witness the changing of the guard at the Governor's house across the road when you visit. After eating we made our way back down Main Street and on to Ocean Village Marina where we met a lovely English lady who had not long moved to Gibraltar after breaking up with her husband. She advised us where to go for cheap cocktails and that was just what we wanted to hear. We returned to La Linea and had dinner at the hotel with drinks in our room from the duty free we had taken through

from Gib. We had never seen the other side of the rock from the urban side, so decided we would take a bus round there from the entrance to Grand Casemates Square. We left the bus at lovely Catalan Bay and had a glass of cider in the Seawave Bar. It can be thirsty work exploring! After climbing up to the road we continued walking until we came to Sandy Bay. The rock is very steep on this side, so different from the populated one. There were chalets dotted all along Sandy Bay but no shops or bars, just a lovely beach. We headed back by bus to Casemates and had a bite to eat in the square. Once again we had dinner in our hotel and left La Linea on the bus after breakfast. We were to meet up with Eileen and Russ at a bus stop near Sotogrande. Sure enough, they were waiting for us at the stop. It was good to see them again and we had a nice lunch at their house before they dropped us off at Estepona bus station where we got a bus for Fuengirola. . Our Hotel in Fuengirola was the Villa de Laredo on the front and not too far from the bus station but we decided to take a taxi this time. We stayed here for 7 nights. The hotel was being refurbished when we had visited in February to check it out, but it was looking good now and spotless. We got a room with a sea view and across the road on the beach there was keep fit equipment. It was funny watching people trying to figure out how to use each of them. We had dinner in an Indian restaurant in Calle Moncayo (Fish Alley) on the first night. We had been told about Fish Alley as it is a street full of restaurants, Indian, Italian and Spanish etc. On Saturday we headed for the Feria or International Festival of Fuengirola. It opened on a Thursday and closed on Monday 1 May. My friend Bob Bradley (Bob the Bass) had told me about this as he usually went to Spain for it. He wasn't going this year as he had heard the British section wouldn't be there due to the fact we were leaving Europe. On the Saturday there was a parade to the fairground where it was held leaving Plaza de Espana at 11.30. We missed that but got to the site as it arrived. There were sections from more than 30 countries and regions, spread across the five continents with cuisine and folklore from all of them. Some of them had performances as well as bands and dancers making for a real fun day. The next day, Sunday

30 April was Helen's seventieth birthday. I knew that Eileen and Russ were coming to celebrate with us but Helen didn't know. They weren't making a full day of it as they had to come a long way and they had to drive back home so they arrived in the afternoon. With the Feria still being on parking wasn't easy, but when they arrived they managed to park at the marina. Helen was delighted to see them. We found a nice Italian restaurant at the marina and spent a couple of hours enjoying the food and drink. They left and we sat for a while at a bar that had a band playing outside. The evening was

spent at our hotel bar. The rest of the week we relaxed at the hotel pool, eating out and listening to singer guitarists.

Pauline, me, Helen, Tracey and Louise

The next meeting of CTF was at the Clutha on 5 May 2017 but I was unable to attend. By this time it had changed to the first Friday

of the month. Helen went to Benidorm with the girls from 22 – 27 May staying at the Ambassador Hotel. I was 70 on Sunday 12 May. Helen's brother George got married to Ellen Fleming on Saturday 13 May 2017. Frank and I played at the reception in the Neptune Masonic Lodge. I went to the 9 June meeting of CTF at the Clutha in Glasgow and it was well attended. We were given fast food at 3pm, a good arrangement. By now electric guitars were being used and we used the house pa which was terrible.

We must have liked Fuengirola as we returned there on Tuesday 20 June for a week, staying at the Hotel Agur. The hotel was situated near to the train and bus stations. On Friday 23 June, we would find out from our hotel receptionist that today was midsummer's eve and San Juan's bonfire night was being celebrated all along Malaga's coast. We were advised to get down to the beach before midnight and take food and drink with us. We were also told us that the Beach Boys were playing at the castle in Fuengirola the

following night. We went to the tourist information and tried to book two tickets using my phone but were unsuccessful. The girl who tried to help us told us just to go and we would get tickets at the venue. On the Friday night we got pizzas and went down to the beach with our bottle of bacardi and large bottle of coke. Spanish families were all along the coast lighting fires and cooking food. There was a great atmosphere all around. We just enjoyed the moment, although we couldn't understand all the babbling around us. At midnight, fireworks were let off all along the coast and everyone walked into the water, including us. This is their way of celebrating the arrival of summer. The following day we were looking forward to hopefully seeing the Beach Boys. How lucky we were on holiday to find this out. They were performing in Sohail Castle at the southern edge of town, over the Puente de la Armada and up a hill. We ate at an Indian restaurant on the way and got there in plenty of time. Outside the castle entrance was a wooden hut which was the booking office. I asked a lady if it was possible to buy 2 tickets and that I had tried to do so online the day before. I also asked her if it was possible to get a discount as I was a musician who had played at the same time the Beach Boys were formed. She told me to go to the back of the hut and then ran away. When she returned we got two seating tickets for a total of £80 when it should have been £90 each for standing tickets. So in we went, got a couple of drinks and were shown to our seats facing the stage and open to the clear night sky. What a setting! Helen had her bacardi miniatures in her bag and a waiter kept staring at us. Fortunately, he was watching us to take our drinks orders. Eventually the Beach Boys

came on and did all their popular songs, 39 in total. They started with Surfin' Surfari and ended with Fun Fun Fun. It took me back to my Five Interns days in the sixties when we used to perform Beach Boys songs. When they were finished playing, the crowd were dancing to the sixties music that was played through the PA system. We left the castle and went down to the beach front which was busy with young people enjoying life with bonfires, music, food and dance. It was a fantastic night and rounded off a great holiday!

Our granddaughter Rosslyn won the gold medal for her age group in the 2017 art competition in Glasgow's Art Gallery. When she went to collect her medal, she found that she had also won the Dr T.J. Honeyman Snr award for her drawing.

My sister Christine was sixty on Friday 29 September, the same day as our daughter Pauline turned 48. She was having a party, so Helen and I, Tracey and Pauline all went. We were flying from Glasgow to Cardiff in the evening so Pauline met us at The Last Post next to Paisley Gilmour Street train station where we had dinner. Our niece Bryony met us at Cardiff airport and took us to her mum's at Glynogwr near Bridgend. My cousin Irene and husband Billy Tees also flew down to Bristol and were at my sister's when we arrived. Chris and partner Mark had booked a cottage nearby for us all to stay in for 2 nights. We brought a block of square sausage and a block of black pudding with us for breakfast. The cottage was wonderful and had four bedrooms. By the time we got there, it was straight to bed. Bryony picked us up after breakfast the following day. We spent the day preparing for the evening party but it rained all day as we put up the marquee at the back of the house. Chris and Mark have many friends, some of whom we had met before at Mark's fiftieth party. They had a singer guitarist on in the marquee and I did a spot with all my original songs. It continued to rain all night, but it didn't deter everyone from enjoying themselves. I can't remember who took us back to the cottage where we continued drinking. In the morning, we were all feeling rough when Tracey and Pauline came down the stairs in their swimming costumes. There was a Jacuzzi in a windowed extension at the back of the cottage and they went straight in. We got picked up again to go and dismantle everything we had put up the day before. Tracey and Pauline flew back that day to Glasgow, and so did Irene and Billy from Bristol. Helen and I didn't go until the following day. I can't remember if they all left together or who took them to their airports, but sometime later while we were sitting having a drink with Chris and Mark, I got a call from Billy. He said that they couldn't find Irene's passport and they had to pay again for an oversized bag to be put in the hold. Billy thought that when he paid for it on the outbound flight, it was also for the inbound one. We all searched for the passport but couldn't find it. Billy phoned us to say that they had it all along. Chris and Mark's Jack Russell had died months before and they got another Jack Russell pup, Meg. While we were sitting that night, Meg was running all around the room in circles.

A week later, on Monday 9 October we went on another David Urquhart trip, this time to Dornoch where we stayed at the Dornoch Hotel. On Tuesday we visited Wick, John o' Groats and Thurso. After spending time in Wick, we continued up the coast to John o' Groats. Finally, I got there in my seventieth year! On Wednesday we headed for Tain passing Glenmorangie Distillery. We could have disembarked for time in Tain but everyone told the driver to carry on. Our next stop was to be the Falls of Shin so we headed for

Bonar Bridge. Following the Kyle of Sutherland shores, not far after Invershin we left the A836 and took the A837. After crossing the River Shin we should have went right on to the B864. Instead, we continued on the A837 all the way across the country to Ullapool. The driver was funny and said he would probably get paid off for taking us so far but no one complained. On Thursday we decided along with the driver that we would go to the Falls of Shin instead of the planned trip. I'm glad we did as it was so beautiful. We had coffee and scones in the tearoom and I went off into the forest trails. We carried on to Lairg passing The Wee Hoose in the River Shin. We turned right on to the A839 and followed it all the way until it met the A9 at The Mound, then on to Dornoch. We got back early so we went down to the beach. After dinner Helen and I went to the Coach House Bar for the night. The next morning Friday 13 October, we headed home to Irvine.

It was our Golden Wedding on 28 October 2017, so we had

a party in the Neptune to celebrate. We asked people to donate to MacMillan Cancer Support instead of giving us presents but most of them gave us money, so we pooled it all together and donated a total of £600 to the charity.

My artist friend Stuart McAlpine Miller invited me to the opening of his latest work at Castle Fine Art in Queen Street, Glasgow. I asked him if I could bring my daughter Pauline and granddaughter Rosslyn. He said I could so I met them at the gallery. I had arrived before them and was looking for a glass of wine; I couldn't believe my eyes when in front of me there was a bar with four different single malt whiskies on offer. I managed to get through them during the time I was there. Aside from that, Stuart's paintings are fantastic. His latest style is kind of comic book characters, pop stars and cartoon characters, layered with text. Really clever stuff! His wife Nicky had a dress on that had Stuart's work printed on the fabric. They have a brand already, and it really is perfection. After a while there were small bowls of stovies, haggis neeps and tatties. By that time Pauline and Rosslyn had came in. I had admired Stuart's work since I first saw an exhibition of his in Eglinton Country Park in the early nineties. In fact, a painting of the Eglinton Tournament still hangs on the walls of the park's visitor centre.

Frank and I played in Grangemouth Railway Club at Hogmanay. CTF had been meeting in the Clutha the first Friday of the month since moving there from the Scotia in May. It was always a brilliant day out, great music from all the guys, good company and whisky. Long may it continue! Five Interns rhythm guitarist Andy Neil and deceased drummer Allan Craig's wife Cathie met with Helen and I at the CTF Clutha gig on Friday 5 January 2018. This would be the first time since January 2005 that Johnny Campbell hadn't met up with me.

We went to Benidorm on Wednesday 28 February for a week staying at Oasis Benidorm Apartments; every one had a sea view. Our flight was at 6am from Prestwick airport and coincidentally the "Beast from the East" was to appear in the UK that day. While we were in sunny Benidorm, Scotland was put on alert as the country was battered with heavy snow. We got to the apartments around mid day and checked in with a Spanish lady who did not speak any English. This often happens but I always tend to get by with my Spanish. The apartment was lovely with its sea view looking onto Oasis Beach Club and the area next to Torre Principado which once had two old Spanish Villas. We got a ten per cent discount at the Beach Club because we were staying at the apartments. After getting settled in, we walked out on to Mediterraneo and immediately noticed a couple coming towards us. It was Ian and Ann Fulton and I recognised them from our CTF meetings. We arranged to meet them that night and on

other occasions that week. Meanwhile the UK was in turmoil, trains were cancelled, shops closed and hospital operations postponed. Schools were closed and the M8 ground to a halt as they tried to get lorries moving. One night while we were with Ian and Ann, their daughter phoned them saying she couldn't get home from her work because of the snow. Fortunately it all came good in the end but it was a worry for them not being able to help her. On Sunday 4 March Ian arranged for us to meet them at El Cisne Flea Market on the outskirts of Benidorm. We caught the 10 bus to Camping Benisol and headed for the café inside which had entertainment and good food on a Sunday afternoon. Don't miss it! We saw some sights there, while we enjoyed the day's music and dancers. The wee woman collecting the glasses in between dancing was called Jeanie and was from Maryhill, Glasgow. The four of us left there and got the bus to Alfaz train station where they held a jam session on Sunday evenings ran by Nicky Chapman. Currently, Nicky runs the jam session at the Church Irish Bar, Albir. It was a good session with some fine singers and musicians. I eventually got up and did Dance with Me, The Trinidad Man and Blowing in the Wind. One night the four of us went to see my friend Shuggy Mcdevitt at Yorkshire Pride 2. Ian and Ann stayed at a lovely apartment on the point which separates Levante and Ponent beaches. They had a great view which looked right along Levante beach. We went to see their apartment on our last night then went for tapas in the old town. We then had a few extra large whiskies in a Scottish bar. We were home on Wednesday 7 March 2018 to find that there was only a light flurry of snow in Irvine which didn't last.

On the fourteenth of March I went for lunch with Davie McCallum, Tommy Gordon and John Williams in Glasgow. My son in law Martin Tierney came to the CTF meeting at the Clutha on 6 April. Ex Beatstalkers vocalist Davie Lennox also came and did a couple of songs. On Friday 12 April, Helen and I had dinner at Glasgow's Hard Rock Café courtesy of my sister Chris and partner Mark as part of their Virgin Experience gift voucher they got us for our Golden Anniversary. After finishing dinner we went to the Clutha for the launch of The Beatstalkers book. A lot of my CTF friends were there and it was good to see the band guys after all these years. CTF had another mid month meeting beginning in March 2018. This would be known as "Tommy Gordon's Real CTF" or simply, "Tommy's Day" and

held in The Winds, just along the road from the Clutha.

Helen and I went to stay the night with our friends Steve and Senga at East Kilbride on Tuesday 8 May. We had a good Tommy's Day at The Winds on 18 May with Frankie Murray, Jimmy Oakley, John Sutherland, Jimmy Campbell, Bob the Bass Bradley, David McCallum and of course Tommy. In the audience was the late drummer Alex Stenhouse's wife, Linda, Sheena Bradley and her sister Liz, Frances Speirs, Tony Howard and big Drew. This wee gig would also grow over the months. The 1 June CTF meeting was a great one and we wore t shirts which we'd had printed. Being such a lovely sunny day, most of our time was spent socialising in the beer garden outside with John Hannon, Gordon McIntosh, John Sutherland and Hugh Boyd. The venue was really getting too small for our gatherings. Frank and I played an open air gig at Tweedbank Gala Day, Galashiels on 2 June in the afternoon. It was quite a run there and back via Edinburgh, but we went down well. There was light rain all afternoon but we were covered and people were dancing on the grass. A brilliant day! We played at The Trust Inn Kilbarchan on 15 June 2018, Dundonald Bowling Club on the 16th and the Tea Gardens Paisley on the 17th. Dougie Murray, Elaine Graham, Linda Gillies, June Paul and Ray Jones all came along to see us. Dougie Murray borrowed Franks' guitar and we performed Apache and Wonderful Land with Dougie

harmonising on guitar.

Chapter 18

On Monday 18 June 2018 Helen and I went to Liverpool for three nights. We travelled there by by train and it was a pleasant journey with my hip flask full of Laphroaig and Helen with her bacardi miniatures. We disembarked at Lime Street station and our accommodation was only a ten minute walk away. Our granddaughter Louise had been and knowing we hadn't gave us money along with Tracey and Pauline for our recent birthdays to pay

for the trip. We stayed at Brownlow's Inn across from the Adelphi Hotel and the pub had accommodation in the floors above. It was a strange arrangement as we had a key for the outside door, so we could gain entry even if the pub was shut. The bar would be all shuttered up in that case. There was a locked door from the bar which gave you access to the rooms. Our room was tiny but it was only somewhere to sleep for three nights. It was my first time in Liverpool at seventy one years old, so where do you think we headed for? Yes, you guessed right, The Cavern, of course, and I wasn't disappointed. It was the afternoon and there was a guy playing guitar and singing. When I went to the bar, I was delighted that they had my favourite Laphroaig and they didn't rip me off with a double. We stayed there a while and listened to the next performer before leaving. We discovered there was a street called Great Charlotte Street quite near to us which had bars and entertainment throughout

the week so we went to Smokey Mo's on our first night. On the next day, we took the tourist bus and got off at Albert Dock.

We found and entered "The Beatles Story" museum. I was in my element there and I found out a couple of things about my musical journey that were similar to theirs. The Beatles began by all strumming guitars and so did the Interns. George Harrison got into the Beatles because he could play the instrumental called Raunchy. I got in to the Interns because I could play Shadows instrumentals. I enjoyed viewing all the guitars which were housed in glass cases, some makes I had never heard of. I read all the graphics, watched movies, and was just taken with the whole experience. Although Helen was with me, it was a different situation for her. I turned a corner and everything was white. There was John Lennon's white grand piano with his glasses sitting on top. To the right of it was his Epiphone semi acoustic, and above it in large letters it said, "This is not here". I just burst into tears! There was no one around to see my reaction but it really got to me. We came out of the museum and headed back to The Cavern for a while. We were told of a small bar located after you exited Clayton Square Shopping Centre into Cases

Street. I can't remember the name of it but it was a crazy place. The drink was really cheap if you didn't bother with brand names and there was a lady singer on. Everyone there was blootered, but it was another experience not to be missed. On Wednesday we went for breakfast at a deli in Williamson Square. When I went in to order, there was a large queue of schoolchildren and surprisingly they let me go in front of them all. We headed for the Albert Dock again. Tommy Gordon had mentioned to me that there was a statue of Billy Fury at the dock so I had to find it for him. The rain came on and it was windy, but I persevered until I found statue while Helen took shelter in the Merseyside Maritime Museum. When I returned and while we were speaking to one of the staff, he told us that there was a John and Yoko exhibition on at the Museum of Liverpool. We went there immediately to find out that the exhibition had been on for quite a while. It was fantastic, well put together and with the appropriate graphics. It was titled Double Fantasy and told the story of John and Yoko, how they met, and all the crazy things they did together. I'm so glad we managed to see this as once in 2013 when we were in Gibraltar; we missed a John Lennon and Beatles Memorabilia Exhibition which was put on by his son Julian. When we came out of the museum we took the "Ferry Cross the Mersey". There were a few stops where you could get off but it was still raining, so we just stayed on the boat until it returned. By then the rain had stopped and we walked to The Cavern for the last time. In the evening we went to a karaoke pub behind our hotel in Renshaw Street. We got home on Thursday evening after a great few days in the Pool.

On Sunday 24 June 2018 we went to see Dougie Murray performing with the Happy Ever After at number nothing Masonic in Kilwinning in the afternoon. Andy Haggarty was also there to see them. They were good and we had a great day. On Monday 2 July Helen and I went to a Hotel in Ayr for high tea as the second part of our Virgin Experience voucher from Chris and Mark.

On 27 July my friend Bill Kerr's sister Mary and husband Billy Black had a Swahovian day in their back garden where they had built a pub and called it The Toby Jug. Sam Stellard and I took acoustic guitars and Bill had a keyboard set up. We provided the entertainment and plenty of Swahovian Mead was drunk that day. Sam was Keur Stashan Yabeesh, Bill was Sidimir Kovlovski and I was Broshnak

Photo by Anne Oldfield

Malakov. We were dressed up for the occasion as were all the other guests. Bill's Father George and partner Sally were there and thoroughly enjoyed their day. Bill's daughter Mairi and husband Chris had the new baby there, only days old. There were loads of people present and one of the highlights for me was Bill giving out prizes to everyone. The food cooked by Mary and Bill's wench Jill was delicious.

I went to see the Trashcan Sinatras on Thursday 2 August 2018 at Oran Mor Glasgow. I met Beith artist Brian Craig and stayed with him most of the night. The band was brilliant as usual and I stayed behind after the gig to get a run home from Davy Hughes and his wife Maree.

Angela Cunningham and daughter Cassandra had come from Wollongong Australia to stay with us for a month. Angela is the daughter of Margaret and Andy Cunninghame, friends of Helen's parents Nellie and Bert who emmigrated to Australia in 1966. Angela, Cassandra, our sister in law Rita and Helen all came to the CTF meeting on Friday 3 August 2018. This would be the first meeting in Avant Garde on the corner of Parnie Street and King Street Glasgow. We had grown out of the Clutha, had membership cards that gave us ten percent off drink and excellent food at three o'clock, all courtesy of owner Billy. Helen and I went over to Brodick on Monday 6 August to meet up with Richard and Betty Robertson. They were staying at the Douglas Hotel, just across from the ferry terminal. Once again just like before at Corralejo,

Richard would not let me pay for anything. We drank good whisky all day and had our dinner before returning to Ardrossan and home. On 11 August we were invited to Helen's cousin Catherine Hester's wedding to John-Paul Percox at Sloans in the Argyle Arcade Glasgow. Tracey, Graeme and Zander, Pauline, Martin, Rosslyn and Helenna were also invited. When we arrived, there was free champagne and various colourings if you wished. After a while we went up one floor to a hall and the wedding. Catherine was stunning and the ceremony was excellent. Back down a floor and more champagne or free bar until the upper hall was ready for the meal. We sat at a table that had John-Paul's mother and father. The food was delicious and the entertainment afterwards was magic. It was a ceilidh band and when they began, the bride and groom came dancing into the room and most people got up to join them. The band was fantastic although I don't dance. Two days later on the 13 August Helen and I took Angela and Cassandra to Glasgow Cathedral and the Necropolis. It was a beautiful day and they were impressed with the Cathedral and the history of the dead Glasgow Merchants in the magnificent tombs. Afterwards we went for a few drinks in the Old College Bar on the High Street. On the afternoon of 24 August I went to the free folk concert in Irvine's Volunteer Rooms as part of Marymass Folk Festival. The main reason for me going was because cellist Wendy Weatherby was playing there with her band. In the evening we went for a meal in The Ship at Irvine Harbour so that Angela and Cassandra could meet the Irvine clan of the Morrisons. Helen's four brothers Jim, Robert, George and Raymond along with their respective wife's, Ina, Rita, Ellen and Catherine were there with Helen and me. On Monday 27 August 2018 Helen, Rita, Angela Cassandra and me took the ferry over to Arran. As soon as we got off the ferry, the five of us got on the bus to do the south of the Island, Lamlash, Whiting Bay, Kildonan and Blackwaterfoot on the west side where the bus terminates. After a short break the north bus took us on through Lochranza, Sannox, Corrie, and on to Brodick. We had a walk around Brodick, went for drinks in the Brodick Bar and onward

to the Ormidale where we had dinner and I had my favourite game dish, venison etc. This was another lovely day out although much of it was spent on transport. At least our guests got to see all of coastal Arran. Angela and Cassandra left for Sydney on 28 August 2018.

On 14 September Frekels members, Ronnie, George, Frank and I went to Jimmy Murray's funeral. Jimmy was a drummer and a good friend that used to come to see us often in the Bier Keller days. I spent a lot of time with him going for curries and drinks on Saturday afternoons. CTF guys, Frankie Murray, Jimmy Oakley, Davey Lennox, Alex and Maureen Borland were also there. We went to the South Western Club afterwards and it was good to catch up with George as we hadn't seen much of him over the last 30 years.

On 15 September 2018 we went to Tracey's old school friend's daughter Erin's wedding to Paul Fallon at the New Lanark Mill Hotel where we stayed the night. Erin and Paul already had three sons, Dominic, Ronan and Nicky and they were all cute in their kilts. Tracey, Graeme and Zander, Pauline, Martin, Rosslyn and Helenna, Louise and Nic were also staying at the hotel. Helen and I were only evening guests so after getting our room we got a taxi with Zander into Lanark for dinner. I don't know why Zander was with us but later we found out that we should have had dinner at the hotel as

part of the deal we were on. We didn't see the actual wedding as it was somewhere at the mill but Erin was gorgeous and the guys were all kilted up. Our granddaughter Louise was a bridesmaid. When we came back to the hotel after dinner we went to our room and all the family joined us for drinks as we had all brought spirits with us. We had our own wee family party before the evening's proceedings. It was a disco and all the young team enjoyed themselves. We just continued enjoying the free bar. Our room was perfect and looked down onto the Clyde. In the morning we had a brilliant breakfast and just strolled around the New Lanark Mill before heading to our respective homes.

Our oldest daughter Tracey was 50 on Wednesday 10 October 2018 and we went to Hamilton's in Irvine for lunch. There was Tracey, Graeme, Zander and Louise, Graeme's dad Stuart and his wife Maureen, Helen and I. We had already given our two girls money when they went to New York with Katy Rafter, Catherine Smith and Louise in late June for a week to celebrate them all being fifty. Pauline's 50th would be the following year and Louise was the tour guide and planner as she had already been to the Big Apple.

On 29 October Helen and I went to Sea World at Balloch, Loch Lomond. We got the train to Glasgow Central, walked to Queen Street station and got the Balloch train. We only went a couple of stops until we were all told to get off as there was a problem up ahead with signals. After a while we got on again, went another stop and were put off again. This time we were told to just make our own way by bus and claim the fare back. We had our bus passes so it didn't cost us but the bus took about an hour and a half. I think all in it took us four hours from the time we left home until we arrived in Balloch. We

walked to Sea World, stayed about an hour or so as there is not a lot to see. We travelled back to Glasgow and went for an Indian curry before heading home.

Helen's brother Robert and wife Rita had their Golden Wedding in the Neptune Masonic on Friday 21 December. Tracey, Graeme, Zander, Louise, Nic, Helen and I went to the Tornyard Indian restaurant for a meal on 24 December, Christmas Eve. Frank and I played Hogmanay at Turnberry Caravan Park. I met up with Interns guitarist Andy Neil at the CTF meeting in Avant Garde on Friday 4  January 2019. This would be the last time I would see Andy. Sam Stellard and I met up at Bill Kerr's for a wee single malt session with me on acoustic guitar, Sam on acoustic bass and Bill on Accordion. We did a video of their song, "Wee Clootie Dumplin'".

On Tuesday 22 January, I actually began painting again. My friend John Hannon who I knew as a bass guitarist was also a mountain climber. He had pestered me for months to do a painting of him on Ben Arthur, Arrochar (The Cobbler). I thought that since I had not lifted a brush since the year 2000 that I should do other paintings before doing his. I started "Balloch" as well as "John Hannon, Mountain Man". Musician friend John Sutherland was having a 65th birthday party at Torrance Bowling Club. Helen and I, John Hannon and his wife Maureen all booked Glazert House at Lennoxtown for the night of the party. We met John and Maureen at Paisley Gilmour Street train station and they drove us there. We got our rooms and had dinner in the hotel along with a few goldies before getting a taxi to Torrance. Just our luck, there was a bridge closed on the road from Lennoxtown to Torrance so we had to go all the way into Kirkintilloch to get there. There were many of us there from CTF and John was knocked out when he and Roberta walked in to see so many people. What a great surprise! His band, "Senior Moments" were all there and the room was full of musicians who all went up for a couple of numbers, including me and Dougie Murray. I had left my phone in the taxi and the number I was to call for a taxi back to the hotel was in my phone. I couldn't take any photos as the phone was also my camera. We did manage to contact the same taxi company and when we got to the hotel, the driver phoned the office

to find that my phone was there and could be picked up on the way home the next day. The office was in Kirkintilloch, so we picked it up and Tracey met us at McDonald's in Helen Street for the ride home to Irvine. During February I was painting Rome's Colosseum, Pantheon, and Ronda's Puente Real, as well as John Hannon's in between. The CTF meeting on Friday 1 March was really bad as the power kept cutting off after Billy had a noise limiter installed. Louise and Nic got engaged and had a party at Beechams Social Club, Irvine on Saturday 6 March 2019. Louise asked me and Frank if we would play for an hour and they both decided from our repertoire what we would play. It was a brilliant night, and to my surprise, my sister Chris, partner Mark and niece Bryony were there. We went down a treat with our hour spot; all in all, it was a brilliant night. Frank took the gear back to our house and at the end; we were left behind as all those that could drive were all gone. Helen's brother Robert came back for us.

On Tuesday 5 March David McCallum and I visited Barras Art and Design and St Lukes & the Winged Ox as we couldn't see how we could solve the sound problem at Avant Garde on our CTF days. It

looked like we were going to have to move again. By this time we had around 300 coming on the day and these two places ideally should be able to accommodate us. I went to the Winds on Friday 15 March for Tommy's day and had a good time listening to all the guys and performed Shadows instrumentals with Dougie Murray.

On Monday 1 April 2019 Tracey and Zander, Helen and I drove down to Lakeland near Cark in the Lake District. We met Pauline, Martin, Rosslyn and Helenna at Tebay Services just off the M6. We had lunch there and decided to meet at Haven Lakeland Leisure Park at Flookburgh. Since alcohol was cheaper in England than what it was in Scotland, we took a detour into Kendal to stock up on drink and some essentials which we hadn't brought with us. Tracey had taken Graeme's big Vauxhaul Insignia instead of her small Suzuki and found the narrow roads terrifying. When we arrived at the park, they had already checked in to the mobile home we would be staying in for four nights. Just outside the park was Skydive Northwest where our friends George and Geraldine who we met at Fuerteventura in 2017 did their jumps from. I phoned George to say that we were staying next to Skydive Northwest and he said that they had just left there not long before we arrived and headed home to Blackpool. We took a walk right round the site in the evening. The next day we went up the east side of Lake Windermere passing

through Bowness and Windermere to the quaint town of Ambleside. I would find out later that my friend Polly Hamilton was brought up in Ambleside. I took lots of photos there as it is an impressive place and I really liked the colours of the stone in the buildings. We had lunch there and Zander bought some geodes from a specialist shop in the town. We then went back to Lakeland for dinner and a night at the entertainment lounge. On Wednesday we headed for Holker Hall. The present house was rebuilt in the neo-Elizabethan style in the eighteen seventies. The cost of a ticket was well worth it as we got to see most of the house which contained great paintings, furniture and a rich history. There were great views of the estate from some of the upper windows, and from one I saw the massive herd of fallow deer in the deer park. The gardens were beautiful with some really old lime trees in the grounds including the 400 year old "Great Lime" having a girth of 7.9 metres. The house was home to the Cavendish family in 2019. We had taken a picnic with us and there was a covered in area where you could enjoy your own food. Zander and I walked all the way to the deer park but we couldn't get anywhere near them due to restricted areas. If you are ever in that area at any time I would recommend a visit to Holker Hall. It was our friends Bill and Jill who had encouraged us to go. On Thursday we all went to Go Ape at Grizedale which is situated between Lake Windermere and Coniston Water. It was a good run there and the roads are mostly single track which wind through fields and forest. Tracey, Graeme, Martin, Zander, Rosslyn and Helenna all went onto the treetops. They were up in the canopies of the trees crossing from one tree to another, and there were five different locations, each with a zip wire which took them to the next one. One thing I noticed at the entrance was a sculpture of a wood cutter, similar to one that was made at the Glasgow Garden Festival of 1988. While they were all having fun in the canopy, Helen and I sat in the café drinking coffee and enjoying the home baking. We left Lakeland on Friday 5 April but just missed George and Geraldine who had arrived at Skydive Northwest just after we had left. We headed up again through Windermere and Ambleside, and stopped for a while at Grasmere where we bought some art materials and local cheeses. We carried on to Keswick where we spent some time before heading home.

On Friday 26 April 2019, George and Geraldine McGuinness arrived at our door in their campervan. We had a great chinwag reminiscing about our times in Caleta de Fuste and they told us all about their skydiving. George has done around 3,200 skydives and Geraldine packed the chutes. I had said that I always wanted to experience jumping out of a plane and George said, "Would you do it for charity"? "Of course" I said. George replied, "Right you're on". They would not stay in our house that night saying that they preferred the campervan. They came to see us playing at Forehill Bowling Club in Ayr the following night. My granddaughter Louise said that she would do a tandem jump with me so I booked us for Saturday 17 August thinking that would be a good time weather wise.

We registered with Ayrshire Cancer Support and got Sponsorship forms. My friend Bill Kerr was 65 on 30 April, the same day as Helen's birthday. I did him a painting of Bridge Cottage where we all stayed in 2016.

CTF moved to BAAD on Friday 3 May 2019. The PA system is huge and the mixer is operated by its owner. This venue was bigger than Avant Garde with its glass roof making it very warm on a sunny day. The drink at the bar was a different price each time you went for the same round. We were supposed to get ten percent off the drink, but I was never sure if we did. We also got food at the interval which wasn't as good as Avant Garde. Brian Lawrence kept us entertained with his acoustic while we ate, and he always does a fine job. We also had a charity day on Sunday June 23 with four of our bands performing for free. I went to see the band Escapade in the Ship Inn Ayr on Sunday 30 June. This has been Rab Reilly's band for many years with a number of member changes. Rab was on lead vocals, Willie Scott on bass, Jim Husband on keyboards, Stevie Arrandale on

drums and Darren McLelland on lead guitar. What a great band and a brilliant repertoire.

On Friday 5 July 2019 we finally got permission to take Bert's ashes to Ibrox. There were eleven of us on the day, Helen's older brother Jim and younger brothers Robert, George and Raymond with their wives, Rita, Ellen and Catherine, Helen and I, and Bert's mate Willie Laing with his wife Margaret. Although I had never been interested in football, it was an enjoyable day which began with us going through the tunnel to the ground, after being told not to go over the touchline into the playing area at any time. I couldn't believe the quality of the grass on the field. It was just beautiful and looked so soft. The hallowed turf! We went round the outside of the field, behind the Broomloan Road side and carried on to the centre opposite the tunnel where there was a hole in the ground. The young man giving us the tour said that we should put Bert's ashes into the hole and the next time the park was being returfed, the ashes in the hole would then be spread in the park before the new turf went down. After we did that, we all went up to where Bert's seat was for many years to have photos taken. Later, we visited the impressive trophy room. I really loved all the portrait paintings which were all over the board room and corridors. Some of the rooms in the building were being refurbished so we probably missed some of the tour. If I was interested in football I would be able to tell you more but I have forgotten much of what we were told. The main thing is that Bert is laid to rest in the right place. When we got back to Irvine we went for a meal at Riverside Lodge to toast Robert Morrison (Berty).

That same year I had a painting of the Colosseum in the North Ayrshire Open Art Exhibition at the Racquet Hall, Eglinton Country Park.

Our friends Bill and Jill had booked a house at Portnahaven Islay from Saturday 27 July until the following Saturday. Once again, they asked us to come and stay with them for as many days as we wished. They were going by car and took our bags while we got the bus from Buchanan Street bus station Glasgow on Monday 29 July 2019. It was a three and a half hour drive to Kennacraig and then another two hours twenty minutes on the ferry to Islay. I think we arrived at Port Askaig around 6pm and our two friends were waiting for us. We arranged that we would go for dinner as soon as we arrived so went to the nearby Ballygrant Inn; seemingly it used to be a band gig back in the day. Just as we pulled into the Ballygrant we heard a loud bang. Helen and Jill saw a sign and thought it was a target and that we were near a shooting range. The Ballygrant bar has to be the best stocked single malt bar I have ever come across, and I did my best to savour some of them before and during dinner. When we were leaving the Ballygrant there was another bang, probably a motorbike backfiring and the girls still thought it was from the firing range. When Bill got closer to the target, he noticed that it was the national speed limit sign. From then on every time Bill came across one of these signs on our trip he would say, "There's another shooting range". It was cloudy when we arrived on Islay but as we approached Portnahaven, the clouds broke and we arrived there in sunshine. The house was situated on a hill and the level on entering from the street had the kitchen, bathroom and lounge. Downstairs were two bedrooms. I was surprised but delighted to see a classical guitar on its stand when I walked into the lounge, and the views of the harbour and beach from

the lounge windows were fantastic. They had found the guitar in a cupboard and had set it up for me. We managed a few wee single malts that evening sitting in the evening sun. Bill and Jill had worked out a loose itinerary for the week and on Tuesday we headed up through Port Charlotte, Bruichladdich, and left the coast road a bit further on when we took the B8018 and headed for Kilchoman Distillery. Helen and I went in to the visitor centre for a look since we were there. The girl who was giving samples out was young and by her accent, a local. I asked her if she knew Stephanie Fraser from Bowmore and she did. I said that our granddaughter Louise went through university together with Stephanie and they shared a flat in Glasgow during that time. The girl said she knew Louise as she had came over to Islay in the past with Stephanie for some special events. I couldn't believe that in a distillery right off the beaten track, Louise was known. She must be taking after me! What I liked about this distillery was that they had a barley field next to it and they did their own bottling. The other

distilleries on the Island send their whisky to the mainland to be bottled. We had a look around the ruined Old Kilchoman Parish Church and Jill went to investigate Kilchoman Military Cemetery; I don't think she was impressed. We left there and Bill took us to the spectacular Machir Bay. We spent time there taking photos and just enjoying the scenery. . Our next stop was Saligo Bay further up the north west coast. We had to walk though a field to get to the sea and there were thousands of butterflies all around us. We then went on to Gruinart passing Loch Gorm on the way and stopping at RSPB Loch

Gruinart Visitor's Centre. There is a viewing platform where you can watch the wildlife on the wetlands in front of you. We made our way back to Portnahaven stopping at Bruichladdich mini market for cheese toasties. It was another fine evening so we sat outside on the patio. Bill and I enjoyed my Islay Mist that was a gift to me from Louise when she was last on the Island. Helen had her bacardi and coke, while Jill went off on her travels to photograph the harbourside, the lighthouse etc and as we enjoyed our refreshments and we could see her on the far side of the bay. Helen and I had a wee nap as we sat in the sunlight.

I had booked the tour at Laphroaig distillery on the Wednesday. It was quite a drive from Portnahaven so we headed off late morning so that we could take our time for my 2pm tour. We stopped off in Bowmore for a look around before carrying on to Port Ellen and on to the distillery. When you buy a bottle of Laphroaig, inside the tube is a little booklet with a number. If you go to the Laphroaig web site you become a Friend of Laphroaig when you submit the number. This entitles you to a plot measuring one square foot of land in a field across the road from the distillery. When you visit the distillery you can claim a dram rent for your plot. You can also go and plant something on your plot if you wish and they will give you a waterproof, wellington boots and a spade. Bill dropped me off well before my 2pm tour and immediately I saw two healthy looking rabbits on the lawn. It must be the air around here! I went in, said that I was there for the two o'clock tour and was given a lanyard with a small glass attached and inscribed with the Laphroaig logo. From the lanyard hung three vouchers which could be used for drams after the tour. I gave my plot number and said that I wanted to claim my rent and was given a miniature of Laphroaig 10 year old. Then I was taken to the tasting bar and given a special dram. I then purchased a couple more; all three were different tasting Laphroaig drams. Then it was time for the tour and at the time there was no production. We had a very helpful and friendly tour guide, but it would have been more interesting if the distillery had been in production. After the tour your vouchers were used for drams. You could use one for the 10 year old, two for a more expensive dram, or three for an even more expensive dram. I went back to the bar for some more whisky which I hadn't sampled, such as Lore and Cardeas. When I left the bar with my first post tour dram, there with his wife Dee, family and friends was my artist friend Eoghann MacColl. We artists seem to know that the best whisky in Scotland has to be Laphroaig. While we were having a good old blether, Bill, Jill and Helen turned up and had tea and coffee as it was free on tap. As I was a bit tipsy leaving Laphroaig, I was attempting to get on another pair of shoes at Bill's car when a gentleman asked if he could help me. As soon as he spoke, Bill said, "I know you, we have met before". Seemingly when Bill was parked up at Glenfinnan in 2016, he had got out of the car and this person had been driving a 12 seater tour bus that had Rabbie's on the side. They got talking and he said that he was taking his passengers to Skye. His name was Euan MacLeod and he was from the North East of Scotland. He had long hair and was wearing a kilt. He told Bill a story about when he was driving a 25 seater bus; he wanted to take all his family on a tour. His boss let him have the bus for a week and all he had to do was put fuel in it. He filled the bus with his family and fuel and they all had a great tour of Bonnie Scotland. When Bill related this to Euan outside Laphroaig, he knew then that they had obviously met before. We had intended to have dinner at Ardbeg distillery but by the time we got there the cafe was closed. We went by Lagavulin distillery to get photos of it and then went into Ardbeg for a look round the outside. On our way back to Portnahaven we stopped for dinner at an Indian restaurant in

Bowmore. We had noticed posters in the village which advertised there was to be a coffee morning at 11am on Thursday in Portnahaven Parish Church which was just across the road from us at Hillcrest House. The Church was built in 1828 and is an example of the 32 "Parliamentary" Churches that were built with a Parliamentary grant of £50,000 in the years from 1823. These Churches could be found in many parts of the Highlands and Islands of Scotland and were designed by Thomas Telford. Port Wemyss built in 1832 is next to Portnahaven and didn't have a Church, so they had to use the one at Portnahaven. The Church has two doors, one for residents of Portnahaven and the other for the residents of Port Wemyss. When you enter the church the pews have a partition in the centre, keeping the residents of the two villages apart, although both

faced the pulpit. We were hoping to get a coffee and some home baking before our Thursday trip, but typically, the Church was still empty at 11 and we just took off on our journey. That day we headed towards Port Askaig where we arrived on the Island, but turned off at Persabus and took the road for Bunnahabhain Distillery. On the way there we noticed Ardnahoe Distillery which we didn't know existed. We thought we should investigate the new distillery. Again, Bill sat in the car while the three of us went into the visitor centre. It is modern looking on the outside and very spacious internally with a well laid out shop, beautiful café, and at the bar we sampled a lovely 12 year old Laphroaig. The distillery was completed in late 2018 and only opened to visitors in April 2019. We carried on to Bunnahabhain and what an impressive sight that is as you approach the distillery with the Paps of Jura in the background. Bill parked the car and as he had been there before stayed in it while Jill, Helen and I walked to the visitor centre. Knowing that Black Bottle comes from this distillery, I was just into the place when I blurted out, "What have you done to the Black Bottle"? Immediately, one of the young men in charge said that it was nothing to do with the distillery, it was owners Distell. At least they seem to agree with me that since the recipe was changed, and the bottle went from green to the original black in 2013, it

wasn't the same. To me, they destroyed the brand. Every sample I got, Jill got one and gave it to me and I think we had four each. Leaving Bunnahabhain we returned to the main Port Askaig Bridgend Road where we took the Glen Road at Ballygrant. This took us into the wilderness and at one point we came to a house which had a cut out wooden guitar on the entrance gate. Bill had known about this and didn't mention it to me beforehand. We came out of the Glen Road at Bridgend and continued on the coast road back to Portnahaven. I said to Bill that we hadn't visited the village pub yet. He asked Jill if he drove down to the pub, would she pick us up later. She agreed and off we went down to An Tigh Seinnse, the local. Bill noticed the Lagavulin 16 year old so we had one of them, then another, then another until the bottle was finished. Helen and Jill came and when we were leaving, I went across to the harbourside for a look and there was my friend Eoghann MacColl sitting sketching the lighthouse with his friends and family all around him. After dinner, we carried on drinking when we got back to the house and this would be our last night.

Next morning after breakfast we decided that it was too long a journey for Bill to drop us off at Port Ellen where we would catch the ferry for Kennacraig. He dropped us at Bridgend where we got the bus, free using our bus passes of course. The ferry was on time and the crossing was dead calm. We had quite a wait at Kennacraig but the sun was scorching. The three and a half hour bus journey back to Glasgow was tiring, even though the hip flask was emptied.

We came into Buchanan Street Bus Station and got a bus to Irvine via Kilmarnock. This was a CTF meeting day at BAAD and drummer George Francey and his wife Sylvia who were at the meeting were on the bus. It was his birthday and he wanted us to go for a drink with them in Kilmarnock, but we were shattered and just carried on home. What a wonderful holiday, thanks Bill and Jill!

Louise and I were meant to do our skydive on Saturday 17 August but it was predicted to be a rainy weekend so it was cancelled. We rebooked for Saturday 19 October 2019. I had booked the return on the train for the Monday as Louise intended to drive back after the jump. The next CTF meeting at BAAD was on Friday 30 August and during the afternoon there was a really heavy rain shower. There was rain pouring in from everywhere and people dashing around to avoid it. Luckily it was nowhere near the stage and all the equipment and instruments. This made me think of Louise's upcoming wedding in July 2020. What if this happened during her day as we would be there most of it? I gave my friend John Hannon my miniature Laphroaig that I got as rent for my plot at the distillery. I felt sorry for him as he had never been to Islay before and Laphroaig was his favourite whisky. Bill, Sam and I had one of our mad single malt days on 4 September. Sam and I went to see the band "Hot Banana" at Irvine Watersports Club on the afternoon of Sunday 8 September. The guys were all members of CTF. CTF had another charity day with 4 of our bands performing for free. I finished a painting of my friends George and Geraldine skydiving on 22 September. This was a gift for them as they were paying for my video when I did my skydive. On Friday 4 October Bill, Sam and I after much whisky recorded a video of their song," The Lavvy in Kyle". This is a song about the public toilet at Kyle of Lochalsh, so if you are ever up that way remember and call in. I went to Tommy's day in the Winds on Friday 18 October and had taken portraits I had painted of Joe O'Sullivan and Dave Jordan with me to give to them.

Saturday 19 October 2019 was the day of our skydive. Louise picked up Helen and me at 8am for the drive to Flookburgh near Grange-over Sands in the Lake District. We stopped off at Tebay Services to have a coffee and sandwich and arrived not long before our expected 12.30. We saw our friend George McGuinness and got checked in. The weather was fine here but it had rained most of the way down. Eventually we went for our training, jumpsuit and harness fitting. I struggled when I was hung up and told to hold my legs up by grabbing the suit at the outside of my thighs. It was a lot easier on the actual jump. By this time we had also seen Geraldine who had been packing a chute in the hangar. We sat in the sun awaiting our turn as we watched the plane load up with divers and watched them as pinheads getting larger as they came down to land. Eventually, around 2pm it was our turn, so off we went walking to the plane over a soggy field. There was a step to get on the plane and when I stepped up, the draught from the propeller made me lose balance and I nearly got blown off. Louise and her instructor were last on and my friend George was behind my instructor. It seemed to take forever to get up to 1400 feet. Louise was nervous so I think that is why they let her out first so that she would not be watching others leave before her. The camera person goes out first and hangs on at the side of the door. I was already hooked up to my instructor, put my head back onto his shoulder, whoosh, and we were off. I find it hard to explain the feeling as we plummeted at 120 mph. There was no feeling of breathlessness or strain on the body; it was just really fast and exciting. The chute opened as we were going through the clouds and I didn't notice any difference now we were going so much

slower. I remember being able to see the whole of Morecambe Bay and Blackpool Tower. Coming in to land it was easy holding onto jumpsuit to bring my legs up so that we would land on our bums. I remember seeing Helen waving to me as I came in to land. I was absolutely buzzing and it stayed with me all weekend. What an experience, I would highly recommend it! We went for a coffee and Louise waited for her video which was put onto a memory stick. We watched it on a laptop and she left not long after for the long drive home. She phoned us to say she was home at 7pm. We were staying on until Monday in George and Geraldine's caravan while they slept in their campervan. In the evening Geraldine runs a soup kitchen to provide food for all the Skydive members and Instructors who stay there over the weekend. We had brought square sausage and black pudding with us so that was also in the mix. They had asked me to bring an acoustic guitar and we had a session and drink on the

Saturday night. On the Sunday morning we had bacon rolls at the café on the campus. It was getting busy as they take students from universities and train them to do solo jumps and there were many young people there. We spent some time watching the jumps and then walked into Haven Lakeland which wasn't too far. George and Geraldine were busy all day. In the evening Geraldine did the cooking again and the rain came on. After eating we moved into the parachute centre and had a few refreshments. On Monday morning after breakfast we got a run to Cark train station for our journey home. I found it strange that our first train of the day was to Ulverston going towards Barrow-in-Furness. This was the opposite direction to where we wanted to go. The next was Ulverston to Lancaster, then Lancaster to Glasgow, Glasgow to Irvine. What a great weekend we had. Never to be forgotten!

Tracey took us to the Vic and Vine in Prestwick for lunch on our Anniversary on 28 October 2019. At the CTF meeting at BAAD on

Friday 1 November my skydive video was shown on the big screen and I announced that Louise and I had made a total of £2,600 for Ayrshire Cancer Support. Frank and I were approached by one of the audience in the Ashton bar Helensburgh. He said he was thinking of having a party on Saturday 9 November and asked me if we would play at it. I gave him a price and he said he would contact me nearer the time. I hadn't heard from him and phoned his mobile on 29 October. When I said who I was he said, "We are actually in Antigua in the Caribbean on honeymoon and were talking about you today".

He said that the party was still on and he would call me when they got home. He did call and asked if we would play from 7pm until 9pm. There would be an acoustic guitarist in the afternoon and disco after we finished and it would be in the Helensburgh and Lomond Civic Centre. We arrived on the day for their wedding party so we set up and kicked off at 7pm. Someone had mentioned to me while I was at the bar that Martin Clunes was there and while we were playing I spotted him. We also noticed Joe Absolom who was also in Doc Martin and has also been in Eastenders. It was a great gig and when we finished, Frank and I got our photos taken with Martin and Joe. Seemingly the groom is involved on the television production Doc Martin. He and his new wife Mairi complemented us

on our playing and we were given more than we had asked for.

The Last CTF meeting of the year was on Friday 29 November 2019 at BAAD and most probably the last time we would meet there. We had been leaving some equipment underneath the stage to save transportation and we were told to remove it. The food had deteriorated and there were always queues at the bar with a different price every time you paid for the same drink. The quality of sound had improved and it was great to be on the stage. After our meeting some of us went to a pub round the corner to have a session as Brian Lawrence was there with his acoustic. After looking at various venues and suggestions we settled

406

on Ivory Black on Oswald Street for the third of January meeting 2020. We thought that it was time to get away for a break before the winter sets in. Our friends Steve and Senga were in Spain at the time and they were always asking us to come over. While I was booking

our flights with Ryanair to Alicante, I only had to hit the confirm button. I had been trying to call them to make sure it would be fine and I wasn't getting through. I hit the confirm button meaning we would be going on Monday 2 December and returning on Friday the sixth. As soon as I did that Senga phoned and said that they were coming home on Friday 29 November. I just booked accommodation and transfers to Benidorm. We stayed in a one bedroom apartment above the Centauro car hire at the triangle in the Rincon end of Mediterraneo. It was good to get a break and although it was cold it was not as cold as Scotland. We did manage to get some sun on a couple of days. Many entertainment venues were also closed. My mate Shuggy Mcdevitt wasn't playing but we bumped into him one night while we were going out for dinner. We ate mostly in the London Bar next to Yorkshire Pride 2 which was closed

We went to the Neptune on Sunday 15 December for the pensioners Christmas Party as Helen's brother Robert was the Master of his lodge. Frank and I were playing at Ayr United's ground for a friend's mother's eightieth birthday party from 2pm -6pm. Our friend Neil, who we had known from the Anchor bar Ayr let us finish early as I had said my wife was in Ayr hospital and we were going to visit her after the party. We went to see Helen and she was doing well. Tracey and her friend Katy had been with her all afternoon and Pauline, Rosslyn and Helenna visited while we were there. Helen got out on Christmas Eve and we had our usual Christmas dinner with the family. We went to Rosslyn's sixteenth Birthday Party on 30 January 2020. I had ordered an acoustic guitar for her on behalf of her mum and dad and she was delighted with it. We  would meet her boyfriend Mihai for the first time. Rosslyn and her friend Arlene entertained us for a while on her new guitar.

Helen's cousin Ian Morrison passed on 28 February 2020 and his funeral was on Friday 6 March at Craigton Crematorium. CTF moved to Ivory Black in Oswald Street and I missed the January and February meetings. Ian's funeral was the same day as the meeting but I decided that I could go to the meeting for a couple of hours and then take the train to Cardonald station where it is only a short walk to the Crematorium. I didn't intend to get up to play but Jim Keilt shouted me up and I performed Dance with Me and Blowing in The Wind. I got to Craigton in time where I met Helen and the rest of the family. We went on to Neilston Bowling Club and I spent time chatting to Billy Young who was Ian's friend from way back. Ian was my mate in the shipyard as well as Helen's cousin. Frank and I played our last gig before lockdown in the Anchor bar Ayr on Saturday March 7.

Sam Stellard, Helen and I went to see Benny Gallagher in the Lounge Largs on Sunday March 15. By this time there was talk of a virus called Covid 19 going around the world and because of it the event was poorly attended. We met Danny and Fiona Anderson from Irvine. Danny had not long graduated as a lawyer; he also set up PA systems for concerts and corporate events. He used to be the bass guitarist with the band Harmonica Jones in the nineties. Benny was great and Sam and I had a dram with him when he'd finished and while we were waiting for Sam's son Barry to pick us up.

From Monday 16 March 2020 Helen and I were on Lockdown to stop the spread of Coronavirus.

The Five Interns guitarist Andy Neil passed on 4 May and I couldn't go to his funeral although I did see the service on the Maryhill Crematorium video link. Sad times!

Pauline, Martin, Rosslyn and Helenna came down to us on 25 June and sat in the back garden well away from us and used Tracey's toilet next door. On another August day Bill Kerr, Sam Stellard and I had a single malt session in our back garden as we were allowed to for a while. The following day, Tracey, Zander, Helen and I went down to Luce Bay with my sister Gladys' ashes. We had held on to them for five years. It was a lovely day but a long drive down and back. Gladys had spread her husband's ashes at the rocks by the sea at Luce Bay when he passed in 1990. I had some photos which were taken then and we tried to find the same spot thirty years later. I hope we succeded! After spreading Gladys' ashes, we went for a drink in the Cock Inn across from Lucebay Holiday Park. We had a fish supper in Stranraer before heading home.

Two days later, on August 11, Louise took her mum Tracey, brother Zander, Helen and I for lunch at Kilmaurs. On 15 August on our way to Steve Cosgrove's seventy fifth birthday party in Hamilton, Tracey dropped us for a short time at Pauline's for drinks in their back garden. She then drove us to Steve and Senga's at East Kilbride as we would be staying the night there after the party. It was good to

411

see Steve and Senga as it has been a long time since we saw them last. Twenty twenty was a strange year!

While on lockdown I recorded 78 songs on video and put them on Facebook. I built four Stratocaster type guitars from parts and wrote and recorded 10 songs. My friend Bill Kerr wrote two instrumentals for me called 'Isolation' and 'Forging Ahead'. CTF had a book published with stories from 25 musicians including myself. There is also a DVD free with the book including my original track called "When will we ever get to play"? I wonder if I ever will!

COVID-19

My life has been frozen by covid nineteen
I've been stuck in the house since March sixteen
Passing the time making music all day
Creative activity from home, not away

Things were going good for this septuagenarean
Now I have to do things to stop me from wearying
Hopefully soon I'll get let out to play
In a future so different from the past, dare I say

A lot to be answered by those with the power
My generation has suffered leaving a taste that is sour
Many have passed leaving life all alone
If you are old and get through it, you were in the right zone

To the heroes in the front line it has to be said
If it wasn't for them many more would be dead
They have put their lives in danger for others
Sisters and Brothers, Fathers and Mothers

Two thousand and twenty I'll never forget
If I ever get through it as it isn't done yet

I pray for the victims of covid nineteen
Good luck to you all, If you know what I mean.

© Jim Collins 2020

Photos

Page

52. Shopping in town.

54. At the Barras.

59. Our Manager Billy Grainger's list of bands.

60. Five Interns.

62. Alastair Neil, me and Andy Neil.

64. Our wedding outside St Convals Pollok.

70. Jim Nelson, The Windmill at Rottingdean near Brighton

72. Tracey and Pauline.

74. Me in the Bier Keller and

75. Frekels in The Vega., Union St, Glasgow.

76. Me and my girls at Battlefield Caravan Park, Inveraray.

78. Frekels

79. Tracey and Pauline at Pinmore Street.

83. Mum and dad

84. Me and Mary Stavin, Miss World 1978.

87. Frekels.

92. The girls with Aunt Peggy.

95. Striking and arc.

96. Frekels. Ronnie, George, me and Frank.

100. "The Talking Horse". John Mitchell, Plater.

102. Tracey and Pauline

103. Helen and I on a bus heading for Blanes, Spain.

105. "Govan Shipbuilders Ltd". Oil on canvas.

107. "Canada Marquis" Oil on board.

109. "The Art of Shipbuilding" Oil on canvas.

112. " Norsea" One of three of the ship under construction for North Sea Ferries technical Offices, Rotterdam. Oil on canvas.

114. Norsea aft end. Oil on canvas.

115. "Launchday" Norsea at Govan Shipbuilders Ltd. Oil on canvas.

117. Helen and I in Florence.

119. Frekels.

120. The Norsea under construction. Oil on canvas.

121. Helen and me on the Norland.

122. Bert and Nellie in Jocky Wilson's car.

124. "Glasgow Cathedral". Oil on canvas.

197. "Destruction" and "Not Too Deer". Oils on canvas.

198. "Slaying of Snilloc", "Transformation of Snilloc", "I Had a Dream". All oil on canvas.

201. Refuge. Oil on canvas

202. Study for "Caitlin". Charcoal. "Caitlin". Oil on canvas.

208. "Figurehead". Oil on canvas.

209. "Industrial Plant". Oil on canvas.

210. "Dreaming of Dad". Oil on canvas.

211. "Planet Football" Oil on canvas.

212. Cave Dwellers. The Duct Keel.

213. "Rusty, The Shipyard Pet". Oil on canvas.

222. "Spirits of Air and Sea". Oil on canvas.

223. Me Louise and Bert on the ferry to Belfast.

234. Louise at Tracey's bar Londonderry.

226. Backdrop for Jesse Garron.

232. "The Hambone", Pastel.

234. Tracey and Graeme's wedding.

235. www.paintingmusicathome.ok Mixed media

236. Louise at Pauline and Martin's wedding.

237. The granary. Oil on board.

238. "Sovereign of the Seas" at Puerto Rico..Oil on canvas.

244. Helen and Louise at Santa Eulalia, Ibiza.

244. Louise and Helen on a boat from Es Cana Hippy Market.

248. Mum in Darnley Court Nursing Home.

249. Frank and I playing in Darnley Court, George and Ann Marie Nimmo looking on as George's Dad was also there.

252. "Caulker". John Black. Oil on canvas.

267. And so to bed. Oil on canvas.

268. "Dry Dock". Norsea at Greenock. Oil on canvas.

278. Bow Assembly. Oil on canvas.

278. "The Thinker". "Rewiring a Crane". Both oil on canvas.

279. "Portrait of me by David Reid.

284. The Twist. Sea Flowers.

285. Louise me and Bryony at the back, Pauline Rosslyn and Tracey in the front at Eglinton Country Park.

286. Me at Benidorm, 2005.

288. Tusk, Frank and me..

289. Tusk top, Ramming out bottom.,charcoal.

297. Bert and his brothers.

298. Jeff and Ann Love.

299. Four of the Five Interns in 2010.

300. Maree and Davy Hughes with me and Helen in the Porthead, Irvine.

302. Donnie Morrison, Ellen Ingram, Bert, Joan and Jim Moody in Gibraltar.

304. Family at the Biopark, Fuengirola..

307. Frank and Helen Cusack's house at Ciudad Quesada, Spain.

309. Early Morning Launch

310. "Carcassonne" Oil on canvas.

311. Zander and Bert at Sliema Malta.

312. Bert and me at Xlendi, Gozo.

313. Helen and I at Can Pastilla, Mallorca.

315. Bert and Billy Laing. Helenna, Zander and Rosslyn.

316. Helenna,Zander and Rosslyn. Sir Alex and me.

318. Pauline and Helenna, Tracey, Louise, Helen and Gladys at 120 Braidcraft Road Pollok.

322. Gladys.

323. Helen and Jill on the same journey as us.

324. Me and Bill on the train from Fort William going to Mallaig.

325. Helen and her Dad at Port de Soller, Mallorca.

331. Bert and Helen at Can Pastilla.

332. Berty Morrison. Helen, Sir Alex, Bert and me.

333. Wreath from Rangers Football Club.

335. Robert and Rita Morrison, me and Helen, Joan and Jim Moody at Torquay.

336. View from our bedroom window looking down Greenfield St.

337. "Bridge Cottage,Benmore Estate, Mull" Oil on canvas.

338. Helen looking for the nudists on Mull.

339. Me in Riga.

340. The Bull Ring, Ronda, Spain.

342. Gibraltar

342. Eileen and Russ with me and Helen at La Linea, Spain.

343. Pantheon" oil on canvas.

344. "The Colosseum. oil on canvas

346, David McCallum, Charlie Taylor, Charlie Sands and Tommy Gordon.

347. Me in the infinity pool in Albufiera a week before Christmas.

348. My CTF portraits.

349. Interns and wives.

350. Friends at Caleta de Fuste, Fuengirola. Legends, Caleta de Fuste.

351. Helen and me at Caleta

352. Me and Kevin Grenville.

353. Sitges.

354. Indian restaurant, Sitges.

356. Top of The Rock, Gibraltar.

358. Me and my girls.

358. CTF Buddies: Rab Munro,Frankie Murray, deseased, Gordon Macintosh, Tommy Goron, John Wightman and me. CTF Clutha.

359. CTF Clutha.

360. Ticket for the Beach Boys.

361. Granddaughter Rosslyn Tierney getting her prizes at Glasgow's Art Gallery.

363. "The Inn at John o' Groats". Oil on canvas.

364. Tommy Joe and me at BAAD. Corona build strats and me.

365. Family at our Golden Wedding. Helen and I with our girls.

367. With Ian and Ann in Benidorm.

369. CTF Clutha

370.. Me and Dougie Murray, Me and Frank and just me.

771. The Beatles Story, Liverpool..

372. Me and Helen at the Cavern.

373. John and Yoko's Double Fantasy Exhibition.

374. John Lennon's gear in The Beatles Story.

376. Swahovian day at Mary and Billy Black's Toby Jug.

376. Love this photo by Anne Oldfield.

377. Rosslyn, Helenna and Zander.

378. Helen and I with Angela Cahill.

379. Helen and I with Cassandra Cahill Cunningham

380. Frekels at Jimmy Murray's funeral in 2018 .

381. Pauline, Catherine McAree, Katy Rafter and Tracey at Erin and Pauls wedding in New Lanark.

382. Tracey, Graeme's Dad Stuart, his partner Maureen and Graeme at Tracey's fiftieth birthday lunch.

383. " Balloch" Oil on canvas 2019.

384. "John Hannon on the Cobbler Arrochar" Oil on canvas 2019

385. Me with my sister Chris, her partner Mark and Louise.

386. Family at Holker Hall estate, Cark, Lake District.

387. Ambleside.

389. Escapade.

390. Family and friends laying Bert's ashes at Ibrox.

391. Colosseum, Rome.

392. Me and Bill enjoying Islay Mist that Louise brought me from Islay, only to take it back there to enjoy. Slainte!

393. Portnahaven.

394. The round church in Bowmore that has no corners for the devil to hide.

395. Laphroaig Distillery.

397. Sampling the water of life at Bunnahabhain Distillery.

398. Jill, Bill and Helen waiting for their cheese toasties.

399. George Francey, drummer.

400. Louise and I with our skydiving certifficates at Skydive Northwest.

402. "George and Geraldine". Oil on canvas 2019.

403. George McGuinness and me.

404. Helen and I on our fifty second Anniversary 2019.

495. Frank and I with Martin Clunes, and with Joe Absolom.

406. Dougie Murray and me at BAAD, Glasgow.

407. Helen and I in Benidorm during December.

408. Rosslyn, Mihai and Arlene at Rosslyn's 16th Birthday party.

409. Sam and I with Benny Gallagher.

410. "The Roman Forum" oil on canvas 2019. Three auld Swahovians.

411. Family photo from summer 2020.

412. My Gibson Les Paul Studio that had to go during 2020